Praise for

IMPLOSION

". . . poetic and incisive . . . Many readers will see aspects of their own family histories in this powerful saga of trauma and healing. An alternately wistful and searing exploration of a troubled legacy."
—*Kirkus Reviews* starred review

"In *Implosion*, Elizabeth Garber has voyaged far into the complexities of memory, navigating the treacherous currents of shame and confusion, and returned, rowing stroke by stroke, sentence by sentence, with a beautiful, clear, heartbreaking tale. Courageous, horrible, terrible, and wonderful, this is a dark and tragic beauty of a memoir that could only be written by someone determined to be fiercely honest in her remembering and her art."
—Richard Hoffman, author of *Half the House* and *Love & Fury*

"*Implosion* is a remarkable feat. Garber allows us to revile her brilliant and destructive architect father as fully as she did when she was coming of age in the 1960s. She also allows us to forgive him as she ultimately does in this wise, searching book. Her story is an echo of the tumultuous cultural revolutions that define her generation. As an architect does, Garber constructs her story room by room, filling the space with both shadow and light. This is a beautiful book written by a new and exciting writer."
—Meredith Hall, author of *Without a Map*

"Elizabeth Garber's elegant and limpid prose resembles the transparency of her father's stunningly beautiful house, where moments of tyranny and abuse creep upon us with a shock."
—Patrick Snadon, Architecture Professor Emeritus, University of Cincinnati

"Elizabeth Garber writes with searing clarity about the years she spent living under the oppressive reign of her father. But this isn't just a book about a deeply troubled father-daughter relationship. Rather, it's a story about a family, an art form (architecture), a generation, and a decade in American history that we're still trying to understand. By reading *Implosion*, one not only gains access to the intimate, tragic details of Garber's broken youth but also to the public world outside her father's realm: one of parallel turmoil, complexity, and yes: implosion. A finely wrought narrative by a brave, unflinching writer."

—Jaed Coffin, author of *A Chant to Soothe Wild Elephants: A Memoir*

"Elizabeth Garber's memoir drives as well as her dad's fine sports car. Sleek, modernist sentences, high-power clarity of perception, bold telling it like it was. Garber never loses touch with the forms of pain caused by her dad's illness. She honors the vulnerability of the whole family, including him, while they are in its grips. In the end, at the heart of the matter is compassion and the kindness of unconditional love, in spite of it all, and the simple beauty of gathering stones found on a clean, sandy beach."

—Alexandra Merrill, international women's leadership consultant

". . . the story of [Garber's] escape, her fight to regain control of her life and to become a loving mother. It is a beautifully written but heartbreaking tale."

—*Pur Sang* magazine

IMPLOSION

IMPLOSION

A MEMOIR OF
AN ARCHITECT'S DAUGHTER

———•———

By

ELIZABETH W. GARBER

SHE WRITES PRESS

DEDICATED TO

my mother, Jo,

and my brothers, Woodie and Hubbard

Revisiting modernism today is like visiting a foreign culture— . . . the past's vision of a Utopian world can hardly be grasped or understood. For many, modernism was something visited upon them, unasked, unloved, and unmourned when its demise was prematurely announced in the 1970s.

—ADA LOUISE HUXTABLE, *On Architecture*

We are all fixing what is broken.
It is the task of a lifetime.

—ABRAHAM VERGHESE, *Cutting for Stone*

CONTENTS

———•———

Woodie and Elizabeth
on Nantucket, 1959

PROLOGUE

The Architect's Daughter 1959

Space and light and order. Those are the things that
men need just as much as they need
bread or a place to sleep.

—Le Corbusier

ON A VAST SMOOTH BEACH ON NANTUCKET IN 1959, my father slipped a grey stone into my hand, saying, "Close your eyes. Feel the stone." The stone was cool and silky like Grandmother's kid gloves. He asked, "What color is it?"

Any child might say grey, or think this was a silly question and say, "Oh, Daddy, let's run" and laugh as she left footprints in the sand. But I was not any child. I was Woodie Garber's little girl, a modern architect's daughter, and I knew he did not want a simple answer. At five years old, I had already found comfort in the private way we saw the world. I had to discover a magic answer that would please him.

I scrunched my eyes together. How could I feel a color? My fingers stroked the stone but all I could see was a flashing darkness behind my closed eyes. I searched for any color in this little rock the sea had pulled across the sandpaper beach day after day. Suddenly I saw in my mind the colors of the sunset I had drawn the night before with thick oily pastels on textured paper. Confused and amazed, I opened my eyes wide and gasped, "It's bright red with orange streaks!" Behind his black-framed glasses, his eyes beamed approval into mine.

Breathless from this discovery, I ran into the wind, my hair whipping across my face. I scanned the beach until I found my own sea-smoothed stone. Running back, I took his hand and placed the stone into his palm. "Close your eyes," I said, my voice urgent and serious. "Tell me the color you feel." I watched his wide thumb moving in a small circle over the stone. I stood beside him, my tall father in white shorts and a Mexican woven shirt with carved bone buttons. I wanted to see what he saw.

The others were far ahead, my mother with her short wavy hair holding the hand of my three-year-old brother, little Wood. Our friend Ruth carried Hubbard, our healthy new baby. Two months before, Ruth had called my mother. "You are worn out. Bring your family here for a rest. The ocean will do you all good."

My mother had said, "I can't leave our sick little girl at home."

Ruth said, "Someone can take care of her. She'll be fine. All of you need a break."

At home in Ohio, we tossed on sweaty sheets, the summer heat keeping us awake. In a bassinet next to my bed lay my two-year-old sister, Bria, who never grew or moved. She was a limp bundle like a baby Jesus in the crèche scene at Christmas. Her grey-blue eyes fell into mine. I put my finger into the curled petal of her palm. Her tiny fingers flickered against mine.

"Hi, Bria." I spoke softly. Her lips fluttered in what I knew was her smile.

I felt my mother's presence behind me. "Saying goodnight?"

I nodded. "I wish she could talk to me." Mommy had told

me Bria had a hole in her heart and would never grow up.

My mother nodded wearily. "She's our little angel." My mother was so tired. All day long she steadied herself by talking out loud to me. "Where did I put my wallet? Hold onto your brother's hand. Hand me the bottle for the baby. What would I do without you? You are so helpful." She managed objects, children, and food. We were fed, warm, and clean. But I wasn't interested in her ordinary world. I was smart, learning to read fast while she struggled to read and mispronounced words. I was filled with hubris, the pride of being my father's favorite.

On Nantucket I woke to the breathing of the waves sliding across the sand, in a house where everything felt fresh and cool. In 1952, my father had designed for Ruth and Bob the first "upside-down" modern beach house on Nantucket. The living room was on the second floor, high above the dunes, while the bedrooms on the ground floor were quiet and shady, tucked in between the dunes and surrounded by windswept tall dry grasses. Under wooden ceilings, we leaned into a white couch while the sound of the waves smoothed us like the stone my father slipped in my palm.

Back home in Cincinnati, in our 1860s Victorian house, our life was confined by hallways, French doors, a formal dining room with a chandelier, a library with a medieval paneled ceiling, bookcases behind glass doors, a pantry, and back kitchen. There, my father's voice boomed with excitement when he talked about Modern Architecture. As a child, I knew there was an exciting time coming, when no one would build cluttered, decorated buildings anymore. Everything would be designed with clean elegant lines. I listened closely to my father. Modern was Truth and Simplicity, and it followed Rules. When we stayed at the house on Nantucket, I knew we were living in the Modern, where the roof lifted up like a wing to glide over the long beach below.

One evening on Nantucket, when the others washed the dinner dishes and my mother put my little brothers to bed downstairs, my father and I lingered at the table as the room grew dark. Beyond the glass floor-to-ceiling windows, the sand beach and sky streaked blue-purple on a forever horizon. "This is what we want to create," he said as he gazed out the window. "Spaces with no boundary between the inside and outside." The wooden structure holding the windows in place became a grid of black lines framing blocks of color: the dark sea, foaming white surf, and indigo sky.

I suddenly remembered an artist who painted like this, black lines and squares of colors. My father brought home to us little booklets on Modern Art that he set on a stand at the kitchen table at home, so we could turn the page each day to a new painting and study modern art at meals. I could identify Miró's happy floating shapes, Picasso's sad blue faces, Modigliani's lovely ladies, and Kandinsky's jagged lines and bright colors. I turned to my father. "It looks like a big Mondrian painting."

My father roared with laughter, patted my back. "That's my girl!"

I lived for these rare moments when I basked in his attention, these moments he claimed me as his special child. From the way everyone else looked at my father when he spoke, I knew he was special. I once heard someone say he was brilliant. I wasn't sure what that meant, but I knew the room felt electric when he walked in and everyone turned to listen to him. I hungered for the moments when he shone his brilliance on me. I was my father's daughter, a devotee, a serious girl studying what he loved: the radiant play of light and space in architecture and art, the thrill of riding in sports cars and appreciating tiny sips he gave me of fine wines.

When we stood on the beach that day, my father holding my stone, he knelt down so his head was even with mine, his knee touching the dry sand. He ran his fingertips over the surface, his eyes closed. I studied his big face, the mole on his cheek, his bald sunburned head. I waited for the color he saw in my stone.

He smiled, opened his eyes, looking into my face. "It's turquoise, Navajo turquoise with a streak of silver in the groove." I nodded, smiling into his beaming gray-blue eyes. Oh, my Daddy. I felt more alive with him than with anyone else.

Garber family: Wood, Woodie,
Hubbard, Elizabeth, Jo, 1961

WE RETURNED HOME to the house where our family had lived since the 1870s, where, soon after my father was born in 1913, his mother went to bed in a darkened room for three years. Forty-five years later, at the end of her life, ghostly and addled, she had drifted from room to room, pulling down shades to hide from imaginary strangers, until my mother, home alone with four small children, couldn't take it any longer. My grandmother was moved to a home for the elderly until she faded away.

In that house, in the room at the top of the stairs, I fell asleep, as I had for two years, to the faint rustle of my little sister's breathing. Yet that winter Bria grew weaker until she could no longer take in formula. My mother decided not to have our baby kept in a hospital. Bria began to starve, etching the hallway with her tiny whimper, until she became too weak to make a sound.

One day the doctor came to our house. His shoes slowly brushed up the stairs. I watched as he held the silver stethoscope to my sister's crumpled chest. He told my parents, "She is still a tiny bit alive. It will just be a matter of time."

My tall bald father gazed out the window, his thin lips pressed. He glanced at his watch. There was important work to be done. He was designing the Modern world. His polished shoes rushed down the steps. Far below, I heard a zoom in the garage, before his red Alfa Romeo backed out and he drove away to his office in the city.

My mother and I stood together looking down into Bria's translucent face in the bassinet. My mother held onto the wicker edge as if to hold herself up. Finally she turned, gathered up a pile of laundry and walked downstairs. The washing machine began to shake the old wooden floors of the house. I smelled coffee and knew she was sitting at the kitchen table with a cigarette.

I continued to stand in the pale grey light next to my sister in the bassinet. Outside the tall window, a light sprinkling of snow coated the ground in our village of old houses. I stared as a white horse crossed our backyard, coming to stand below the oak tree, before looking up at me inside the house. I gazed at the horse's white mane, the long curving back, the hooves in the snow-flecked grass, while I listened for any trace of my sister's breathing.

When I went downstairs, little Wood drove a truck on the rug, making vroom noises next to baby Hubbard, who gnawed the railing on the playpen. I continued down the dark basement steps to help my mother. When we climbed up the bulkhead steps to the backyard, carrying the basket heavy with steaming clothes, the horse and snow were gone. I pulled diapers out of the basket and handed them to her one at a time. Our hands grew red and stung with cold. She pushed down the wooden clothespins until we emptied the basket.

IN THAT HOUSE of tall ceilings, I grew used to mysteries I didn't understand. In that house with heavy curtains, my father sometimes went to bed and stayed there for weeks. Reading, sleeping, not talking, not going to work. Other times his heart pounded so hard and irregularly that the bed shook and he went to the hospital for days or weeks. My mother explained to me that the doctors were trying to get his heart to go the right way.

But one night, a year after my sister died, the doctor called to say they had tried everything, but our father had thrown a clot. I watched her talking on the phone. Her eyes grew wide and her face looked white. Each time he said something, she repeated it. She spoke slowly, like she couldn't understand what the words meant, repeating what he said. "The clot can go to one of three places, the heart, the brain, or the lungs. If it goes to the first two places, he will die."

I had learned the heart pumped blood, brains were inside our head and lungs were how we breathe. She said with a strange thin voice, "Call me when you know something." She sat so quietly. I took her hand.

Then she said to herself, "Okay, now. I've just got to buck up." She looked at me and smiled a thin smile. "Let's give those little boys their bath." I helped her get them undressed and filled the tub with warm water. They splashed, holding the red tugboat under water and then laughing when it splashed back to the surface. We thought about my father but we didn't say a thing. I was a girl who had to help her mother.

When I went to bed, I watched the hall light, and prayed, "Please don't let my Daddy die." And he didn't.

But after that, I felt responsible for keeping him alive. I was no longer a girl who simply adored her father; I was the girl who had to save her father. I would keep him alive and happy by talking about what he loved: art and architecture. I knotted myself into a strange bond of loyalty, binding myself to him, no matter what happened, for the rest of his life.

In the Victorian house, my father and I waited for the

Modern. I believed him, that the Modern would release us from the smothering confines of the Victorian world, not knowing what legacy would follow us, even into a glass house.

Garber house under construction, 1965

THE GLASS HOUSE

1965

*Every house ... should be a fruit of our endeavor to
build an earthly paradise for people.*

—ALVAR AALTO

WE BROKE GROUND IN 1965 IN GLENDALE, OHIO, A
village built in the 1850s for commuters to Cincinnati fifteen
miles away. It had been the first planned suburban community
in the U.S., with winding streets that followed the shape of
the landscape instead of imposing a grid plan. Now protected
as a National Historic Landmark, the center of the village is
dotted with enormous houses on vast plots, built primarily in
the late nineteenth century, with diverse architectural styles
as if picked out of a catalogue, from Queen Anne to Gothic
Victorian to southern Plantation-style colonnades. Needless
to say, my father's radically modern design, the first of its
kind for miles around, shocked the neighbors, who called it
"The Glass House."

Set on three acres in a valley above a creek bed, the house
is enclosed by a horseshoe of towering white-barked syca-
mores and a giant hornbeam tree, with long thorns which
cast shadows across the flat gravel roof. The house floats like
a gleaming rectangular volume of light set into the landscape.

Vertical posts create a series of five framed squares the length of the house. Long porches on either side shadow the long, glass-walled Great Room from the sweltering summer sun. The flat roof appears to hover above the living room by a line of clerestory windows on each side, which allows diffused light and air to filter in from above.

For years, when drivers turned down the hill at the brick Italianate-towered fire station and saw our house, they inched by, staring. We called them "rubberneckers" and planted a screen of hemlocks that grew over the years to block the view.

In May 1966, we moved into a construction site. My father declared we would save a lot of money and have the "time of our lives" finishing the work ourselves. At this point, the house looked like a plywood packing box set down onto a muddy field, dwarfed by mountains of topsoil and yellow clay subsoil. Viewed from the hill above where the old mansions line Sharon Avenue, we were the sore thumb. The exterior walls were plywood. The windows and exterior walls of sliding glass doors were installed. The flat roof was tarred and sealed. Inside, the walls were insulated and plastered, and there was a plywood sub-floor. There were no cabinets, interior doors, trim, built-in desks, or closets. We had a stove, refrigerator, and a plywood surface to cook on.

Mom's friends asked, "How will you manage?"

She laughed. "We have running water, electricity, and flush toilets. It's no biggie, really. Lots of people get by with less." She'd grown up summers on a farm; she was strong and resourceful, and tried to make the work fun.

When the phone company came to install the phone, they asked, "Where do we put it?"

She said, "Nail it to this two-by-four in the kitchen."

Our three kids' beds were placed in a row, with a sheet hanging to divide our space from our parents' half of the bedroom. We each had a box for our favorite books or toys. Our clothes were hung from a rack or folded in boxes. Everything else we owned was stored in the basement. This arrangement was supposed to last a few months, but it would be nearly a year before we could move into our own rooms.

Garber Family, 1966

On Saturdays, the alarm blared. Our father's voice boomed. "Six thirty. Rise and shine." His voice barked commands. "The carpenter will be here any minute." He wouldn't stop until Sunday night. "We've got to be ready for him." We were twelve, nine, and seven years old, pulling on stained work clothes, eating our bowls of cornflakes before our father called impatiently from the two bedrooms that had been made into a shop. The table saw whined as an older carpenter taught our father how to rip plywood sheets to size, to construct what would become structures for cabinets, closets, desks, drawer faces, and cabinet doors for our kitchen, bathrooms, and four bedrooms. The "shop" room was a maze of tools: sawhorses, jointer, router, sander, drill press, and stacks of piled plywood. My mother, brothers and I were told what to do. Stack scraps, vacuum sawdust, and sand every single surface, inside and out. Rub on two coats of hot linseed and tung oil. Steel wool between each coat. Wipe off the dust. Every weekend—when we weren't outside clearing brush, tilling gardens, or weeding.

We learned to work; our muscles ached, then grew stronger. Our tender palms blistered and callused. This was our father's plan. He lectured us on the evils of our generation, lazy from constant television exposure and permissive parenting. He announced, nodding at our mother, "We believe that our family should be the center of our life. Work will instill discipline and good work habits. I certainly hope to see some initiative in each of you." He added with enthusiasm, "Remember, this is fun! You'll remember this for rest of your lives and you'll be grateful." We nodded, smiled obediently, and got back to work.

The cabinets were built of walnut plywood, and every unfinished edge showed a cross-section, like the brown and white cream-filled waffle cookies they gave us at Girl Scouts. My mother clamped each piece of plywood into a vise. My brothers sanded the rough edges of the plywood. My mother and I cut strips of walnut veneer and brushed on a coat of thick yellow glue. While the glue dried, I painted glue on every plywood edge. The next step was challenging. I unfurled the strip of sticky veneer along the glued plywood, leaving a little edge on either side. If I didn't hold it straight enough, the narrow strip of wood veered off, showing the plywood raw edge. I had to start over and rip the two sticky edges apart. I got it right more and more often.

I used a block of wood to smooth down the veneer, pressing out any air bubbles. I leaned close, pulled an X-Acto knife towards me, trimming the edge flush along the plywood. I had to focus or risk cutting into the wood or my finger. With sandpaper wrapped around a block, I sanded the edges of every drawer and cabinet door until they were smooth. I stood up straight, stretched my back, and kept going. My father announced I was the Queen of Edging. My mother and brothers then oiled each cabinet door.

Our dad set the table-saw blade for cutting out a slot in the drawer sides. He showed my youngest brother how to measure. "Do you know how to read these little lines?" He wrote on a block of wood each of the fractions to explain to Hubbard. "We want ½ inch. Now we lock the blade in place. Help me hold this board so the board doesn't kick. That's my boy." My little brother held the board carefully as it moved through the saw. He carried it to a stack, picked up the next board and handed it to his father. They continued through the whole stack. My dad clapped Hubbard on the back. "What a great worker you are."

When friends dropped by, our father announced one of his many rules: no outsiders were asked or allowed to help. We could say hello for a few minutes but then we had to go back to work. They could visit with us as we worked. Friends of my parents came by to see what was happening on the construction site. My father loved to give the tour, explain his philosophy of how families should live and work together. The kitchen and Great Room were the center of the house like farm kitchens, where we would can and freeze food, from May strawberries to applesauce in the fall. No longer would the family be separated. No longer would the mother be slaving away in a back kitchen; no, we would all work, cook, and play together.

Then he explained to our guests, "We thought we'd be done a lot sooner, but this is really great fun for all of us. It's almost like a second childhood for me." As he steered them toward the sliding glass door, he asked, "Have I told you I got a bulldozer so I can finish up the grading myself? I named it Peanut."

They walked out onto the porch to survey the two acres around the house. He explained, "I planted soybeans this summer. This fall, I'll till it under and plant rye and vetch for the winter." His voice boomed with his huge enthusiasm. "The soil will be dynamite after a few years of this nitrogen building!" His voice faded as they crossed the field and we continued to stack lumber in the shop.

My best friend Linda lived across the field from us, and came over to visit all the time. We were skinny girls with mousy chin-length hair and plastic glasses, mine tortoise-shell ovals, hers turquoise with points like Cadillac fins. While I brushed on glue, she told me what she'd seen at the shopping center. "You've got to see the cool paisley fabric I got for sewing a skirt. How soon are you going to be done?"

"That's a good question." I looked at my mother, who shrugged, glancing at my father who had come back in after saying good-bye to our cousins. My brother's friends were riding their bikes up and down the earth mounds, shouting my brothers' names, calling them out to play. As the afternoon light poured in from the west, my little brothers, in first and fourth grade, asked, "Please, Daddy, can we go out now?"

My mother would have let them, but our father's voice sliced through our plans. "What do you think? Not until every tool is put away, every block of wood is picked up, and every bit of sawdust vacuumed are you going anywhere." We started cleaning up, hoping our activity would cut the lecture short. But he wouldn't stop. "I don't care about your homework or your friends; a job isn't done until it's done. When are you ever going to learn good work habits?" We set our jaws, glared at the floor as we did what we were told.

Mommy spoke quietly while our dad started running the sander. "Let's make a race and see how fast we can get this place cleaned up." As soon as we finished sweeping, while the sander roared and our dad had his back to us, my brothers raced downstairs to get their bikes.

Linda said, "Come on." We dashed out the front door down the stone steps, across the drive and up the hill, across our acre field of vegetable gardens, to reach her tidy ranch house to look at Simplicity sewing patterns.

That fall the outside of the house was finished. A crew arrived with a flatbed truck loaded with panels to cover all the plywood wall sections of the house. These were my father's invention, solid panels with crushed milk-white glass pressed into epoxy. The rough sharp edges sparkled in sun and moonlight. He'd been experimenting with new materials for exterior cladding on his buildings. The schools he designed had panels with white stones set into epoxy. For our house, Woodie explained he wanted an exterior that would not require painting, would not absorb dirt, would be self-washing with the rain, would be highly heat-reflective, yet be fun to look at. We looked at them up close, touching our finger tips to the ragged chunks of white glass, their edges as thin and sharp as razors.

The crew used a crane to lift them into place and they wore heavy leather gloves and canvas jackets for protection as they installed them. My mother said she was too scared to watch them work, afraid someone would get hurt. But my brothers and I sat on the muddy hillside and saw when a young man's arm was ripped open by the flash of glass as the panel slipped, blood splattering the sparkling white panel. They scrambled, wrapped his arm, and tied a tourniquet before an ambulance took him to the hospital. The crew continued working, slower and more carefully. They sprayed the blood off with a hose. For years, my mother was frightened by these panels, worried someone might fall or be pushed against the walls of sharp-edged glass.

By late winter of 1967, after our hand-built cabinets had been installed in the kitchen, bedrooms, and bathrooms, the carpentry shop moved to the basement. Wide wooden flooring was installed on top of the plywood sub floors, sanded, and finished. Movers delivered the grand piano from storage. Now was the time to really move in.

In the Great Room we unpacked and placed furniture as if we were arranging a set for a play on stage. My father had been buying and storing things we didn't know about. We rolled out a large woven orange rug in front of the stone fireplace. On one side of the rug we placed my father's black leather Eames chair and ottoman. On the other side, we pulled protective paper off the Womb chair we'd had since I was a baby. My father had had it recovered with a burnt-orange fabric.

I jumped into the chair, running my hands over the familiar shape arc, like a round-backed throne around me, drawn in with a flat area on either side for my arms. "Oh, Daddy, I love this color!!" I gave the eye to my brothers, teasing them, "This is mine. Mine since I was a baby, right, Dad?"

"You grew up in that chair. I'd come home from work, settle into the Womb chair and give you your bottle."

Maybe I only remembered because of the black and white photos in the album, my dad beaming at me, tossing me in the air, and us laughing. He'd lost his first daughter in a divorce when his first wife took her and disappeared without a trace. After he married my mother, she had three miscarriages and they thought they couldn't have a baby. They'd tried to adopt, but their age difference of eighteen years was too great and they were told they were not acceptable parents. Then she got pregnant with me, had complications and had to rest in bed for months. When I was born, he always said, "I was the happiest man alive."

Setting up our new house made our dad very happy too. It was the culmination of years of planning, and he knew where everything went. We kept bringing up boxes and packages that had been stored in the basement for the long year we'd lived in a construction site.

On either side of the stone fireplace were walls of bookshelves. My dad's boxes of jazz records filled two long shelves. Next came rows of books, and above them our dad's collection of Mexican pre-Columbian sculptures he'd been buying in Mexico and sneaking across the border since the late forties. Their Mayan and Olmec clay and stone faces stared out into the Great Room.

Woodie set up the new stereo in a walnut cabinet in front of the stone wall, and ran wires to the biggest speakers on the market, three feet by two feet, placed high above the room, on top of the kitchen cabinets. The sound permeated every inch of the house. He piled a stack of his favorite records on the record player, the honored saints of our childhood. We started with our favorite, Dave Brubeck, followed by Duke Ellington, Benny Goodman, Count Basie, and Harry James, to celebrate our day of unpacking after a year with no music. In the Victorian house, we had listened to them on what were then the newest stereo speakers, little boxes whose sound filled only the library.

Now the music reverberated through us, sound bouncing off the glass walls, down from the heavy beamed ceiling high above us, and we were caught in the center. Our dad was turned on, bebopping with the music, saying "Oh, yeah" with the beat, as he hauled a stack of chairs into place. Calling out on a favorite song, "Damn, I heard this when I was at Cornell! Seems like it was just yesterday." When night came, the music mellowed down a notch to the cool of Archie Shepp, Art Blakey, and Pharaoh Sanders.

Above the stereo, he hung a new painting none of us had seen, an abstract in reds, oranges, blues of a bull fight, the matador's cape a blur of red. Above us, circling the entire room below the beams and the ceiling, was a two-foot-wide panel painted my father's favorite color, a deep Chinese red.

We set the rest of the modern furniture into place: an Eames molded round coffee table, Knoll international lounge chairs with orange leather slung on wooden frames, a Danish teak rectangular dining room table with stacking metal and molded walnut plywood chairs, and a round Formica breakfast table surrounded by smaller stacking birch veneer chairs. All in the Great Room, all placed under their respective ceiling lights, all according to my father's plan.

Woodie was radiant, his voice loud and filling the room, as if he were lecturing to students. "I'm sure the thought of one room for cooking, dining, play, living and everything else will be absolutely shocking to many of our neighbors, but this is the wave of the future!" We nodded and kept bringing up boxes. To us it was a great adventure, a scavenger hunt; opening each box was like Christmas.

But we were also daunted by this magnificent room that had suddenly changed from the sawdusty construction site piled with lumber where we had camped out for a year. We were still the same midwestern kids in beat-up work clothes, yet we were turning our house into a showplace, a museum of the modern, that gleamed and shone and revolved around us.

Garber House Great Room,
two hanging Bertoia sculptures

In the kitchen, we unpacked Woodie's collection of copper pots and pans, some small enough for one fried egg or melting butter for artichokes, increasing in size and shape to huge pots big enough for a dozen lobsters. Woodie snagged them onto a series of hooks hanging down from a long metal beam with welded arms bolted to the ceiling high above.

Then my mother, the boys, and I pulled open the walnut-veneer cabinet doors and the deep drawers we had built and filled them with dishes, staples, cooking utensils, following Woodie's chart of where everything went. He was too excited to focus; he kept hauling boxes upstairs for us to unload, and kept walking around, looking at the house from every angle. His masterpiece, his dream house, was coming together.

The finale was unpacking Bertoia sculptures from wooden crates, like opening heavy bronze Christmas ornaments to set around the house. My dad commissioned sculpture by Harry Bertoia for several of his buildings. Every time Woodie visited his studio to talk about their work, he brought home a small new sculpture for us.

There were two made of short bronze rods of equal length welded to a central hub to form a 'bush.' We set the larger one on the Eames coffee table and the smaller one on the dining room table, where the light from above made silhouetted patterns through the rods onto the table.

My father played with the tall sound sculpture, made with three-foot-long bronze rods welded in a grid attached to a ten-inch-square base. He grasped the rods together and then released them all at once, so they swayed and collided against each other, making a cacophony of sound. Placed onto the piano, the clashing of the bronze rods rumbled through the body of the piano.

Another sculpture, made with thin aluminum rods, was held together like a fistful of wires thrust into the metal base. This 'bouquet' of silvery wires floated around with only a faint whisper as they touched each other. My brother Hubbard set this in front of the stone wall on the edge of the fireplace hearth.

The stone fireplace wall was painted a gritty white. Suspended from the ceiling, a cable hung down for Dad to attach a three-foot-long black metal-framed sculpture, with wires attached to the top and bottom that held squares painted bright colors. It was a model for a screen that had been built, life-sized, for the St. Louis airport. Woodie had seen the model gathering dust in Harry's studio on a visit, and convinced him to sell it to him.

My father asked me, "Do you remember why Harry chose this set of colors for one side and these for the other side?" He swung the sculpture, showing me the side with red, orange and yellow squares. On the opposite side, the squares were painted blue, purple, black.

"Of course, Dad." I rolled my eyes. "You taught me this when I was almost a baby! They are 'hot' colors on one side and 'cool' on the other."

"Just wanted to keep you on your toes, Sugar."

I grinned. "Don't worry about me, Daddy!"

As night settled, my brothers and my father played with the lights, tapping and turning the dimmer switches, trying to remember what light lit up what part of the room. Finally they left them all on full and bright, and the room spun around us, a dizzying flash and flare of reds, copper pans, walnut cabinets that gleamed like coffee beans, paintings, and driving jazz rumbling through it all.

I was setting the table. My mother was making a supper to celebrate, steaks with crushed garlic were ready to grill on the new broiler that had just been installed, scones in the new oven, corn heating in a copper pan on the stove. My father called out to her, "Dinner can wait. We have to go outside and walk across the field to see the house from outside."

The entry closet stood like a big box when you entered the great room from the front door, making the visitor pause, our father explained, before they entered. We pulled on our coats and hats, and stepped into the muddy boots we had left in a row on the porch. The house was still surrounded by vast bulldozed fields waiting for our landscaping. It was raw, late winter as we walked across the sticky clay mud of the fields, across the drainage ditch and up the road so we could see down the hill towards the house.

This was the first night the house became what it was designed to be. We stood together, my little brothers holding my mother's hands, and I leaned against my dad, his arm flung around my back, as we looked at what we had created. The darkness hid the mud field. The house shimmered like a white mirage in the valley, the crushed glass wall panels sparkling, while the Great Room blazed as if on fire, red, orange, and wood reflected and glowed inside the long glass walls. We were dazzled by my father's vision. We had all worked together to make it happen. He clapped us all on the back, heady with delight. "We did it." We nodded, smiling, repeating his words, almost stunned by this magnificence, never dreaming what would happen to us living in this blazing cauldron.

We walked down the road together in the dark, turned onto the gravel drive that cut through the woods and followed the creek. There, on the crest of the hill high above us, the house sailed like a moonlit ocean liner. We walked up the driveway, proceeded under the inset ground-level entryway, and mounted the wide stone stairway leading us back to the Great Room, the heart of the fire.

Woodie (professional portrait),
circa 1960s

THE MIRROR GLASS TOWER

1967

*Every time a student walks past a really urgent,
expressive piece of architecture that belongs to his
college, it can help reassure him that he does have that
mind, does have that soul.*

—LOUIS KAHN

THE FRONT DOOR FLEW OPEN. "BOY OH BOY, does that smell good!" In his fifties, Dad was a bull of a man, bald and big-chested, with a booming voice that filled the Great Room. "I've got exciting news once we get dinner on."

In the narrow galley kitchen, our pretty mother, in her late thirties, lifted a steaming beef tongue out of the pressure cooker, filling the house with the smell of bay and pepper. Her black hair was cut short, setting off her dangling Mexican silver earrings. My dad had convinced her to wear skirts above her knees. He said, "With legs like yours, it's a crying shame not to show them!" She'd felt shy about it, but he insisted. He bought fashionable clothes for her when he went to New York City for meetings.

The floor-to-ceiling sliding-glass walls of the Great Room became mirrors at night, reflecting me and my two younger brothers as we laid out the silver on the glowing teak table. Now aged seven and ten, the boys looked like skinny twins, with buzz cuts, wearing button-down shirts with jeans.

Dad shouted to us playfully, "Come give me my kiss." Even though I was thirteen, I didn't mind running up to give him a kiss on the cheek when he got home from work. He wore big black glasses, a plaid bow tie, a white shirt, and a boxy Brooks Brothers suit. My brothers ran up and pecked his cheek before running back to set the table.

"Lilibet, turn around and let me see your outfit!" I beamed with pleasure to show off my mod orange-and-yellow-striped top, yellow miniskirt, and orange vinyl belt he had given me for Christmas. I was skinny and shy at school, but looking at myself reflected in the glass walls under a grid of ceiling spotlights, I felt like Twiggy, the British model, with my short haircut.

He added, "I brought home the new *Vogue* for us to look at after dinner."

"Wow, cool!"

"You look great in those colors. That's my girl." He patted my butt. "Now get back to work and help your mother."

The night my father would first tell us about the tower, Mom skinned the tough outer layer of the tongue before settling the huge savory chunk of meat on a wooden platter. She carried the platter to the table and we followed with serving dishes of green beans and corn, frozen last summer from our garden. I sliced her homemade whole wheat bread on the cutting board.

No one else I knew ate tongue. It seemed everything we ate was unusual, different from the kids at school. Brains sautéed in white wine, kidney pie, marinated herring, ratatouille from our vegetables in the garden, and on Christmas morning, sweetbreads, cooked in cream with capers.

My brother, Wood, with sensitive eyes, carried white china plates to the dining room table. My dad barked orders with enthusiasm. "Hubbard, don't forget the butter or the horseradish!" My little brother brought a small bowl of our dad's favorite horseradish. Our dad switched into his German accent. "Have I ever told you about the summer I worked for my uncle on his horseradish farm?"

"Of course!" My brothers and I rolled our eyes. "The horseradish stung your eyes so bad it looked like you were crying." We were sure we knew all his stories. We sat down at the table and started loading our plates.

Dad interrupted us. "How many times do I have to tell you? Do not start eating until your mother lifts her fork!"

Our mother waved her fork in the air, good-heartedly, as if she was making fun of the rule. "I've lifted it. You can start eating now." Then, to distract him from his namesake, she asked, "Now Woodie, tell us your exciting news."

"It's final. I got the commission for a new high-rise dorm at the University of Cincinnati. It will be called Sander Hall." He served himself a large slice of tongue, slathering it with horseradish before taking a big bite. He chewed with great appreciation before he continued. "I'll be designing a great way to live for college students. A place they can really feel at home." He warmed up, slipping into the teacher voice he used when lecturing student interns. "When I studied architecture at Cornell in the 1930s, we stayed up late in bull sessions talking about modern designs coming from the Bauhaus architects in Germany." He winked at us. "Sometimes you learn more outside of the classroom than in lectures! You need to have places to talk." He looked at us, expecting us to nod like his students, showing that we understood before he continued.

"It's all about social interaction." His voice filled the long room as he explained. A California study had showed that students benefited from housing that supported social interactions. He didn't want to build another monstrosity with long dark halls, with everyone going back and forth to use a single large bathroom. "That's what the University wants because it's cheaper to build. But no way am I going to submit students to that impersonal layout!"

He made a quick sketch of his plan on a paper napkin. Clustered like little villages, were five double rooms, a shared bathroom, and their own pajama lounge. "They'll have a big lounge downstairs where they can hang out too. I'm going to fill it with modern furniture."

Designing this dormitory tower was completing a full circle for my dad's career. My father said he became an architect because he grew up under a drafting table. In 1913, the year he was born, his father's Union Central Tower in downtown Cincinnati, at thirty-eight stories, was the tallest building in the world outside of New York City. Covered in marble and white terra-cotta, the tower was crowned with a cupola of a small Greek temple of the type you might imagine finding in a forest glade, but which was equipped with an aviation beacon for the modern era. At night the illuminated skyscraper was a symbol of the up-to-date city on the banks of the Ohio River.

CINCINNATI WAS BUILT in the heart of the Ohio Valley, a crossroads where the East separated itself from the West and the North defined itself as different from the South, a place that had wrestled with the dynamic tensions of these factors since its beginning. The city's shape is defined by the ancient river that had carried native people for centuries. Settlers were intent on building a fine city on a fertile plain, cupped by an amphitheater of steep hills. Steamboats plowed the thick river, mills sawed the dense forests, industrialists built factories, and skilled craftsmen arrived to construct a booming city in the early nineteenth century.

The Queen City, as it was called from its earliest days, would be compared to Rome's seven hills, and architects were the means to these grand visions. Cincinnati's architects designed Greek- and Roman-inspired edifices to rival the greatest European cities. An influx of German educated refugees settled in the Over the Rhine area of the city, building brick and stone churches, homes, and businesses in Greek Revival and Romanesque, Gothic and Italianate styles. Fueled by ingenuity and industry, the city expanded rapidly, moving out of the crowded downtown into the hills. The Miami canal and trains transported materials and passengers to planned suburbs, including the village of Glendale, where my family settled. In Cincinnati's expanding years, architects were revered and their work set out to define culture and improve society. My grandfather and father had both answered the intoxicating call of architecture.

My grandfather's firm, Garber and Woodward, was the most influential and prolific architectural firm of the first third of the twentieth century in Cincinnati. As my parents drove us through the city, they would point out elegant buildings of stone and brick, towers, schools, and homes. "Your grandfather designed that building."

———·———

MY FATHER, WOODIE Garber, learned the building field from the bottom up, as a hod carrier and day laborer on his father's construction sites until his father's career and fortune ended abruptly with the Depression. Relatives helped Woodie with tuition as he worked several jobs to pay his way through architecture school. When he emerged from Cornell in the mid-thirties, fired up with the prospects of designing modern buildings, he was lucky to find any work. He was fitted for a linen smock and joined the legions of draftsmen in John Russell Pope's office in New York, where they designed the classically-inspired National Gallery in Washington, DC. He spent days drawing specs of Doric columns and vaulted ceilings, while by night he studied Le Corbusier and the Bauhaus architects who were escaping from Germany to the US.

For over fifteen years, from the Depression in the early 1930s to the end of World War II, hardly any new buildings were commissioned in the US. Sigfried Giedion's Harvard lectures from 1938-39, published as *Space, Time and Architecture,* became the bible for a young generation of architects who waited for America to begin building the modern age.

As the war ended, there was a demand for many new buildings, and modern architecture led the way into the post-war
age. Materials developed during the war for airplanes, metal,
glass, and plastics offered lower-cost options for the new
buildings, instead of the more expensive traditional stone and
brick Beaux Art buildings that copied designs of the past.

During the war, my father had been a civilian engineer
and architect, designing engines and low-cost, quickly constructed, flat-roofed, air-cooled barracks for troops. When,
at the age of thirty-two, my father finally opened his own
practice, in 1945 in Cincinnati, his wartime experiences in
utilitarian buildings would influence his work. He submitted
his first major design for a competition, a glass tower for
downtown Cincinnati, which might have made him famous
nationally. It would have been the first curtain-walled glass
skyscraper in the U.S., the first sealed, temperature-
controlled office building, as well as the first office tower
with movable partitions. The drawings of this elegant
weightless tower, the Schenley building, graced the cover of
the inaugural issue of *Progressive Architecture* with a twelve-
page spread for this revolutionary design. My father's design
addressed many of the issues of glass buildings for decades
to come. He planned for double-pane glass to reduce summer heat and to conserve heat in winter. There would have
been radiant floors to heat or cool the building. This tower
design preceded all the famous American International Style
glass and steel skyscrapers.

56 PROGRESSIVE ARCHITECTURE—Pencil Points, OCTOBER, 1945

Drawing of proposed
Schenley Building, 1945

But the glass tower was opposed by Senator Robert Taft, Sr., of the Republican political family of Cincinnati. My father was informed that no modern building would be built in 'their' city, and the glass tower was never built. But this didn't stop my father from continuing to lead the battle for Modernism in Cincinnati. His strident, unwavering belief in the Modern way would mean that Woodie Garber's career would be marked by a fight for nearly every building he designed.

IT'S DIFFICULT NOW to imagine the magnitude of the general public's shock and fury on first contact with Modern Art and Architecture in the early twentieth century. There were riots in response to early art shows, and some early modern buildings, made of concrete, metal and glass, were picketed or vandalized. Many planning boards moved to forbid modern buildings from ever being built in their towns. Yet, the radical designs and concepts of early Modernism were welcomed by many connoisseurs of art and design. Perhaps for many, appreciation of Modernism was a trained (or educated, or even privileged) admiration, yet there still lingers a conservative backlash against and hatred of Modernism. Even today, early modernist buildings are being torn down at an appalling rate.

My dad's work finally took off in the early 1950s, with his design for the Cincinnati Public Library, the first modern library in the U.S. following WWII. Distinctive for its open stacks, glass walls, and enclosed garden behind a brick serpentine wall, it was featured in *TIME* and *LIFE* magazines. His buildings were striking and unusual. Over the next two decades, his firm designed modern flat-roofed schools, with open-plan classrooms filled with light. His design for a Frisch's hamburger restaurant had rippling roofs, inspired by the poured-concrete hyperbolic/parabolic roofs by the Spanish architect Félix Candela that my father visited in Mexico. His cantilevered entryway to a glass, metal, and stone addition to the Gothic-designed Episcopal church shocked the village of Glendale. Proctor Hall, at the College of Nursing and Health at the University of Cincinnati, had moving panels that blocked the sun through the hot Ohio summers. And there were so many homes. Woodie designed stunning personal modern homes for discerning Cincinnati clients and their families.

Maybe every architect dreams of building a tower. Woodie's first tower had not been built, but now this college dormitory gave him another chance. He explained to us at dinner that night how he would clad the dorm with a newly developed mirror glass. By 1967, glass towers had been around for quite a while, but mirror glass solved a lot of energy problems, conserving heat and helping with cooling. In Boston, I.M. Pei's firm was designing the John Hancock Tower, which would begin construction the next year. My father's dorm would be the first mirror-glass tower in Cincinnati. Towers saved land and gave everyone a terrific view, and reflective glass meant you could control light and temperature.

He was determined to make the dorm living spaces elegant and functional like a modern home. He would choose every piece of furniture for the lounges: Knoll International metal-framed chairs slung with leather, and Bertoia chairs. The ground-floor lobbies would be light and airy, as dramatic as the finest modern home. He said, "These students won't have to live with broken-down couches, heavy desks, and uncomfortable chairs. They'll have built-in desks along the room-length windows just like us."

I thought about this. "That means my room is just like a college dorm room. Cool!"

"That's right, Sugar."

"How tall will it be?" Hubbard asked.

"It's twenty-seven stories. In '65, when I designed the Master plan for the University, I'd planned for three low-rise dorms, but to save money they want to put 1300 students in this one building."

My mother looked concerned. "That's a lot of students in one building."

"I've got it worked out." He explained that the secret to this building was that it would really be two dorms stacked on top of each other. The boys would be on the upper stories and girls on the lower levels. They'd have high speed elevators going to each section so they wouldn't have long waits. He was confident. "It will work out great."

He added that it would have crushed milk-glass panels all the way up the side of the building, just like ours. "Can you imagine how it will sparkle in the sun and moonlight, high above the city? Rainstorms will keep washing the panels clean of the city's dirt."

"Wow, Dad, it will be twins with our house," I said. Our

home was the only other building so far built with these panels. "That is so groovy." I was trying out the new hippie expressions I heard on the radio.

Dad rolled his eyes, "Groovy?" We both laughed.

———.———

AFTER DINNER, AS my brothers helped my mother wash dishes, my father put on a new Dave Brubeck Quartet record and settled into his black leather Eames chair with a pad of paper and pencil. I curled up in the orange Womb chair with *Vogue,* each of us reflected in a spotlit island of light on the dark opaque walls behind us. The long room ended in bookshelves on either side of the white stone wall with a fireplace. My father had placed theatre spotlights on the ceiling to shoot beams of red, yellow, and deep blue through the hanging Bertoia sculpture. Colorful shadows moved across the white stone wall and the bullfight painting. Circling the entire room high above us was the continuous gleaming stream of red. At the other end of the long room, in the kitchen, my mother wiped down the Formica counter. The grain in the plywood walnut cabinets moved in patterns.

Brubeck's friendly piano circled the room, punctuated by Paul Desmond's lilting sax, with a deep bass and steady drums in the background. Dad leaned back, reading liner notes on the album. He called out comments. "Would you listen to that!" My dad had taken me when I was a little girl in pajamas to see them at a club. I'd grown up playing their red plastic 78s. Listening to Dave Brubeck was my best lullaby.

My mother and brothers played a card game at the kitchen table. The music was a lively stream flowing around all of us in that big room, tucking us in with its syncopated rhythms. I looked around the room and imagined students living in a modern tower, with glass walls reflecting them as they hung out in lounges on chairs like ours. They would learn to be Modern, like I had.

My father sketched the dormitory layout, made notes, and murmured to himself, "It will be a perfect building. They'll just love it."

Villa Savoye à Poissy,
photo by the author, 1973

VILLA SAVOYE

1967

The business of Architecture is to establish emotional
relationships by means of raw materials.

—LE CORBUSIER

MY FATHER AND I LAID OUT OUR MATERIALS AND
tools on the long built-in desk in front of the window that
ran the length of my parents' bedroom. He'd always said you
can never have a big enough desk. We were working on my
end-of-the-year eighth grade French project. Some kids were
making French bread, or a model of the Eiffel Tower out of
toothpicks, or cheese fondue. We were building an architectural model of my favorite building by the French architect,
Le Corbusier: his Villa Savoye.

At the architectural supply store I had spent my entire
babysitting savings of thirteen dollars, earned at $0.50 an
hour, on basswood dowels, white mat board, special glue,
gray rough-textured sandpaper for the driveway, and a bag of
green lichen to glue on the board at the end to appear to be
grass surrounding the house. Over years of visits to my dad's
office, I'd seen many scale models. I couldn't believe we were
making one together.

For years when my mother ran errands downtown, she

would drop me off at dad's office in a tall brick house with a small round tower near the University. I'd climb the long carpeted stairway, holding onto the carved banister, before entering the bright white drafting room where angled tables, like boats with sails, flew above my head. Long wooden T-squares, clear triangles, and mechanical pencils littered vast sheets of paper, covered with lines, tiny arrows and careful printing in pencil. I'd sniff the sharp ammonia from the blue-print machine in the next room.

On one occasion, I slipped through a circle of men to find my dad gazing at a roll of blueprints. He'd picked me up so I could sit on a tall stool and see the heavy roll of paper they were studying. He pointed with his finger as he talked. Then he looked at me.

"Lilibet, see if you can help us out. What do these double lines signify?" His voice was warm and booming. I squinted down at the grid of blue lines, my face serious.

"Those are walls."

"And what are these cross lines?"

"Windows." I could feel the young men in their white shirts, sleeves rolled up, smiling as they watched me, Woodie Garber's daughter. And I could feel the pressure of the history of architecture in my family weighing on me.

"Good. And this?" I peered at a series of parallel lines and suddenly I wasn't sure. I could feel my father's held breath, his steady eyes, and in my own eyes, the sting of tears. I had to know the answer. I had to prove myself to my father.

He made a little movement with his fingers, like a little person climbing steps, and I knew in an instant. "Those are stairs going down to the next floor we can't see!"

He patted me on the back with his big warm hand. "That's my girl!"

Over the years I absorbed their language of special words: clerestory, cantilever, reinforced, transparent. I loved the names of architects they murmured reverently: Walter Gropius, Mies van der Rohe, Alvar Aalto, and my father's favorite, Le Corbusier, whom he called Corbu. Le Corbusier's complete works, a series of white books, were placed prominently on a bookcase next to my father's desk in his private office.

As the years passed, I'd make a bee line to sit on the metal Bertoia chair next to Corbu's books. Bertoia said his chairs were mainly made of air. My father was the first architect to commission Bertoia's sculptures to go with his buildings.

I'd turn pages in a Corbu book, looking at old photographs of white buildings and drawings. My father would pause between phone calls to stand next to me, pointing to a photograph or drawing, admiring details of a line of windows, a curving roof garden.

Every year there were architectural scale models of his newest projects. I walked around the model for the proposed Cornell University Library on a large table next to the window. My father came over and crouched down so he could look at eye level with me. I peered in the little windows and doors, touched the pretend trees and scratchy bushes. Tiny faceless people walked on sandpaper sidewalks, looking like they knew where they were going. Two long walls were covered by an attached sculpture by Harry Bertoia, a jigsaw puzzle of colorful panels. My father pulled shades down over the windows and turned on a light inside the model. I imagined being a student going to the library at night, looking through the trees at warm window light glinting through the red, blue, and yellow panels on the sculptural wall.

My father explained to the students standing next to him. "They loved the design but they didn't want the sculpture attached to the length of the building. But that Bertoia sculpture was absolutely key to the whole design. I told them, 'No way. You take it as it is or you leave it.'"

I turned to look up at him as his voice grew more forceful. "Never!" his voice punched and his eyes pierced. I was a little afraid because he sounded so angry. "Never capitulate or change your concept to meet design-by-committee!"

My father launched into one of his lectures. "Some people are so damned narrow-minded and are afraid of modern architecture." Then he eyed me. "You know you don't use swear words!"

I nodded yes. I knew that.

He said so many people in America wanted buildings that looked like Greek temples or brick palaces, monuments on pedestals. He loved what was clean, clear, and elegant. He said, "What happens inside the building must determine the shape of the building. A building should support how people live inside it, not control how they live."

I listened carefully, intent on becoming his finest student. I went back to the white linen book of Corbu's buildings. When I was eight, I showed my father my favorite, a house that looked like a sculpture of light and shadow set in a meadow.

He pronounced the French name for me, Villa Savoye,

near the town of Poissy. "You are something special, Lilibet. It's my favorite, too."

I leaned against him and he put his arm around my shoulder as we gazed at the photographs.

I loved sharing architecture with him. I was usually stranded in a world of chatting children and practical mothers. I longed for the importance I felt when the intensity of his attention beamed on me like a spotlight. Most days, I was a quiet, awkward girl who helped her mother and told her brothers when to pick up their cars. But with him, I entered another world. The two of us enjoyed discussing the colors Bertoia chose to paint on square discs on the sculpture hanging in front of the stone wall in our living room. My mother might look at a Kandinsky abstract lithograph my father had bought during the Depression, and ask awkwardly, "Is that a boat in a storm?" In contrast, father and I would glide like figure skaters, effortlessly discussing the play of texture and intensity in the lines and spaces. I became fluent in my father's languages, yet away from his world I floated adrift, often unable to speak with other kids on the school bus. Standing in the sun on a baseball field, I was the gangly girl who was teased for never catching the ball. A desperation and yearning built in me for his company, his conversation, his attention.

I was enthralled, charmed, and captivated by my father's world, his mind and his affection. But to be in thrall comes from the Middle Ages: to hold in slavery. Being enthralled locked me to him.

As we started building the architectural model, it was much more complicated than I had imagined. My father said,

"First we line up all our tools so they are ready to use." I already had my own half-size drafting board, t-square, clear plastic flat triangles, mechanical pencil, and a professional metal compass with little tubes of replacement lead and metal points. When I was in fifth grade and we still lived in the old Victorian house, I'd asked my parents for a compass for Christmas. I didn't explain I wanted to know how to find my way if I was lost in a forest.

My father had assumed I meant a drafting compass and bought me a complete beginner's set of drafting tools. On Christmas morning, when I opened the large pile of unusually shaped presents, I was thrilled. Now I could draw plans like my father.

"Anything you draw," he said, "I'll take to the office and bring you home blueprint copies."

After Christmas dinner with our aunts, the bald uncles, and older cousins, I showed them my drafting compass with pointed legs. But I confessed, I didn't know how to tell directions with it. This brought great gales of laughter, becoming a story to be repeated as a joke on my father.

My father had taught me that Christmas day how to use my drafting compass on transparent graph paper. Pinching the compass lightly at the top, he touched the point through the paper until it pierced the wooden drafting board. He twirled the compass which pirouetted like a ballet dancer, one long thin leg pinned to the board and the sharpened lead toe stretching in a circle across the page. We drew a compass flower, with intersecting circles that etched five identical petals. I spent all of Christmas leaning over my drafting board, teaching my wobbly dancer how to twirl in circles until my technique became as precise as my father's. I glanced up at my father in his red and black plaid shirt and knew he was happy that I loved my presents.

By the end of the afternoon I announced to him as he leaned back in his Eames chair, "I want to be an architect too."

His face darkened. "I wouldn't wish that on anyone, especially you, Sugar. It's just one battle after another. You have to fight for every goddamned inch of progress you make in a town as narrow-minded and conservative as this one. I should have become a lawyer for all the fighting I've had to do in my life." He shook his head at me and his adamancy silenced my ever thinking of being an architect.

———.———

NOW, AS MY father and I set out additional tools he'd brought home from his office, I felt serious and important. His father's triangular scale ruler looked like it was made of ivory, with little lines and numbers along each edge. A sharp X-Acto knife for cutting mat board. Drafting paper and the white book in French with Corbu's plans. "First," he said, "we have to decide what scale model we want to make." He showed me the scale on the side of the paper, and turned his trisquare so it would measure centimeters. "Because the building is French, the designs are in metric scale. A hell of a lot easier to deal with than our inches, which are a pain in the butt, if you excuse my French!" He laughed as he calculated on a scrap of paper what scale we should use.

We decided that the model should be roughly about one

foot square on a two-foot-by-two-foot piece of plywood. I picked up my compass and twirled it on the board. I said, "I guess we won't need this today, building a square house."

He smiled. "We sure do need it! Look again." He pointed to a curved round wall on the ground floor, and then to a tiny circle with lines.

"What's that?" I asked.

"It's a spiral staircase, running up through all the floors. You can stroll up the ramp or climb up the spiral steps. It's really quite elegant. You'll see."

I leaned against my dad's shoulder as he plotted out the dimensions of the ground level of the house on the plywood base and explained the design.

The *pilotis* were metal posts that supported the structure. My father explained, "Corbu revolutionized how we think about exterior walls." If the posts carried the weight, walls could become nothing more than a skin over the building with cut-outs for windows, allowing a building to feel light and open. From round dowels we cut posts with the X-Acto knife and glued them in a grid, equally spaced, five posts in five lines, forming four cubes by four cubes for a square house.

It was a house designed for the modern age. "You drive up to the house and straight into the garage," he said. His fingers pretended to drive a car under the house, and turn into the garage. I imagined my father's new XKE Jag pulling in, snug in place, a sleek modern design that matched the house. His two fingers walked like little people getting out of the car and ascending the ramp into the middle of the house.

He asked, "Do you remember some of Corbu's principles for Modern buildings?"

I offered tentatively, "Make a house a Machine for Living in and Form follows Function?"

"Good girl, exactly!" He nodded, patting my arm, but he corrected me. "Not many people remember that Louis Sullivan, the grandfather of modern architecture, said 'Form ever follows function.'" That's one of the reasons my father hated Frank Lloyd Wright. "Frank Lloyd Wrong in my book," he said. In my father's view, Sullivan taught Wright everything and Wright had not honored his teacher. "But don't get me started on that!" he'd say.

He ran a hand over his bald head. "Once you get your car out of view, and come up the ramp, what do you see?" He swung both arms out in a sweeping motion. I walked my fingers onto the second floor garden of our model where it opened to the sky. Thin walls enclosed the house inside and out like white ribbons, with strips of windows that framed the meadow, woods, and Paris in the distance. He said, "You live above the cars or roads." Looking out my parents' bedroom window, my line of vision went straight over the driveway below to our vegetable gardens and trees, where clothes that hung on the line were drying in the wind. The land around our house was still raw, weeds rising out of bulldozed earth where it would eventually be landscaped with ground cover, lawns, and gardens.

Garber house, 1966

I could see the principles he had applied to our house: the garage below, the house cantilevered out on posts, an open plan of rooms, and exterior and interior spaces under the same roof. The structure was divided into equal sections by posts approximating the geometry of Villa Savoye. We parked the sports car and VW bus in the basement, the hardworking part of the house to be used for practical things. A Machine for Living in.

Our chest freezers were stocked with corn, peas, string beans, strawberries, and applesauce. The wine cellar built into the earth kept the dusty bottles cool, and the root storage room was lined with bushels of potatoes, onions, apples. The shelves were laden with home-canned tomato sauce, stewed tomatoes, relish and pickles, golden globes of peaches in syrup, and rows of jams and marmalade. The vast room of the garage was divided into sections for storage units, carpentry shop, tractor, and gardening tools. With the functional spaces hidden underground, the living space floated above like a sculpture of light and shadow surrounded by gardens, a Machine for another kind of Living.

Villa Savoye was a square divided into a grid of sixteen squares, roughly sixty feet by sixty feet. I asked my father, "How many posts do we have in a row on each side of our house?"

"Think about it."

On either side of the Great Room was a pair of long porches, each edged with three white posts, equally distanced, with an overhang at the end, just like Villa Savoye.

I had to figure this out. I ran out of my parents' room, past the galley kitchen into the Great Room.

I called out, "Where's a tape measure?"

"In the tool drawer. Make sure you put it back!"

I grabbed the measure, followed the glass wall to the heavy wooden front door. Outside, the earth smelled warm from the spring rain. At the edge of the porch, the decking was wet under my bare feet. I measured from the middle of one post to the next. Thirteen feet and a few inches. I ran down the stone stairs to the entry area under the overhang held up by another post. I measured from the *pilotis* to the wall of the house, about thirteen feet. I measured the first bay of the garage. Thirteen feet again. I walked across the gravel driveway. I looked up at the line of four bedrooms. In the end room above me a spotlight shone on Daddy's head as he leaned over the model, gluing pieces into place. Each bedroom section was the same, four in a row, all about thirteen feet wide. So our house was a grid of four sections by five sections. I walked up the grey stone steps, leaving wet footprints.

I sat down next to my dad to figure it out on paper. "Why did you make the lengths between our *pilotis* thirteen feet?" I practiced pronouncing the French word correctly. "Isn't thirteen bad luck?"

He looked at me over the top of his glasses. "Was it thirteen feet precisely?"

I shrugged sheepishly. I had rounded out the extra inches. He corrected me, "In buildings, every measurement is precise. The dimension is thirteen feet four inches from the center of each post. Now why would I do that?"

I had no idea. He reassured me that plenty of adults couldn't figure it out either. He smiled, "The secret of our house is that it is really built in meters." I remembered from school, when they taught us that someday we would use the metric system for everything like in Europe. A meter is three feet four inches, or 40".

Then my father quizzed me, "How many meters are in 13'4"?"

"Four! So our posts are four meters apart." He made a quick sketch of our grid, pointing out that our house had a narrow overhang on our east and west walls. I looked at the plans for Villa Savoye; it had overhangs on the north and south walls. He wrote out the math. "Our dimensions are sixteen by seventeen meters, or 53'4" x 56'8"."

Our house was just a little smaller than Villa Savoye. The miniature grid of bass wood posts became more real to me. I imagined I was a little figure in the white cardboard house looking out the window towards Paris. My father guided the X-Acto knife along the ruler edge, his face in the shadow, his eyes behind thick trifocals, his mouth pulled tight.

My father had never seen Villa Savoye or any of Corbu's buildings. History had restricted his generation. Getting out of architectural school in the 1930s during the Great Depression, he couldn't afford to go to Europe. Then there was the war, and it was a wonder Villa Savoye survived the Nazis. They hated modern architecture and used the house for storing hay for cows and horses that were kept in the garage. After the war, when Europe was rebuilding, my father was becoming an architect with little income and had a young family. He hoped someday to get to Europe. There were some buildings he'd like to see in person someday.

No wonder he liked going to Mexico. On a small budget, he could drive to see radical modern architecture that hadn't been stopped by the war. I imagined someday I too would leave Ohio and go to Mexico and France.

We continued working on the main floor of our model, cutting out pieces of mat board, gluing the walls into place once we cut out windows. We glued the ramp from the first to the second floor inside the house walls. The ramp continued from the second to the third floor outside, in the enclosed patio open to the sky. On the top floor, freestanding walls curved and opened to form private outside rooms full of daylight. I loved the roof garden. I asked, "Why didn't you design us a roof garden?"

I watched his pale eyebrows rise as he laughed behind his black frames. "I didn't have the budget that Corbu's clients had. And you forget how hot it gets here in Ohio!" He had raised the middle of the roof over the great room to have clerestory windows for airflow, so our house was filled with filtered indirect light in summer yet kept out the muggy heat. In winter, when the sun was at a long angle, sunlight streamed in from the high windows.

I cut out grey sandpaper for the driveway leading to Villa Savoye, under the overhang, and curving to the garage door. Woodie showed me how to brush on the rubber cement and shake on crushed lichen so it looked like grass. "We better open a window so we don't get woozy!" He stood up and put his arm around me, hugging my shoulders. "Are you happy with this, Missy?"

I leaned my head against his chest and nodded, yes.

"I'll drop you off at school in the morning on my way to work."

I could smell our favorite Sunday dinner, melting aged cheddar with beer to make Welsh Rarebit, to scoop onto toasted homemade bread. My father said, "I'll put our tools away. Go help your mother."

"I will, Dad, I just have to go to the bathroom first."

"Don't close that door, Missy." His voice was friendly but firm.

"But Dad, I'm thirteen. I need some privacy from the boys."

"Don't be ridiculous." His voice was more forceful. "Leave that door open! We aren't a bunch of Victorians who have to cover every inch of our bodies!"

"Okay, okay." I kept my voice upbeat.

I ran into the bathroom and glared at the cold walls of polished tiles of green marble stones set closely in grout. My father declared that, as a modernist, we were forbidden to close the doors, and chastised us for false modesty if we tried to sneak the solid birch door shut. The brushed steel door handle's precise click would give us away. Then I shook off my irritation, remembered the model we'd built, and hurried out to the kitchen.

In the Great Room, under one spotlight, my brother Wood was setting the table on the teak dinner table, and under another spotlight, Hubbard was writing at the round Formica kitchen table. I was excited. "Mommy, you won't believe what we made. Corbu's house is so beautiful."

My mother squinted at her recipe. She said, "That's great, Elizabeth," as she stirred melted cheese in the copper double boiler. "I just know this Rarebit is going to lump up. Do you think I need to put in more beer?"

After we cleared dinner away, I set the model on the table for everyone to admire. Spotlights shone on the little mat board house, where blocks of light and darkness floated on *pilotis* above a green field. I pointed out to my brothers and mother how people walked through the house. Then my brothers washed dishes. My father played Dave Brubeck and I leaned forward on my elbows to look through cutout windows, imagining living in my little house on *pilotis*. I turned the plywood model to see the house from every angle.

In their newest version of *Take Five*, the insistent piano rocked my head back and forth, building up a driving tension until the sax smoothed it out. I looked up. The night had turned our glass walls to silvery dark mirrors, reflecting the little white house on the table and my face above, short hair and tortoise shell glasses. My mother and brothers worked on homework at the kitchen table. Record over, the needle skipped and jolted at the empty center. "All right everybody, time to go to bed." My dad stood up and stretched. "It's been a good day."

———

THE NEXT MORNING, I stood in the driveway, holding my model house on its plywood base, while my dad backed the Jag out of the garage. From below the row of bedroom windows, I studied how our house was built into the hillside. Standing in the drive, you could see our house had two stories like Villa Savoye. I turned the model around to the side where it looked like an abstract mask, with long dark eyes above and two sections like a dark open mouth. I looked at our house and it was almost exactly the same, without the roof garden. Our ground floor had two garage doors, with empty space on either side and *pilotis* at the corners. My father took the design of Villa Savoye and slid it into the earth like a long drawer. Had anyone else ever seen this? I was shocked. My father had copied Corbu.

Woodie got out of the car and came around to my side so he could hold the model as I got in. The red leather bucket seat was a snug fit with the model on my lap. My dad smelled like shaving soap, one hand on the wooden steering wheel, the other on the wooden stick shift knob. As he shifted into first gear he said, "Hold the model carefully so I don't bump it."

I was nervous and spoke carefully. "Our house looks just like Villa Savoye from this angle." I showed him that side of the model. It was so obvious.

He reassured me. "That's what architects do. We study other buildings and their concepts, and develop them to meet the needs of the site. I took Corbu's points and made it work for our family. Good eye." He patted my knee.

———————

MY FATHER PULLED into the driveway behind the buses at Princeton Middle School on a hill overlooking Interstate I-75. He came around to my door and carefully maneuvered the plywood base out of the car. I climbed out of the low leather seat, straightened the sleeveless A-line dress I'd sewn, and took the model from him.

Some boys walking by yelled, "Man oh man, was that some kind of Corvette Sting Ray, or what?"

As I walked down the crowded hallway, past slamming narrow lockers, a group of guys in skinny black jeans, white socks and short ankle boots turned and stared. They usually never talked to me, but one guy asked, "What is that, a space ship?"

"Uh, no, it's a modern house, in France. It's for French class."

A shorter guy—I noticed his bad acne—joined in. "How could that be a house? Where's the door?"

"Well, you can't see it at first, but it's here, under the overhang."

"Sure, Four Eyes. It looks like a lot of sticks to me."

I continued on, untouched by their snickering. I was carrying The Modern like a cake, like a prize on a platter, filled with my father's pride. I couldn't see that we were all living in a kind of suspended 1950s, where the impact of the 60s had yet to arrive. Even though it was 1967, my mother still wore white gloves when she went shopping in the city. I still wore skirts to my knees at school except on pants day, which came one day a year. In Cincinnati we read about the 60s in *LIFE* and *TIME,* where we studied black and white photos of Civil Rights marchers, long-haired rock and roll bands, sit-ins, protests, like it was a story going on far away.

We didn't know that by the end of the year, cities across the country were about to shatter into violence. The social changes of the 1960s were about to slam into our privileged Midwestern backwater with an intensity none of us could imagine.

But we still felt untouched in a life that seemed un-changeable. I couldn't imagine that my father wouldn't al-ways charge into the house with his big plans and that we wouldn't always do his bidding. I thought we were already radical, which meant "modern." We lived in a glass house, for heaven's sake. We'd already changed. We'd left everyone else behind in the dust as we zoomed ahead in our father's Jag. How much more could we change?

RIOTS

1967

Architecture or revolution!

—Le Corbusier

THE CINCINNATI ENQUIRER WAS SPREAD ACROSS
the breakfast table. My parents leaned over the front page.
My father's face was tight, his lips pinched. The headlines
blazed: *Race Riots Continue 3rd Night.* A large black and white
photo showed a car on its side, burned out, windows shattered, on a wide street with stately old houses. Behind the car
I saw a brick house with a round tower. I peered at the photo
more closely. The glass door. The brick tower. That was my
dad's office, behind the wrecked car. I stared at my father.

He looked at his watch, "I left my office less than ten
minutes before those Negroes pulled a white man out of his car."

The paper explained that rioters had beat up a man who
had driven down William Howard Taft Road right in front
of my father's office, only three blocks from the University.
Then they set the car on fire. My father's car had been parked
in a small garage behind the office. He had slipped out
through the back door. He shuddered. "When will it be safe
to go back to the office?"

My father paced, looking out the glass windows across

our gardens. His voice was loud again. "I've got a gun. If anyone crosses my lawn that I've just seeded and tries to get to our house, I'll shoot them."

My mother's voice was quiet. "They are burning the places where they live and work. Things must be really bad for them to do that. They have no interest in coming out here and crossing *your* yard."

For weeks the paper had been full of talk about riots. It was a new word for me and seemed to have been taken out of a history closet, shaken out and ironed, leaving it fresh and ready to go. It slipped from lip to lip like sips of coffee over breakfast. We read about riots breaking out across the country, like an epidemic with doctors grappling with a disease, and bringing in the government who knew how to take care of it. The paper reported on quarantining the disease. Separate the outbreak from the unaffected people and it will burn itself out. But the epidemic leapt across the country, and had arrived in our city.

My father recounted what had happened the night before. He stood in the shadows of the glass doors to his office with a baseball bat. He peered out, watching the crowds surging down on the street. He smelled smoke from fires a few blocks away. Police in riot gear marched by, followed by the heavy thudding of a tank. What if someone threw a Molotov cocktail through the door where he was standing? He imagined the smashing of glass, gasoline leaping into flames racing up the stairs, setting his stacks of blueprints, plans and books ablaze. An architect's life work lives on paper until it lifts off into form.

Suddenly he decided he had to leave. He raced down the

basement stairs to the underground garage to start the Jag, a quiet rumble under the long white hood. He opened the garage door onto a back street below his office, cautiously pulling out. He quickly shut and locked the garage door, then slipped away as fast as he could. Headlights off, as if that could hide that sleek car's perfume of privilege. The back street was vacant, yet the night air was electric with shouts of rage, smashing glass, gunfire, and smoke.

He noted the time on his watch, before the car whispered down the emptied streets of Avondale, lined with sturdy three-story brick houses that had been built by German families a hundred years before. In a city under curfew, he skirted past Corryville's paint-peeling row houses jammed with students, fraternities, and families. Neon signs glowed red and blue inside darkened liquor store windows, barbershops, and corner groceries in nineteenth-century brick storefronts. Reaching the strangely empty Vine Street, he accelerated down the curving road designed by urban planners to propel suburban traffic from the densely populated hills of the city to the Interstate.

Once on the highway, adrenalin racing, he gunned the engine, letting that baby rip, eighty, ninety, up to 110 miles an hour, past the industrial wastelands of factories in Ivorydale pouring out the slippery stench of soap and detergents. Past GE factories lighting up the sky with round-the-clock shifts making bomber engines for Vietnam. Past the sprawl of new suburbs with twigs of trees propped in each identical front yard. Past every car and truck on the highway until his exit, when he slid back into the safety of the old village where he grew up, where towering oaks and elms covered the sky.

He crossed the tracks, cruised past the parade of dignified homes stepping up the hill, until he turned right at the brick firehouse. As the Jaguar curved down the hill, he gazed at the white sculpture of a house he had created, like Brancusi's finely chiseled marble Muse on a pedestal at the Guggenheim in New York. At this late hour only a few solitary spot lights glowed within, like a candle inside a lantern, waiting for his return.

This was his monument to all things modern. This was his slap in the face to the world of Victorians, to the Greek-columned edifices of his father's generation of architects, to all the narrow-minded people who tried to get in his way. This was his battleground for what was right and true. He would not lose it, no matter who he would have to take out to defend his creation.

The riots sparked a fury in my father. The Modernist radical would now pit himself against the new revolutionaries, blacks fighting for jobs and justice, women fighting for their voice, and long-haired anti-war protestors setting out to bring down the old order. He did not realize he was pitting himself against his own wife and children who, almost inevitably, each in their own way, would be joining the revolution.

———

FOR ME AT thirteen, reading the news about the riots rumbling through the city was like sitting up late on a hot summer night waiting for a tornado. Not that tornadoes were common in this part of Ohio, but when the winds blew wilder than before any thunderstorm, when threatening thunderheads turned purple and the bruised sky turned yellow, we knew something bad was coming. When night fell, we would sit out on our porches, listening to cicadas in the dark trees, radio on low, playing music quietly. The announcers would break in with bulletins, reports of sightings and touchdowns. The familiar shadows of enormous trees turned ominous. But then soon everyone would go off to bed, the storm past and out of mind. By morning our life in the suburbs seemed to continue unscathed by the riots. I left to catch the bus to school.

I crossed the field to Linda's yard and entered her mother's spotless chrome and linoleum kitchen. Her mother, with perfectly coiffed grey hair, dressed modestly in a buttoned blouse and A-line skirt below the knee, stockings and flats, was always polite and welcoming, yet I felt she was wary of me. I came from a strange modern world that had landed in the back meadow behind her house. For six years, I arrived daily, crossing her kitchen to walk with Linda to the school bus. Linda's mother scanned us like a detective, as our fashion styles changed from careful to daring, our skirts from below our knees to short, then long, while our hair grew short, then long and longer. Linda and I perfected a secret language of raised eyebrows and hidden smiles to hide our plans.

Linda and I studied our skirt lengths like advanced geometry. On the way to school, Linda would roll up her waistband so her skirt was as short as mine. Two awkward girls, we'd walked down tree-lined street like nuns, our heads bowed towards each other, our backs curved forward to carry our books, as we conferred over everything essential: how to keep knee socks from falling down, our latest sewing plans, and boys, of course.

But we were most engrossed in the study of our town, like staring at a crowded chess board, a constant study of class and race, changing block by block. On the bus to high school we noted the different parts of town: the rich mansions with a black maid or cook, the small village center with brick store fronts, upper-middle-class streets that abruptly changed mid-block to working-class whites. When the bus rumbled over the train tracks, we crossed to the "wrong" side of the tracks with working-class blacks on the right side of the street and middle-class whites on the left. Hidden beyond the trees on the edge of town were a few more mansions on sweeps of land. Studying our town's caste system, we completely forgot the city fifteen miles away, where one hundred firebombed businesses smoldered. Hundreds of rioters who had been arrested would be sentenced to serve their time in the century-old Cincinnati Workhouse.

ON THE THIRD day of the riots, my mother shifted the gears on her faded old VW bus to labor up the hill into Millvale, dreary Cincinnati public housing designed with only one road in to keep poverty hidden from view. The projects were considered so dangerous that ambulances refused to go in there at night. My mother had started volunteering at the Millvale Head Start Montessori School four years before the riots. My youngest brother, Hubbard, was three when she started taking him along with her to play with the other children while she helped the mothers.

My mother was one of the legions of upper-middle-class women in Cincinnati who joined the Junior League or the Women's City Club to "do something," to put their brains to work, to organize, to plan, to feel competent. She didn't know any women who went to a job and worked, except the one single mother we knew who was a nurse—besides, of course, the black women in Glendale who took care of white women's babies and served food at their dinner parties. These private social organizations provided myriad options for a woman to channel her energy: fashion show fundraisers to organize, panels for discussions on social issues, or hands-on volunteering. My mother felt shy and uncomfortable with the stylish women at the Fashion Show, and somehow found her way to Millvale where she preferred volunteering. At dinner my mother would tell us stories about the students and their families.

With a new edge of confidence in her voice, my mom explained how the school didn't have money for the fancy Montessori equipment that private schools spent a fortune on. She admired the teachers who made their own sand trays, letters, numbers and measuring materials out of what they had lying around. They called her "the white lady" since she was about the only one they ever saw in Millvale. The teachers asked her to figure out ways to involve the mothers who had to volunteer or take a class at the school while their kids were in the program. She kept trying to think of interesting places to take them.

She told us, "These moms don't have cars. Their girls get

attacked on the way to school. They are stuck there." In our VW bus, she took the mothers to Findlay Street Market downtown to show them how to buy fresh produce and meat cheaply instead of using canned food to feed their families.

Some of her stories were funny, like the field trip to the whiskey factory. The mothers went through the whole tour hoping to get free samples at the end. The factory didn't give samples, but they did give visitors a full sit-down lunch. The mothers were hiding food in their purses to take it home. "The factory people asked me not to bring any more field trips." My mom laughed, "We had a great time."

Around the small kitchen table, when we sometimes ate early with our mother, long before our father got home, she'd tell us about the world beyond our village of Glendale. She shrugged, "I'm so naïve and I don't understand a lot of things, but I do ask questions."

When she wondered why some people had sheets or blankets covering their windows, one of the black women, a mother at the school, looked at her like she was crazy for not knowing. "That's a drug house." Our mother found out that people boiled down Paregoric—a medicine we'd taken when we had tummy aches—because it had opium in it, and then they'd shoot it up with a needle. When she was interviewing families for Head Start, she'd go into apartments where all they had for heat were the gas burners on the stove.

In one house where children were crying of hunger, she observed their grandmother putting a white powder in their mouths. My mother asked, "Why are you feeding those babies cornstarch?" My mother repeated a line that came to her as if from a dream: "Waitin' for the red clay of Georgia." Startled, the grandmother looked at her, "How you know that, white lady?" My mother shook her head, didn't know how she knew, but it must have been a story from Cora, the black woman who had raised her.

During the riots, when my mother arrived at the Millvale Head Start to volunteer for her usual shift, the teacher looked up and asked, "What are you doing here today? There are riots going on in the city!"

My mother shrugged. "I didn't think you'd be closing school, so I came."

The teacher was firm. "I think it would be better for you to go back home."

As she walked to the VW, a few young men ran up to her. She asked, "You aren't going to hurt me, are you?"

"Oh no," they answered, friendly. "You're the white lady in the green and white bus. We know who you are. No one around here is going to bother you. We just want a ride downtown." She took them as close to Avondale as she could before they saw lines of police in helmets with heavy billy clubs. She dropped them off a block away, saying, "You be careful." They smiled back at her, "You too."

THE RIOTS CAUSED a seismic shift that split our community. I slowly realized my parents had slipped onto different sides of a widening divide.

My father's booming voice announced regularly how liberal he was, how he hired a Negro architectural student to work in his office before anyone else had hired a Negro student, how pleased he was to design the addition to the Negro church in Glendale. When he talked to Negroes in the village, they called him, Mr. Garber. He'd say, "Just call me Woodie." When Rena helped serve at dinner parties, he told her and anyone listening, "We're just like family. We go back together a long time." He'd explained that she had been a teenager when she started taking care of his father as he was dying. She smiled and nodded in her crisply ironed uniform, "We go way back, Mr. Garber. We sure do."

In southern Ohio, the village of Glendale seemed to me like places I had read about in the South. When my father had grown up in the village, many of the big houses in the village had Negro ladies in well-ironed uniforms who "lived in." Others had "day help." Now there were just a few houses where Elsie or Louise would answer the door when my mother paid a call to older ladies. As children we called all adults Mrs. or Mr., except these dark-skinned women with warm voices who brought out trays of food and ran the workings of the household. Everyone white, even children, called these Negro women by their first names. But to my black friends at school, they were "Mrs." They had never even heard their first names until we said it.

The Negroes lived on the other side of the village in a few blocks of modest houses. Since I'd been a little girl, I'd gone with my mother when she bought chunks of homemade lye and lard soap from Rena. Her children and I had looked at each other shyly, standing next to our mothers' dresses as they talked. But when Rena had helped at my house when new babies came, or for dinner parties, she called me her "special girl." She'd taken care of me since I was a baby.

———

AFTER THE RIOTS, my mother went to Rena's house to check in on her. They sat and talked on Rena's porch swing. Rena told her, "No one dared go out on the streets the three nights of the riots in the city." The black neighborhood was only a handful of streets, but the police were cruising heavily. "We were hiding in our houses, waiting it out. We didn't want anyone to think we were like those hot-headed city blacks who call us Uncle Toms."

She shook her head and smoothed her apron. "We like how things are here in Glendale. Everyone knows their place." Rena explained that they weren't happy about the *new* Negroes, who were moving in on the new street into big split-level ranch houses. "They don't know their place."

———

THAT SUNDAY AFTER the riots ended, my mother, brothers, and I walked up the hill for the ten o'clock service at the Episcopal Church. Some white men standing in front were saying in loud voices that they needed to get a machine gun to protect their church and village from "those Negroes." The next week my mother met with her friend, the Episcopal Bishop of Southern Ohio, Roger Blanchard. He told her how he wore his black shirt and white collar as he walked and talked with rioters on the streets, the only unarmed white man out on the streets, night after night, as the city burned, and tanks rolled. A few weeks later, he came to our church to give the sermon. Before he began, I heard some older people grumbling that *some* Episcopalians were getting too radical for their taste.

A strikingly tall man with a shock of white hair, his melodious voice filled the gothic arches above us as he told stories about what he heard on the streets those nights. "These men and women are rioting because of racism and poverty that we have allowed to continue." When he had confirmed me, I'd felt a shock of energy as he made the sign of a cross on my forehead. Standing at the carved podium with an ornate rose window behind him, he seemed to be looking right at me. "We need to make a commitment to make a difference."

He explained that a commitment wasn't just a nice idea, something put aside when it was inconvenient. It was a serious undertaking. He read the definition from the dictionary. "It means to be obligated or emotionally impelled." He told us that he had planned to go on a sabbatical, but because of the riots he was staying here. He had been given an office in City Hall so he could work to improve race relations and economic justice. He looked carefully at each of us, his face scanning the filled pews. "What is *your* commitment?" I turned to look at my mother. She was gazing up at him, nodding, her lips tight and serious.

My mother's life changed after she read what happened when three hundred arrested rioters were sent to the Cincinnati Workhouse. We had always been curious about the shabby castle-like building next to the new Interstate when we drove into the city. Now riots erupted at the Workhouse. The paper inaccurately reported that inmates were banging their metal cups on the bars. *TIME* magazine explained the prisoners were protesting with their pee buckets in cells built for Civil War prisoners. Some demonstrators set fire to their straw-filled mattresses to protest the conditions. Hearing about the prison haunted my mother.

One afternoon, she was driving us home in the VW bus from swimming at the whites-only private club we belonged to, the Glendale Lyceum. She was about to turn right, to go down our wooded driveway to our modern house, but she pulled over to the side of the road and didn't turn. We stopped talking and stared at her.

I asked, "What are you doing, Mommy?"

But she waved us quiet as she sat in the driver's seat staring at the driveway. Though I could hardly know it at the time, my mother was staring at a line only she could see. A line she believed was there just for her.

"Mommy?"

"Shhh. Wait."

She was looking. Thinking. Then she looked at us, at the road, at us again. And then she gripped the wheel, and we were off, slowly crossing that invisible line, toward the beginning of something––what, she did not know. But it was the end of something too; that much she did know. The end of waiting.

She knew she had to research the Workhouse, and then do something about it.

The next day she headed down to the Cincinnati Public Library. They let her go into the stacks and unwind the rolls of hundred-year-old newspapers to read about the building of the Workhouse in 1869. Eventually she started going to the Workhouse to interview women inmates, and later organized volunteers to go into the Workhouse, the beginning of her work in prison reform.

At home she told us what she was doing, but didn't tell our Dad. He often made comments about how she didn't know what was going on in the news, and told her she should read *TIME* every week like he did. She was afraid to tell him about her research, afraid he'd say it was silly. Much of the time that was easy; she stayed quiet at dinner, and Dad dominated most conversations with his frustrations dealing with the University about designs and safety regulations for Sander Hall. That dorm seemed to be wringing the joy out of architecture for him. Meanwhile, she decided the safest path was to avoid any arguments and keep what was important to her secret.

Elizabeth, Hubbard, Wood, 1968

MONDAY NIGHT

1968

We are caught in an inescapable network of
mutuality, tied in a single garment of destiny.

—MARTIN LUTHER KING, JR

ON A MONDAY NIGHT IN MAY, AS MY BROTHERS
and I set out plates and silver at the round Formica breakfast
table, Mom said, "I decided to try out these frozen French
fries I saw at the grocery store." We looked at her, amazed
she would be so daring.

Our father forbade us to ever eat fast food. "I won't have
my children eating that fried trash. Name me one restaurant
with better cooking than your mother's!" We'd never been to
one of those drive-in places near the highway. Everyone at
high school went to them. I'd pretend that I knew what their
shakes and fries were like.

Every night of the week we had good formal dinners,
except on Monday nights when we ate cube steaks or fish
sticks because every Monday our father went to the Literary
Club of Cincinnati. Formed in 1849, this was a private club
for one hundred men of the city—professors, theologians,
physicians, men of business and finance, politics. Each member
had to be proposed by a member of the club. Once invited,

members were in for life, meeting their requirements for an hour-long paper every two years and short papers on their off years. The year's schedule of meeting dates, readers, and titles of papers was printed on a small card that my father always carried in his date book.

Once when we were downtown, Dad parked in front of a small Greek Revival brick house down the street from the Taft Museum. He pointed out a small brass plate that said Literary Club on the door. I asked, "Has a woman ever gone to a meeting?"

"Never. We don't even let women serve when we have our dinners. Only at the spring picnic meeting are wives invited, when it is held at a member's house." As we drove away, I thought how strange that was, that women couldn't even touch their food. From September to June on Monday nights, our dad never missed a Literary Club. For us, Monday nights were our favorite night of the week.

When our father was home, we followed the Victorian rules of his childhood, with correct table manners and his authoritarian rule. We were becoming tense, obedient, and wary every night he was home, except Monday nights when we could relax and be ourselves. When we were home alone with our mother, it was as if we were almost equal, that all our voices and stories were respected and heard, and that it was more important to be real than to be polite. Our personal liberation began because we were simply having fun instead of obeying. Across the country, many mothers joined their children in turning against the fathers who had been raised to be strict at the dinner table. Battle lines between children and their fathers began to form over the length of hair and skirts, turning the dinner tables into a battlefield. When some mothers sided with their children, the fathers raged at their betrayal.

When Mom brought the hot fries to the table, we each grabbed a handful out of the pan.

"Ugh, they're lumpy," Mom grimaced.

"And dry," I added and shrugged.

Wood pretended one was a cigarette, took a puff and blew out the smoke. We all copied him, even Mom, balancing cigarettes like Brando. We kept blowing pretend smoke at each other as we ate our cube steaks, cottage cheese, and peas frozen from the garden last summer.

Wood looked at me and said, "You so ugly, the tears run down the *back* of yo head." He'd spent the afternoon at The Corner in Glendale, where Jefferson dead-ended into Washington, in front of the uneven basketball court, on the black side of town where long ago "the help" had lived. Wood was the only white boy hanging out and telling jokes with Otis, Artie, Big George, and Wood's best friend Boris.

"Hey, Wood, that is so funny. Tell me some more."

"Yo mamma so fat, she *wishes* she could clap."

I looked confused on that one. He rolled his eyes. "Don't you get it? She's so fat, her hands can't meet." I nodded, now I got it.

"You're the slowest person I ever knew to get jokes. You so smart, you're dumb. Hey, why are you punching me?" He looked up at our mother laughing. "Save me, save me, Jo. Elizabeth's being mean to me."

For years our father had insisted that our friends call him Woodie and then told us to call him that as well. Recently I'd experimented with our mother. "Okay, Jo, I'll fold the laundry."

She had been shocked and spoke to me sharply. "Don't be impertinent with me, young lady."

A few hours later she stood in my doorway as I was working on homework. "You know, calling me Mommy doesn't really work now that you are getting older. Besides, your friends call me Jo, so of course you can call me Jo." My brothers instantly changed over to calling her Jo, even though they were only in seventh and fourth grade.

Our father lectured her for letting the children be "too familiar" with her. She looked at him incredulously. "You've told them to call you Woodie for ages."

WOOD TOLD MORE stories. "Big George was brilliant today. He was doing the Ed Sullivan show. Lots of people can say, 'We've got a really big *shoooow* for you tonight,' but George does the whole show, all the guests." Wood imitated George imitating a Barbie girl, batting eyelashes, teetering in high heels, and talking in a high voice. "We were rolling around on the ground, we were laughing so hard."

George had been in my class since fourth grade, always funny and smart, the only heavy boy in a class of skinny kids. Now that we were in ninth grade, his humor was bitter and angry. I'd grown afraid of him. I was sure he saw right through me, that I was some stupid white girl who didn't have a clue. I hurried off to class, imagining him watching me, shaking his head and muttering, "Pitiful."

I announced, "I have a cool new friend in study hall. She's from Lincoln Heights." Cute with short curly hair, Billie Jean had joined our class when her school integrated with our high school in the fall. Lincoln Heights was an entirely black city that had been built in the 1920s and 1930s to provide housing for Southern blacks who were coming north to work in the big factories along the canal that once connected the Ohio River to Lake Erie. They had their own mayor and police, school, and stores. It was near Glendale, but I'd never known it was there. At school I heard kids say no one white ever drove through it and the town had dirt streets.

"She's as sarcastic as me about all the stupid people at school. When we want to ignore them, we speak French." By junior year, we would name ourselves the Sarcastic Bitches of Princeton High School. Billie Jean was different than the Glendale black girls I'd gone to elementary school with. She seemed more serious, and more confident.

I looked at Jo. "I wonder what it's like to grow up around just Negroes. Even the mayor and police are Negro."

She paused, thinking. She looked at me. "I bet it's a relief. Our country is a really hard place to live if you are Negro." We all nodded, feeling sobered.

She asked with a little smile, "Anyone want ice cream while we watch *Laugh-In*?"

"YES!"

"On one condition: you clear and wash dishes. My scar is really hurting. I need to rest."

We leapt to our feet. "No problem." We cleared the table and put dishes in the dishwasher. She sat at the table cradling her right side with her arm while she read the paper.

That winter I had spent a lot of time sitting next to my mother on her bed after school. She threw up a lot and lay curled up, her belly in pain. She had headaches, had dark circles under her eyes that started to look yellow. The doctor kept sending her home, saying nothing was wrong. I was only fourteen but I knew something was wrong. I sat on my parents' bed with my biology book. I asked her to show me exactly where she hurt. I puzzled over the overlapping clear pages of the organs. I was sure her gallbladder was causing her problems, but her pain wasn't on the right, it was on the left side over the pancreas, an organ I didn't understand. I peeled back the page and showed her the picture. She murmured, sounding far away, "Pancreas. That's what sweetbreads are. What we eat for Christmas breakfast. Sautéed in butter and white wine. Such a strange thing . . ."

A few days later, when we were at school, an ambulance wailed by, taking her to the hospital. They discovered she had pancreatitis from a blocked gallbladder duct. Her numbers were dangerously high. Only a few months before, a man in our town who lived across from the church died suddenly from pancreatitis. Somebody told me my mother's numbers were worse than his. I walked by his house, thinking about his wife and little children. I prayed, "Please don't let my Mommy die." Though I couldn't know it then, she did nearly die.

There was a day when the pain was so bad, she slipped out of her body and floated up to the ceiling. It was so easy. The pain was gone, worries evaporated. She didn't think about us at all. She saw her body down on the table and thought nothing of it. Then a nurse, in the strong black Ohio accent, commanded her: "You are not going anywhere. You come back. You are not going to leave your children all alone." My mother felt sucked down a tunnel and slammed back into her body. The pain was stunning.

She was in the hospital a long time. Once the infection was down, they would take out her gallbladder. When the surgeon set the date, my father said, "Make sure she's better by this summer because we are going to Mexico." He had a big building under construction, a college of nursing at the university, and Sander Hall was in the design stages at the office. He was working long hours. He stopped by to see Jo on his way home. Friends offered to bring us food, but he said, "No, we are doing fine on our own."

The boys and I missed our mother so much it scared us. Dad always seemed mad and in a hurry, if we saw him at all, before we went to sleep. At home, we didn't talk much when Mom was in the hospital. I made dinners and Dad ate in town near the office. The boys and I ate cube steaks and peas night after night. We were listless, waiting. Was Jo ever going to get better?

I washed clothes, packed our lunches, and got us off to school. I was worried and tired trying to keep up with homework from ninth grade. The house was cluttered and dirty. One morning, when I walked across the field and stepped into Linda's perfectly clean kitchen, her mother told me, "I've noticed your clothes have been on the clothes line for eleven days." I felt I'd done something wrong. "Oh, gosh, I haven't been able to get the clothes in."

When Jo got home in the spring, her long scar was painful and it took months to get better. Even as she started to cook and get groceries, something was different about her. She was with us but also seemed far away. Someone had given her a copy of Victor Frankl's *Man's Search for Meaning*. She told me that when Frankl lived in a concentration camp, he paid attention to what happened to people, how some became bitter and lost, while others found meaning. She carried it with her everywhere, reading in the car while she waited for me at ballet, or Wood at piano.

I found the worn paperback shoved under the seat with paragraphs underlined in pencil. I wanted to find out what she was thinking. I read, "Everything can be taken from a man but one thing; the last of the human freedoms—to choose one's attitude in any given set of circumstances, to choose one's own way." In her handwriting she'd written, "What will I choose?"

In mid-April on a Thursday night, Wood and I were doing homework at the kitchen table while our mother took Hubbard to a fourth grade program at school. We heard the VW drive up the drive and then there was a strange sound. Someone was crying. We looked at each other scared. Was our mother sick again? Hubbard was holding onto her as she stumbled up the stone stairs to the front door. When she came inside her face was streaked with tears. "Someone killed Dr. King." She ran past us to turn on the television in their bedroom.

Hubbard's little face was pale. "We were driving home listening to music when a voice interrupted to say Martin Luther King had been shot. Mommy started crying." He looked at us. "I didn't know what to do." We went in and sat next to her on their bed as she stared at the flickering screen.

Underneath our seemingly secure lives, my mother was haunted with questions about injustice. What would she choose?

Her searching questions would begin to propel her out of our father's solar system, into a universe of her own. We had always rotated around his life, his interests, his rules. Almost dying had changed her, breaking the magnetic pull toward all the projects our father dreamed up. She still followed his orders, carried out all the landscaping tasks he put on the list each weekend, but underneath she was thinking, starting to imagine a life with interests of her own. Eventually, when he discovered she had begun to create her own life, he saw it as an absolute betrayal.

AFTER WE CLEANED up the kitchen that Monday night in May, we scooped peppermint and chocolate chip ice cream into bowls, and headed into my parents' room to watch *Rowan and Martin's Laugh-In*. Our father was adamant that we would never watch television on school nights, only on Friday and Saturday nights. Jo wasn't following his rules to the letter anymore. We started sneaking what we wanted to do and made sure he didn't find out. She settled into bed in her nightgown, and we sat in a line along the edge of the bed, mesmerized from the first line, "C'mon Dick, let's go to the party." The characters became part of our lives: the Farkel Family, Tiny Tim, Lily Tomlin as Miss Ernestine at the phone company, Henry Gibson the poet, a weird little guy riding a tricycle and falling over, and a Nazi soldier saying

"Verrry Eeen-ter-es-ting." By the time it was over, my brothers were bouncing on the bed saying "Everybody look alive, 'cause here come de judge! Here come de judge!"

Jo called out, "Okay guys, brush your teeth. Get in bed, and lights out before your father gets home."

As my brothers and I lay in our beds, our rooms in a line, we heard his car rumble up the gravel drive. The garage door opened, the Jag drove in below us. A last double rev of the engine before he turned the key. My brother Wood called out in a loud whisper, "Hey listen to this. Yo mama so poor, I saw her kickin' a can down the street. I ask her what she was doin'. She said, 'Movin'.'"

I lay in my bed, thinking about a poor woman walking across the street kicking a can. I was trying to figure it out as fast as I could. I heard the garage door crash shut, then the basement door closed, and my father's feet were brushing up the limestone steps.

Wood called out, "Don't you get it? The can, that's all she has. She's moving."

"Okay, now I get it. Great joke, now shush, here he comes."

The solid wooden front door slammed shut. We turned on our sides in the darkened bedrooms and pretended to be asleep, as we heard our mother ask, "How was Literary Club tonight?" His footsteps were heavy. I could hear her bare feet as she hurried to kiss him.

"What's wrong, Woodie?"

"It's terrible. There was a fire in a dorm up at Ohio State. Two girls died of smoke inhalation in a high rise dorm tower. It's a damn shame."

I lay in bed, stunned. From my bedroom I could see into the Great Room, a dark cavern except for a spot of light over the entry.

"Oh, Woodie. That's awful."

His voice was determined. "That won't ever happen in my dorm!"

He paced back and forth in the living room, turning on the grid of spotlights. "We've made it so safe. No one will ever die in my dorm!"

"I believe you, Woodie, I do."

His footsteps stumbled on the wooden floor as if he didn't know where to go.

"The press is hounding me, questioning my dorm. Got calls all day. Asking me, 'Will this happen here?' It's a nightmare."

"Oh, Woodie, I'm so sorry. Why don't you come to bed?"

"I can't, not yet."

I heard him drop into his Eames chair and pile records on the stereo. Even on low, Miles Davis's trumpet played a driving blues river with Coltrane's sax the undercurrent, pulling us into a troubled sleep. Those girls, I kept thinking, those poor girls who couldn't escape the smoke in a glass tower.

Woodie rally racing, 1952

RACING CARS AND WINE

1968

*The relationship of Modernist architects to their work
remained at base a romantic one: . . . their domestic
buildings were conceived as stage sets for actors in an
idealized drama about contemporary existence.*

—ALAIN DE BOTTON,
THE ARCHITECTURE OF HAPPINESS

THE SPRING I WAS FOURTEEN, MY PARENTS INVITED
our German friends Frank and Ushi Laurens to dinner. My
father had a surprise to share with them, and we all knew it
had to do with wine. Their Mercedes pulled up our driveway
and we hurried down to meet them. Ushi's voice greeted us
like her fine perfume. "Oh Voodie, your home and your gardens are so bea-u-ti-ful this evening."

Hours before, we had dumped cartloads of weeds on the
compost pile, before parking the muddy tractor and rototiller
under the overhang. Now we saw our work through her
European eyes as the golden light of early evening softened
the raw edges of the landscaping. We saw the spreading
ground covers and not the patches of bare earth. The fruit
trees we'd planted looked like pert school girls in flowering
dresses, and a fresh crop of buckwheat gave the illusion of

grass, hiding the rough clay and stony soil my father sculpted with his bulldozer.

My mother had told me they were Jewish and had barely escaped from the Nazis. In Germany, Frank had worked for a firm involved in retooling machinery that had business dealings with a company in Cincinnati. Someone here sponsored their coming to this country in 1939. They were the only people in their families who survived the Holocaust. Arriving in this country with nothing besides Ushi's fur coat, jewels sewn in the lining, Frank now had his own company. They had become friends with my parents after they asked my father to design a modern renovation for their apartment. Frank and my father loved talking about wine and art.

When I was five, Frank and Ushi took me and their granddaughter to dinner at La Maisonette, Cincinnati's finest French restaurant. We little girls were invited to have a taste of wine along with our dinner. When I took a sip of the French Burgundy, I declared with a quiet sincerity, "I prefer German white wines."

This was met with waves of appreciative laughter and Frank declared, "You are your father's daughter."

Standing in our rough driveway, Ushi wore a tailored light wool suit, her coiffed hair like brandy swirling in a glass. I thought Frank looked dashing in his cashmere vest, dark shirt with gold cuff links, and silk tie. Older than my father, almost sixty, they looked like they had stepped out of *Vogue*. Connoisseurs of everything fine, their contained nods and discerning smiles seemed to anoint our labor with their approval. Standing on limestone slabs my father had set into place with chains, crow bars, and the bulldozer, they looked petite, both wearing the most stylish leather shoes I'd ever seen. As they admired the glossy leafed magnolia sporting its first blooms, my father's voice boomed, recounting how many bales of peat mulch and carts of composted oak leaves he needed to turn clay soil acid enough for his magnolias to thrive. Even though my father sounded confident and certain, I was sure he waited for their blessing. Next to them he was a rough-hewn bull of a man bursting out of his Mexican striped shirt and khakis, his feet naked in sandals.

My mother, in her late thirties, wore a sleeveless fitted dress made from a Simplicity pattern she had sewed on a little Singer at the kitchen table. She had remembered to scuff off her mud-stained Keds at the last moment and slipped on dressy sandals. Her Mexican silver necklace, like chain mail, wreathed her long neck. Her tan face was lovely without a trace of makeup, and her dark hair was stylishly short.

Frank turned his kind attention to my younger brothers with their matching bowl haircuts, button-down shirts and their good jeans, and asked about their plans for summer vacation. Wood, at twelve, with a sensitive face, said he was reading the Captain Hornblower series about life at sea. Turning to nine-year-old Hubbard, already as tall as his older brother, our father recounted how Hubbard had accidentally driven the front bucket on the tractor right through the fiberglass garage door.

My father said, "We were furious with him. 'How could you do this?'"

My mother added quietly, "We had forgotten he was only six years old."

Then Frank turned to me with a kind smile, speaking in

his German-accented voice. "And you, young lady. I think soon you will be needing your first ballroom gown. I promise to give that to you when the time comes." I was tall, and awkward, yet in his presence I felt lovely. I blushed with pleasure.

My father interrupted and led us up the slate steps to the house above. From now on he would be the conductor of the evening with the house as his symphony, and we each performed as if responding to his baton. The sunlight poured across the oak floor and reflected on the walnut cabinets. Chinese red panels circled the room. Pre-Columbian Mexican statues lined shelves next to the fireplace, their Mayan and Olmec stone faces watching us next to my father's small crucifix. Glinting over the piano was a five-foot-long bronze Bertoia 'Cloud' sculpture. With the sliding doors open to the breeze, the house felt like an airy pavilion. The Swedish designer Bruno Mathsson's teak banquet table was set with Mexican woven placemats, German Arsberg china, and paper-thin Finnish wine glasses.

My mother had been anxious about preparing a meal fine enough for Ushi, Frank, and my father's expectations. My brothers and I had picked peas, fresh lettuce, and herbs from the garden. I'd helped Jo blend leeks and add cream to the soup, and while she marinated steaks in Côtes du Rhône and garlic, the wooden salad bowl overflowed with greens tossed with our father's favorite oil and vinegar dressing. The Danish enameled bowl, black with a red interior, brimmed with chilled Vichyssoise sprinkled with chives.

Over dinner, between careful spoonfuls of soup, Ushi asked, "Voodie, Frank tells me you once had a Bugatti. How have I not heard this story?" She turned her lovely face toward his. We all looked up eagerly, as my father beamed with pleasure.

My father always drove sports cars and he had raced cars before I was born. His style was rally racing on gravel roads cross-country, not on a paved circular racing track. As children we learned to recite the names of the cars he'd raced. The Alpha Romeo 2C was an old-fashioned, one-seater racing car. He'd bought the first Jaguar XK 120 roadster to arrive in the U.S. after the war. We had a big black and white photograph from a race called the Bellfontaine Hillclimb, with his Jaguar in the air with only one wheel on the gravel road. Even though he was wearing a helmet, I could see he was smiling.

His favorite car was the last one. He smiled at Ushi. "That was my true love, my purple Bugatti." When I was a baby, he had to stop racing to have time for his family and work. His last Bugatti he would eventually sell to a museum.

His voice filled the room and he gestured with his arms. "Bugattis are truly a work of art. I'd been searching for one for years." He told us the history of the Bugatti family, Ettore and sons, and their skills in design and engines. As he spoke about them he picked up an Italian accent and quoted Le Patron. "'What kind of cars inspire this devotion? Are they dead silent, smooth riding as mobile featherbeds, quick to start in the blackness of zero mornings, so easy to drive that a child can manage them? *They are not!* Most Bugattis are noisy in every way a car can be noisy.'"

Our father had carried a photo of a Bugatti in his back pocket for years. Finally he found one for sale from a guy who had to sell it to save his marriage. Our parents flew to Philadelphia to pick it up and drive home. "We thought it would be a joy ride."

Our mother shook her head and smiled.

Woodie pretended to pull off a tarp and his face looked like the car was in terrible shape. "I was worried your mother would doubt my sanity, but she was loyal." They left an hour later, the car paid for, with an owner's manual in French, even though my father didn't know a word of French. They started on the long drive back to Cincinnati.

Our mother smiled at Woodie. "Within a few miles my feet were burning from engine heat." Green oil started streaming down the fender to her right, and she was scared. "Woodie, what in the world are we going to do?'"

Our dad sounded like he was back in that car, his voice growing louder in the joy of the story. "The exhaust noise was deafening. The fumes were choking us. The water temperature was heading towards steam!" They turned towards New York for the nearest mechanic who could work on sports cars.

Our mother paused to pass the salad. "And then the rain started." She described how the windshield was at such a sharp angle it left a gap between the glass and the hood. It poured a waterfall of oily rain on their heads and laps. Their clothes were ruined. She laughed, "At least the car kept us warm, too warm." She shook her head at the craziness of it all. My brothers gazed at my mother with awe, imagining they were in the car too.

Our father exclaimed, "My left shoe was soaked with burning oil coming from the engine. I had to take it off and put my foot under my right leg to protect it."

He said to us, "The next day was Saturday, your poor mother's twenty-second birthday. She was such a good sport." He reached for her hand across the table and squeezed it fondly, before continuing. Frank and Ushi smiled their appreciation.

My parents spent the day in a garage with a French-speaking mechanic, trying to get him to understand to do just the minimum so they could get home. "We didn't have much money to pay him." Our father nodded for our mother to continue the story.

She explained, "In the afternoon we left with two cases of oil. I'd found us raincoats at an Army Navy store." She spoke to the boys, "Your dad put down a sheet of asbestos on the floor to protect us from the engine heat."

Heading west, they kept stopping because the car boiled over. They had to keep refilling the oil. Then the sun came out. Spring in the mountains of Pennsylvania. She grinned, "It was a perfect birthday."

He continued, "And then the fun began." My father's bald head was glowing with beads of sweat under the spot lights at the table.

A baby blue Cadillac sedan with steer horns on the front and silver stirrups for door handles had pulled alongside them on the highway. That couple thought our parents in raincoats in the purple Bugatti were the funniest thing they'd ever seen this side of Texas. They accelerated to pass. Our father looked at our mother and she nodded. "I put down the accelerator and stayed right with them. The guy in the cowboy hat looked over at us and started to look annoyed. He tromped down on his accelerator with a roar, and we stayed right next to him, effortlessly. Then we sailed on by with a wave. At that moment, we knew the Bugatti bug had gotten us."

My parents smiled at each other like I remembered when I was a child, in a way I hadn't seen them smile for a long time. Our father whispered to us all in a stage whisper, "I didn't tell her that 195 kilometers an hour meant we were going 120 miles an hour." Our lovely mother smiled and pretended she didn't hear him.

Then he looked at me and my brothers sternly. "Now don't you do that when you start to drive." We looked at each other and knew we all wanted to drive fast too, someday.

Ushi clapped her hands appreciatively, "Bravo. What a marvelous story."

———

AFTER MY BROTHERS and I cleared the dinner dishes, our mother brewed coffee and we served dessert. She had ordered an Austrian torte made at Woodie's favorite old-world restaurant, Lenhardts, in Clifton. Countless thin layers of hazelnut cake were layered with whipping cream, laced with slivers of strawberries and topped with whole berries. As we took our first careful bites with heavy three-pronged Stieff silver forks, my father told Ushi and Frank a story about the source of the mystery dessert wine he would be serving.

He had heard of a vast wine collection that had to be cleared from Mr. Jergens' cellar, of Jergens lotion fame. He had died and his mansion was being sold. The wine experts from La Maisonette had deemed the French wines worthless and didn't bother to look at the rest. The executors said whatever bottles anyone wanted, they'd sell for fifty cents a bottle. My father had to check it out. He drove into the city in the VW bus and brought us all along. The wine cellar turned out to be the whole basement, stone-walled, heavy-ceilinged, stone-floored, and filled to overflowing with bottles. We stepped down the stone steps, ducked under beams, avoiding light bulbs swinging on wires. We explored the maze of rooms, all deep-shelved, with heavy wooden structures for carrying their weight in wine. My dad discovered that behind each bottle there were more, going back in time. Wooden and cardboard cases, unopened, were stacked in every corner.

We'd watched our father disappear into the shadows, hunched over to save his bald head from hitting the low beams. His voice echoed through the stone cave, as he enthused, exclaimed, and mumbled questions to himself. Wiping off grime with his now-filthy handkerchief, he squinted through his trifocals as he lifted bottles to the light, checking for sediment, condition of corks, the vineyard, region, and vintage. We heard him swearing under his breath, "Damn, the cork has gone to hell," or "Oh, my god, priceless." He filled boxes steadily and waved for us to lift and haul them up the stone stairs to the van.

Soon my brothers and I searched for treasure of our own. I don't remember who found the stack of cases of 1929 champagne. Our dad was too busy to pay attention, but our mom who was born in 1929, laughed, "What a trip." She pulled one out of the case, pushed back the crimped metal, slowly inched the cork upward with a worried look. She was afraid the cork might pop and hit her, but it didn't even fizz. Nor the second. But the third cork flew off and bounced off the ceiling. We cheered and she handled us the bottle to take a little sip, like we did Christmas morning when we had champagne with sweetbreads for breakfast, or at weddings. We cheered, "Wow, cool. It's bubbling." We carried box after box of our own treasure up to the VW bus.

Woodie spent days in that cellar, filling the VW bus to the ceiling before driving on the highway out of the city to our house. We lugged box after box into the basement, filling his modest wine cellar to overflowing, each bottle an education. His *Encyclopedia of Wines and Spirits* lay open next to his bed, fluttering with marked pages. He was an archeologist sifting back through layers of history. My father was always the hero, delivering his stories as if he had discovered the ancient city of Troy. And we all sat back that night, willing to be enchanted. For tonight's dinner party, he brought out the prize to share with his friends, his fifty-cent trophy, to return the favor of the fine wines Frank and Ushi had generously shared with him out of their wine cellar.

———·———

HE REPEATED A story he'd taught my brothers and me about Auslese wines. "German wines," he smiled to all of us, "as you well know, are grown in a harsh northern climate where the hills are steep and the soil rocky." He explained how, when there is a summer without much sun, there will be no sweetness in the wine. But on a good year, he pronounced, the German wines will be finer than any southern wine. Ushi and Frank smiled politely, knowing my father was making this point because their collection was mostly French. It seemed they had a playful competition between their French and his German wines. But my mother told me that they avoided everything German because of what had happened to their country and to them.

Under the spotlights at the table, as the gardens beyond faded into darkness, the glass wall turned to mirror, reflecting the group of us as my father continued. In the fall, in the finest vineyards, the men who climb those hills for the harvest carry three small bags with them on their chest, in addition to a large sack for ripe bunches of Spätlese grapes. My father gestured like an actor. I watched our reflections, our heads lit from above, leaning towards his sweating face. He mimed a hand picking the overripe grapes and placed them into the first bag on his back. We knew these were to be made into the buttercup-yellow, delightful Auslese we'd had many times.

"The more shriveled ripe grapes, touched by the noble rot, Edelfäule, are placed into the second smaller bag. They are to be made into the golden Beerenauslese." He pronounced the German with gusto, but I worried how his German, remembered from childhood Sunday dinners at his grandmother's table, sounded to Ushi and Frank. "The rarest grapes, raisinated on the vine," he showed like a puppeteer with his fingers, were small and withered. He put them into the tiniest bag over his heart. "These grapes," his voice rose dramatically, "will become the pinnacle of German wines, the rare and treasured," he pronounced it slowly, so we could hear three words put together, "Trocken-beeren-auslese."

He displayed for us a grimy, chilled bottle. The stained label crumbled at the corners. Trockenbeerenauslese. 1929. He had researched this. "A very good year, if it is still fit to drink." He found cases and cases of this treasure stashed away in a dark corner of Mr. Jergen's cellar. We were held spellbound in the wonder of his discovery, a secret he'd saved for this evening. He lifted his well-worn brass corkscrew to the task. My youngest brother held the bottle steady as he began to spiral down through the soft cork, dark and stained at the top, screwing it down to the hilt, as the brass arms rose like wings. My father placed his hands on either side, and gently pulled down the wings, prying the cork away from the surface of the liquid gold it had guarded for forty years. The cork emerged. The wine was intact, unspoiled.

He wiped the lip of the bottle and poured a taste into the first glass. 1929 Gold Trockenbeerenauslese. He handed it to Frank, who held it to the light. I thought it would be golden and clear like an Auslese. Instead it was deeper, darker, like the burnished shell of a chestnut. He swirled it and breathed it in. It was viscous, clinging to the edges of the glass like a liqueur. A tiny sip. He nodded with a look like pain and pleasure at the same time. My father poured all of us a small sip.

My heart was pounding to taste something priceless. The thick weight of elegance slipped across my tongue. I knew I was too young to appreciate it. I didn't know if I enjoyed it. It was difficult and heavy, like a crescendo of chords from Shostakovich. Perhaps it was otherworldly like ambrosia, meant only for the gods on Mount Olympus and not for us mortals. Ushi and Frank looked at each other over their glasses with sadness. I wondered if they tasted a world that had disappeared; a time when they were young and life opened with the freshness of dew in their garden. We raised our glasses to the light and toasted the deep bronze impossible sweetness.

SUMMER OF '68

The modern movement is a story of high hopes,
boundless optimism, innocent social idealism and
considerable hubris in which the artists, architects and
artisans of the world would make it a better place
through a radical new kind of design.

—ADA LOUISE HUXTABLE,
"MODERNISM, IN PERSPECTIVE,"
THE WALL STREET JOURNAL, JULY 12, 2006

MY FATHER'S FIST POUNDED THE DINNER TABLE, shaking the water glasses. "We've run every layout we can come up with to keep our concept and fit the smaller area the University is demanding. They are squeezing all the beauty of the design out of it. I keep fighting them on this, but they won't budge."

After the race riots in 1967, the University had promised the community of Corryville that they would not encroach any more on their homes and businesses. This meant the University had to build high-density student housing for projected enrollments. That's why Dad had to design one very tall tower, twenty-seven floors, instead of three smaller dorms to house all the students. The University Committee said they liked his concept of clustered suites, but it was cheaper and used less space to build a dorm the old way, with long halls and rows of rooms. If Woodie wanted to cluster the rooms, he had to fit them into the square footage of the traditional dorm. He came home discouraged. The doubles were squeezed down to two hundred square feet. His frustration reverberated throughout our house.

Before building permits were given, before foundations were blasted out of bedrock, before the building grew from the blueprint rolls, his design for Sander Hall was already controversial. He slammed *The Cincinnati Enquirer* on the table, day after day announcing each new round of headlines. They claimed the building was a fire hazard, like the Ohio State tower where two coeds died. But after several studies, new headlines blazed. *Sander Hall Judged Safe.* The Building Commissioner was quoted, "I'd let my son live in the dorm."

My father's face got red, sweat gathering in the wrinkles on his forehead under the bright light of the dinner table. His eyes glowered behind his trifocals as he swore about everything he was doing for these kids. Captive to his explanations, we knew not to make a sound or to look away as he shouted, "I designed this building specifically so no smoke can reach the dorm rooms. I have fresh circulating air coming directly into every single god-damned dorm room." His fist hit the table, rattling the silver and china plates, as he punctuated his design points. We nervously nodded our agreement.

Then someone would pass the green beans, ask for more salad, and we'd remember what we were interested in. My brother Wood, who at eleven read voraciously about ships and life at sea, exclaimed, "Did you know the thickness of battleships in World War II were only this thick?" He held his fingers in a narrow gap of air.

Our father immediately jumped on his words. "You're dead wrong."

"But Dad, I just read it in a book. Sure some walls were really thick but some were this thin, so shells would go right through them and not explode."

"Show me the book. That thickness is impossible. Don't you think I know how thick the walls of a battleship are?" When my brother was silenced, the attack continued.

He glowered at his namesake. "You have no work ethic. You never apply yourself." This was an echo of lines we'd heard for years, but his ferocity of attack increased that summer. "You have no integrity."

Wood stared at the table, his shoulders slumped forward. The bowl cut my father had given him was rough and uneven, like a punishment.

Woodie continued, "Why won't you do better in school? Is it willfulness that you don't even try? Why do you sabotage my every effort to improve you?" He demanded, "Answer me."

Wood couldn't speak. None of us could. My mother nodded for us to clear the table. We left Woodie at the table making angry sketches with his marker pen that tore the paper napkins, the ink leaving tiny blots that stained the teak table. We slipped away to our rooms.

———

WHEN WE WERE young and lived in the Victorian house, we all ran to meet Woodie and kiss him when his sports car roared in the driveway. Here we did the same but it was because we were required to, and it seemed he couldn't get away from us fast enough. He had to walk the boundaries of the land, to watch his creation in every angle of light, and to determine what work we had to do next. Beauty became a cruel taskmaster.

Beauty confronted us everywhere we looked, as if the house and gardens had a voice. *I am symmetry. I am elegance. I must be perfection. I am a place to observe the snow falling on either side of my transparent walls of glass. I am an aesthetic experience for watching late afternoon sunlight trace through the clerestory windows.* When we glanced up from weeding in the vegetable gardens, the precise series of windows mirrored everything that was unfinished, the raw incomplete gardens. The house and our father became one, clamoring after us: finish the gardens, finish the spiral granite terrace. I must be complete. The human clutter had to be hidden in drawers or closets. Every surface was to be kept clear to show the sleek design. It was a place for a dazzling life, not the ordinary tedium of homework, housework, or reading the paper. We were trained so we would know how to live in a modern house.

The house was the pinnacle of my father's success, his monument to every concept of modern design and living he revered. Did we both love and fear this house, admiring the lines and perspective the way we had been trained by our father to appreciate a fine racing car, a stunning sculpture, or a priceless bottle of wine? The house was Beauty more than it was Home. Did the house demand his attention so fully, so jealously perhaps, that he couldn't see clearly who lived inside? For the creator of the house, had we become a distraction or a detraction to his monument?

———·———

ONE NIGHT AT a dinner that seemed unusually calm, I made sure I used perfect table manners, as I held the heavy silver fork, keeping my left hand in my lap, while our family ate roast beef and the first salad from our garden.

I had planned my strategy carefully, casually announcing, "Linda and I want to get our ears pierced this Saturday at the mall. I've saved up the money from babysitting so I can pay." I smiled and nodded. Showing him how responsible I was.

I continued, laying the foundation of my argument. "The really great thing about pierced ears is that you don't have to worry about losing earrings. Maybe you want to do it too, Jo?" I glanced at each of my parents. My father gave her magnificent Mexican silver earrings from New York City or from their trips to Mexico to look at modern architecture in the 50s. She had a drawer of polished hoops, dangling shapes, clusters of shimmering droplets, and layered circles like chain mail that matched her necklace. She screwed each earring tightly to her earlobe to make sure it didn't get lost. If one did pull off unnoticed, we searched everywhere, heartbroken over its loss. I'd been given a few simple pairs that I carefully screwed into place.

I added my final points with a flourish, "Since I'm just starting to wear earrings *and* because we are going to Mexico this summer, it seems like starting out with pierced earrings is a sensible choice. Don't you think so?"

That summer, after the garden was planted and we got our vaccines, we would leave for a six-week trip to Mexico. We would be seeing ancient pre-Columbian ruins and modern poured-concrete buildings by the Spanish-Mexican architect Candela, who had inspired my dad to build soaring roofs based on hyperbolic parabolas. But the trip was not just about architecture. Our dad enthused about hand-woven rugs in Saltillo, black pottery in Oaxaca, and described the twisting narrow mountain road to the beautiful little town of Taxco, the silver capital of Mexico. That was what really excited me. I had saved my babysitting money for a year to buy silver jewelry.

At school, all the girls were going to the new shopping mall's jewelry store where they felt a flash of pain and were left with a gold stud imbedded in their earlobe. After weeks of conspicuous ear dabbing, their ears emerged decorated with hoops or studs in bright pink or purple. Nicer girls wore small gold balls or pearls on their earlobes. That's what Linda and I were going to do. All we needed was to get a parental permission slip signed before we headed to the mall.

My father's answer came swift as a stroke of a guillotine. "You will not pierce your ears. Your body is not your own until you are twenty-one. After that, you can do what you choose, even though I don't approve of pierced ears."

I was stunned. My body was not my own until I was twenty-one! It was his? I glanced at my mother, but she was staring down at the table, slowly shaking her head. Claustrophobia closed in around me. The conversation had been closed with a slam.

I looked down at the table, my eyes stinging. Then I

glanced at my brother Wood and rolled my eyes. "He's so controlling," I muttered.

"What did you say, young lady?" His words lashed me.

"I said that you were so controlling."

"You are god damn right I'm controlling." He glared at me and sweat gathered in the wrinkles on his forehead. "I'm an architect. I have to watch every detail every moment on my buildings. If I let down my guard for one moment, if I make one mistake, someone could die or a building could collapse."

I resisted rolling my eyes, and thought, "Yeah, right."

Then he pointed his finger at each one of us. "I watch you kids like a hawk too. For your own good. Somebody's got to do it around here." He glared at my mom. "I don't want you kids going down the tubes like all the hippies I see all day at the University. Getting into drugs. Dressing like sluts. No work ethic. I won't have it. No child of mine will look like that."

My mother became numb and silent at the table. She stared down at the table like we did. We didn't get mad at her, or expect that she should stand up to him or fight. She was our sanity, our safe place, our kindness in the glass house. We were devoted to her, feeling like she saved us from him all the time, even when she went silent and froze up and couldn't help us. Sometimes it felt like she was one of us. She was trying to survive, just like us, trying to keep out of his line of fire, just like us. Her father had also been a tyrant, lecturing at the dinner table, and our mother slipped back into her childhood survival strategy of the invisible daughter. She was one of us, slowly becoming rebels, each in our own ways, against our dad.

Then he glared at Wood. "We've got to cut your hair, young man. It's getting too long."

I was relieved to have the pressure off me, but shrugged at my brother, gesturing "sorry" with my eyes.

In my father's childhood in the 1920s, only prostitutes and lower class women pierced their ears. No one from the middle and upper classes would ever pierce their ears—it was "unclean." Women's clothing and lives were under the lock and key of their fathers. Strangely, my father was fiercely enforcing the doctrines of his childhood. Even though he claimed to be Modern and Liberal and Radical, he was determined to squelch any signs of the new revolution in our family. He kept cutting my brothers' hair too short with his electric clippers.

Under the accelerating pressure of the late 60s, as the Tower loomed over us before it was even built, my father was turning into more than an echo of his patriarchal German father. Our grandfather Frederick was known for swiftly thwacking the back of the carving knife onto the elbow of any son of his who dared lean his elbow on the table. Children were to be controlled and lectured into submission.

I knew I'd complain to Linda about my dad's rules and we'd laugh it off. She'd say, "Your dad is such a character." But the claustrophobia stayed with me, made me feel sick. Years before, when my father showed us the finished plans for our modern house, there was my room, with two single beds, the desk, the closet, the bookshelves to be built in. Even the half moon of a chair was drawn in. My room was all planned out. Everything in this house was his design. Couldn't I have any place that was just mine? I felt the pressure closing in on me as I looked down at the dinner table. My body was not my own, but his. Little did I know yet, what this could mean for me.

Something had happened to our family after we moved to the glass house. Now we were trained to never say no to him. We knew we could not speak the truth. We gave over our freedom, because there was something fearsome in him we dared not challenge.

———

MY FATHER CHANGED the subject and turned to my brothers. "This summer, boys, keep an eye out for ground-hogs. I'll get the gun out so we stay on top of them this year. We can't let them get into our gardens."

My brothers looked at me and grinned.

"Groundhogs," I groaned.

My brother, Wood, had read that groundhogs are hard to trap since they have a lot of tunnels. If you chase them down one hole they are likely to come up any number of other holes. Last summer he'd waited, watching a hidden entrance. When the mother came out and sat on her haunches he put a clean shot through her head with the .22. He ran up to the house, calling to me, "I don't know if I got it. Will you come look?"

I said, "You aren't going to trick me into looking at any dead groundhogs this year." They all laughed, remembering my screech when I saw the trickle of blood and chased Wood back up to the house. Even though he liked playing a joke on me, when he saw it dead, he felt sick about it and stopped hunting them.

My father eyed him angrily. "You aren't going to wimp out on shooting groundhogs this summer, are you? Remember all the work we put into growing all our seedlings and planting them." All spring, between the table and the living room area, my father had set up a huge metal structure, with layers of shelves and grow lights that made it look like a glowing space ship in the window. Dayglo-green forests of baby leaves rose toward the light. He was scientific about their temperature and watered them with special fertilizers. Then we'd hauled all the trays out to the garden, transplanted them and watered them regularly until they got established.

Eight-year-old Hubbard piped up immediately to distract him. "I'll shoot them this year."

"That's my boy." My father patted his youngest son on the shoulder. "You are such a great hard worker, Hub. You put your brother and sister to shame. They just don't have the same work ethic you have." His young face beamed with the compliment yet glanced at us with an embarrassed shrug. We reassured him with a glance. We acted like we didn't care what the Old Man thought of us.

THAT SUMMER WE went to Mexico with another architect, his wife, and two children in a long camping van. We five kids played cards as our parents rotated driving thousands of miles, coast to coast across Mexico. I kept a journal and recorded our expenses and mileage. My mother tried to cook while we drove, but she clutched her still painful scar as my father took winding curves too tight, throwing us out of our seats. We climbed over newly-poured concrete buildings at the university in Mexico City, and over ruins in the Yucatan. We climbed up steep temple steps, and stared at carved faces on stone walls. We bought tortillas by the kilo, bargained at the market, and made bowls of guacamole in our camper bus. I loved my embroidered blouses and silver earrings from Taxco, hoops and dangles with screws to hold them tightly to my earlobes.

WE CAME HOME to August's heat and the 1968 Democratic Convention in Chicago, where protests against the war in Vietnam became a bloody battle against Mayor Daley's police and the National Guard. My brothers and I sat with our mother in front of the television at the edge of our parents' bed every night watching the convention. On the black and white screen, we watched riots, shootings, tear gas, police with dogs attacking long-haired hippies and clean-cut college students not much older than us, who ran away with blood running down their arms and faces.

My father snarled at the television, "Just shoot them all," and stormed into the living room to put on big band jazz, a wall of horns loud enough to drown out the ominous rumbling of soldiers hitting batons against their shields before they turned them on the students.

She stayed up for the eleven o'clock news. I woke up to the muted sounds of gunfire. I stood in the doorway to their room, saw my mother's face, pinched and drawn, shaking her head, her face haunted.

My father listened to the chanting students' voices saying, "Kill the pigs." His voice boomed, "Bunch of freaks. They deserve what's coming to them."

My mother watched him. That was the moment she knew: the marriage was over. But it would take years before she had a plan, the courage to leave our glass cage, and a way that she could support herself and us.

One afternoon, my mother and I were weeding, our backs curved as our legs straddled the rows of green beans. The garden had overgrown with weeds when we were in Mexico. Working side by side, we moved down the row, talking as we pulled out handfuls of waist-high pigweed towering over the beans. She asked, "Remember that game your dad played, where you had to guess the color of the stone?"

A game with stones? I was shocked. I thought the stone game was something he played just with me, something special he and I shared.

"He told me to close my eyes and handed me the stone. How the hell would I know what color it was?" She had started swearing a lot more since I'd become a teenager.

She continued, "So I said 'Green.' But when I opened my eyes, it was this boring grey stone. I just didn't get it. Here I was with four children under six, with three in diapers, a dying child, and he wanted to know what color a stone was when it was clearly grey!" She stood up straight, shaking her head with irritation. She stretched her back to see how many more rows we had to weed.

I felt sick. My favorite childhood memory lurched into an uncomfortable new awareness. I yanked on a tall pigweed and it broke off in my hand.

My mom glanced over from her row. "Pull it slower so you get the roots."

I kept my face down, feeling nauseous. How many people had he handed a stone, asking them "What color do you feel in the stone?" I thought that was our special game. I grabbed and pulled another weed, steady and satisfying as the long roots released. I tossed it in the bushel basket and grabbed another weed. Was this game one of his many tests? To see who could play creatively with him? I had passed my father's test and my mother hadn't. What made me feel sick was that, years ago, I had wanted to win. I wanted my father to think I was smarter and more interesting than my mother. But now I didn't want his special attention anymore. I never even thought to let my mother know what this had become.

———•———

THAT FALL, MY mother started going to meetings about social change and the criminal justice system. She'd leave dinner on the stove for us to eat when Woodie got home from the office. My brothers and I cleaned up the kitchen. He read in his Eames chair and played records while we did our homework. At bedtime, he said good night to my brothers. One night, he stood at the door to my room. "Time to finish up with your homework. You know you need a lot of sleep if you're going to be any good on your test tomorrow." I agreed.

I hurried to the bathroom to brush my teeth and change into my nightgown. I tried to slip into bed and turn off the light before he noticed. But he came back, his white shirt unbuttoned at the collar from taking off his bowtie after work.

He turned the light back on before he sat down on the side of my single bed.

"Let me give you a back rub to help you go to sleep." His voice was thoughtful, like this was a good thing I should appreciate. Back rubs had been part of our life with our father since I was a little girl.

———·———

I REMEMBER SUNDAY mornings when my brothers and I climbed onto our parents' bed. My father and I would look at architectural magazines and the boys would drive their little cars across the covers. One day Dad said, "Let's see how sensitive you are." He took my hand and with the tip of his index finger, he touched mine. "See how your fingertips rise in little mounds. That's very good." I looked at my fingers and saw tiny mountains I have never seen before. His fingers touched my fingertips and I felt little tingling fires in my skin. Looking at my fingers up close I saw little swirls like brush strokes across my skin.

He explained, "Not everyone has sensitive fingertips like you do. Some people have flat round fingers and don't feel much. I always make sure my new architectural students have sensitive fingers. You can't design buildings without sensitivity." I thought of all the things his students had to be good at.

Daddy said, "I know you are very sensitive because of your fingertips." I felt special, but a little worried. What if I didn't have little tips on my fingers? Would he still have loved me?

He taught me. "You can take your fingertips and touch someone's back and it feels really nice." He moved his fingertips across my arm. "See how good that feels. Now you can try doing that on my back." He turned over, naked under the covers, and re-arranged the sheets. I practiced moving my fingers in little circles and lines around the moles and freckles on his back. He said, "That's good, Sugar." But after a while I got bored and looked out the window. He said, "Pay attention to what you are doing. Make your fingers lighter." When our mother came back from the kitchen with coffee, he thanked me before sitting up to drink coffee with her.

When my brothers and I were older, we sat around my father lying down on the big bed, each of us running our fingers over his wide back. Sometimes they ran little trucks or cars over his back, making *rummm-rumm* noises. When they went too fast and started crashing into each other, Daddy would say, "Enough of the cars. If you want to get a massage, I'll time how long you massage me." We built up credit. For every five minutes we massaged his back, we got one minute. It took a long time to save up for our massages. Sometimes on weekends, we got bored and looked at the funny pages with one hand while we made circles and lines on his back waiting for it to be our turn.

When it was our turn, we pulled off our pajamas and lay on our tummies. His big warm hand moved from our head in long strokes down our backs, across our bottoms and down our legs to our feet. He was careful not to tickle our feet. Then we rolled over and he gave us a front rub over our chest and belly, skipping around our pee-pees and going down our legs. Then it was all over. We called out, "Are you sure our time is up?" "I'm sure," he said. Then we ran off to our rooms to get dressed.

When we get older and lived in the modern house, my brothers stopped going in to my parents' room when he lay in bed all day. Then he would call out to me, "Lilibet, come give me a back rub." I always went. I had already learned, without ever being told, that I could never say no to my father.

Now I was fourteen and he said he was going to give me a massage. He said, "Let me help you with your nightgown." He lifted it off over my head. I lay down on my belly, shivering as he pulled the sheet and cover down to my feet. He stroked his wide palm over my back, buttocks and legs in long slow sweeps down to my feet. Even though massages are supposed to be nice things, I couldn't relax. I held myself tight. I hoped it would just be a back rub and not a front rub. But after a few strokes down my back, he always told me to roll over. Of course I did. I was trained to be obedient, compliant, to do what I was told. We all were. Obeying what he told us to do for a few more years.

Now I had to look up, the light above my head shining down on my desk. I didn't want to look at his face. I stared at the ceiling. He sat beside me, his hands stroking from my shoulders down around my breasts over my belly, along my hip bones down my legs.

He said things in such a normal way. "Your body is developing so nicely. Your hips are filling out, which will be good when you have a baby." I tried to shrink my breasts away from his touch. He spoke like he was doing a good thing. "I won't touch your breasts or your nipples. You don't have to be afraid. You have a beautiful body. You should feel good about being naked."

I stared at the ceiling, saying in my mind, I hate this, I

hate this. The voice in my head got louder. Don't touch me. Don't touch me.

His hand circled my belly, and moved close to my pubic hair. I jerked away. "Don't worry, Sugar. I won't do anything to arouse you."

I said to myself, I won't feel anything. I will freeze my body so I don't feel anything. He stroked down my arms, the hollows of my shoulders and back around my small breasts.

I said, "I really need to go to sleep now. Thanks for the massage, Daddy."

"You're welcome, Lilibet." I sat up and lifted my arms so he could put my nightgown back over my head. I pulled the flannel gown down to my ankles. He tucked the sheet and blanket around me, and kissed me on the forehead. He walked to the door, turning out the light. "Night night, Lilibet. Love you."

"Love you too, Daddy." I pulled the sheets and blanket tight around me. I pulled my arms on either side of my body, making my body rigid. I wouldn't feel anything. I stared up at the ceiling, holding my body like a frozen princess. Once I heard my mother's VW come in the driveway after her meeting or class, I fell asleep.

This became a ritual that started when I was fourteen, and continued, when I was fifteen, and continued, when I was sixteen. Each time it happened, I would forget it in the morning. I wouldn't think to tell anyone, never my best friend or my mother. It was just one of the weird things that happened in our family. It was just something I had to endure until someday I would leave home.

AMNESIA

All architecture is shelter, all great architecture is the
design of space that contains, cuddles, exalts, or
stimulates the persons in that space.

—PHILIP JOHNSON

EVERY TIME I WALKED AWAY FROM A BAD EN-
counter with my dad, a strange amnesia wiped the slate clean.
If I had a week away from home or even a day's distance from
my dad, the old script, the memories of my adored father,
stepped in and it was as if nothing bad had happened.

One afternoon when I was angry, I tried to understand
what was happening to me. Why would I forget the bad
things that happened with my dad, the yelling, the touching?
How did my mind wipe those memories clear? I looked up
the word 'amnesia' in *Merriam-Webster's Collegiate Dictionary*:

1. *loss of memory due to . . . shock, fatigue, repression*
2. *a gap in one's memory*
3. *the selective overlooking or ignoring of those events or acts*
    that are not favorable or useful to one's purpose or
    position.

I read the words at my long Formica desk, under the wall
of windows looking towards our gardens. Then my mother

called me to set the table for dinner. By the time I returned to my room later, I'd forgotten my anger, the word 'amnesia,' and the bad things that happened. My mind was wiped clear, again. I had a happy family, I mean really. Sure my family was unusual. We weren't boring like lots of other parents. Our house was amazing. I flopped the dictionary closed, burying the word 'amnesia' into that dark maze of words on thin paper.

———

I TRAINED MYSELF from an early age with two urgent assignments; I had to save my parents, each in a different way. With my mother, I often felt older than her, being a serious little girl watching her try to figure out how to keep house, how to entertain. Now it seemed she was growing up with us. I was helping her, encouraging her independence, taking her shopping, teaching her how to chose her own clothes. I corrected her when she mispronounced words when she read aloud to us. She had left college with relief at twenty to get married, but now she had gone back to college to study criminal justice. I listened to her read her first papers and cheered her on.

With my father it was more complicated. No matter what was happening to me, no matter how bad it was, I still felt a deeply rooted requirement to keep my dad happy and alive. When there were good times between us, when we talked about a new sculpture or about racing cars, I was flooded with an engulfing love for him. I felt like a child gazing at him filled with adoration. A daddy's girl. But when times got bad, I somehow survived by managing my memory. I sorted my memories of my dad into three boxes.

There was the cool stuff that crowded my memory bank, providing me with stories to tell about my life. Driving me and my best friend to school in his Jag. The sculpture he brought home. The Kandinsky lithographs he'd bought when he was poor and living in New York when he was just out of school and paid for them at $3 a week. How he cooked out of James Beard and Julia Child cookbooks when everyone else's mom cooked out of Betty Crocker. Being the Architect's daughter and knowing about buildings. Learning to sail the twenty-five-foot racing catamaran. Never mind that he took us out sailing the first time in gale-force winds, terrifying my mother, who couldn't swim.

As a teenager, that was so cool. I loved the wind. I loved being out on the trapeze slung out over the waves rushing below me. My mother was scared of so many things. She was so scared of thunder and lightning she'd sit on the stairs with us when we were little kids and sing songs. I wasn't. I'd sit at the window and watch it all. My dad wasn't scared. When I was a little kid, he raced cars on weekends, rally-racing on dirt roads across country. I loved the photograph of him, airborne on a curve in the XK 140 Jag. "That's my dad," I'd tell a friend.

There were the "He was kind of crazy" collection of memories. How quickly we erase pain. How quickly nightmares disappear with morning. Oh, yeah, my dad would get down and stay in bed a lot. But other times he was excited about things and was the most exciting, interesting person you'd ever heard. That's how people talked about him. "Oh yeah, Woodie, he's a bit nuts, but what a great architect!" Or they'd say, "You either love him or hate him." I guess if everyone else thought he was okay, then he must not be too crazy. And isn't everybody's family kind of crazy? My parents didn't get drunk and stumble around, like some parents I knew. Now *that* was awful. I guessed we were lucky.

Those times he went to bed, our mother said he was tired, he'd been working hard. He needed to rest. But a weekend in bed became a week, and then longer, and we got used to it. "He'll be better soon," she'd say.

When I was fourteen, our family had been invited to an afternoon party to meet Eileen Ford, the head of the famous modeling agency in New York. My father had known her from debutante parties when he was in college. My mother, my brothers, and I were all dressed and ready to go, but my father lay in bed on his side reading architectural journals and smoking cigarettes.

I felt desperate to meet this icon of fashion, hoping I might be discovered. My mother kept us busy picking up the house, folding clothes, doing homework while we waited. Every so often she would go into the bedroom. I'd hear her cheerful voice say, "It's time to go, if we want to get there in time." Another hour would go by before she tried again, her voice upbeat, pleasant. "It's getting late, we need to get going."

The day of the Eileen Ford party, my brothers and I stayed out of sight, waiting. The afternoon ticked by. More phone calls were made. "We're still coming. We're running late, so terribly sorry." I kept hoping we'd go, until the afternoon light greyed, and the day ground down into dullness. The last call, "I'm so sorry we weren't able to make it." My mother made dinner. We sat quietly around the table and she took his dinner in to him. I passed by his bedroom that night.

At his bedside, a glaring spotlight on a folded-over page, his long shadow stretching out the door.

My mother had explained to me that my father was Manic Depressive, that he had highs and lows. Lows were when he couldn't get out of bed, and highs were when he would say he was as high as a kite, bringing home stacks of new jazz records he'd listen to all night, or the finest Japanese or German cooking knives, a new Bertoia sculpture, or the Jaguar. That's what I thought it was, highs and lows, you get used to it, you normalize it. It's just the way my father was.

Finally there was the weird stuff. But even that fit in with the kind of crazy stuff. He was modern. He was against everything Victorian. He thought we shouldn't be shy and embarrassed about our bodies. That's why we are forbidden to close the bathroom door when we're in the bathroom. That's why he walked naked around the house, even though it's a glass house with no walls in the living room. He told us there are nudist camps and he had wanted us to go. He even showed us a magazine with pictures of nudist camps. Gross. Weird. But other people do that too, so. So.

Well, it must be okay, then, to require us to be naked when we went on vacation on an island in Canada. He said, "Here's our chance to be naked all day, in the wind. It's so beautiful and natural." My best friend Linda said, "That's crazy," and she wore her bathing suit. That night when my brothers and I lay in bed on our stomachs, our sunburned bottoms burning, she giggled.

And when he put his hand under my nightgown every night to slide over my bottom when I kissed him good night, he was checking to make sure I wasn't wearing underpants.

He said we need our bodies to breathe at night. It was all about being healthy. He wanted us to love our bodies and see how beautiful they were. That's what he said, when he gave me a back rub and then a front rub. See how beautifully you are developing. It was weird. I just had to lie there and get through it. He didn't do it to anyone else. I was sure of that. My brothers were okay. Then I'd go to sleep. I never thought to tell my mother. She was off at meetings. The next day, I'd forget it all, chatting with Linda about homework on our way to the bus. I tried not to think about it.

Each time I left home, I'd quickly forget about the crazy and the weird stuff. I'd just talk about the cool stuff. My dad. "Wow," friends would say, "he's so cool." And when I was with my dad, I tried to have a great time like we always did. Tried to keep him upbeat and happy and excited about the things he loved, and then it was better for all of us.

SUMMER OF '69

We shape our buildings; thereafter they shape us.

—WINSTON CHURCHILL

AS I SHIFTED DOWN THE GEARS IN THE VW BUS and pulled to a stop in front of the Corryville Rec Center, a heavy waft of chlorine hit me. At fifteen, with a learner's permit, I'd driven into the city on the highway with my Dad. He looked at me approvingly. "Great job, Lilibet. Once you learn to double-shift down like a racing driver, I'll let you drive the Jag."

"Really? The Jag." I was shocked.

"Someday, Sugar, someday. You've got a lot to learn first."

I glanced at my watch. "Time to go teach my swim class. Bye, Dad. Have a great day." I jumped out of the driver's seat.

He walked around to the driver's side of the bus and gave me a kiss on the cheek before getting in the van. He waved to the director of the Rec Center, walking towards us in front of the crumbling concrete city pool surrounded by ten-foot-high metal fences. He said, "Have a blast!" before driving off to walk the Sander Hall construction site a few blocks away.

"Sorry I'm late, Mr. Flannigan. My first time driving this far! Guess I'm still a little slow!"

"Hey, that's cool, that's cool." A wiry man with a large

afro grinned at me, the skinny white girl from suburbia in a hand-sewn sleeveless dress. "We haven't opened the gate yet." Crowds of kids were climbing up the metal mesh fence and shaking the gate. "They are going nuts to get in the water. Another hot one! That pool isn't going to be much cooler."

"Yeah, it's another hot one." I nodded, blushing. My first day, he guessed I was a college student. I wrote in my journal that he was as cool as a cucumber.

He looked around at his team, two life guards and three of us swimming teachers. "Hey, ready to go?" We all nodded and he opened the gate. A cheer and stampede of kids of all colors ran to crash into the water. As the only white girl there, I was afraid I might say something stupid and offend someone.

At my training for the job, the white woman from the Recreation Commission had said, "You have to keep these kids at arm's length and stay in control." But the kids just wanted me to play in the water with them.

"Miss Garber, look at me do a big ole cannon ball."

"Miss Garber, look at me put my head underwater."

"Miss, Miss, Miss." They climbed on my shoulders, hung on my arms, threw their arms around my waist. "Miss, Miss, look at me!" Mondays and Wednesdays all summer. I taught swimming classes and then they had free time to play.

Two hundred kids in water two feet to three feet deep. All morning in the hot sun. Afternoons we closed the pool for lunch break and the team had a break upstairs in the rec room. The muggy, dark room was lit over the long padded pool table, where teenagers leaned over cue sticks and shot endless games of pool. Miss Jackson taught me to play pool, and I was thrilled when I beat Mr. Flannigan my first practice game. Thrilled by the click and roll of heavy balls slinking into pockets.

This had been my dad's idea, for me to learn about the real world. I had suggested working at our local private club where we swam all summer, the Glendale Lyceum, but he said he didn't want me being treated like hired help in our town. He said people there can be vicious with the help. I thought maybe they might be that way if you were Negro, but I didn't think they'd treat me that way. But he said, "Absolutely not." Then he found me this volunteer job.

In 1969, Corryville was a predominately African American community punctuated by burned-out buildings and empty blocks like broken teeth, remains from the riots two years before. The University had devoured the town block by block, razing whole streets of brick row houses for a stadium, parking, and my dad's dorm. Urban renewal projects tore out more blocks and rerouted roads and plotted highways through the poor neighborhoods. Sander Hall dorm was slowly rising to tower over the community.

Most days Dad drove his new BMW because he had to carry around a lot of architects who were flying in to tour his buildings. As we commuted into town, I asked, "Sorry, Daddy, I don't mean to be rude, but would it be okay if I read in the car? Extra credit summer reading before junior year. It's so thick but I love it."

He glanced over. "What's the name of the book, Missy?"

"*Five Smooth Stones.* Have you heard of it? About a black man growing up in New Orleans."

That summer, it seemed we were all practicing saying "a

black," ever since six Negro men from Lincoln Heights had come to our church to present "The Manifesto Addressed to the White Christian Churches and Jewish Synagogues in America" for five hundred million dollars in reparations for the cost of slavery and racism. I watched the seated congregation, women in summer dresses and hats, men in summer weight suits, some faces serious, some furious, some nodding with concern. The six men read the statement out loud. The funds would be for buying land for evicted farmers, printing presses and TV stations for Black Americans to have an alternative to white propaganda. At the end they chanted "Brothers and Sisters, We are no longer shuffling our feet and scratching our head. WE ARE TALL, BLACK, AND PROUD!" Some people stood up, angry, sputtering, "Who are you to demand money from us? Don't you see all we've done for you?"

I was proud of Dad when he stood up. "We have no idea the kind of violence that Negros face every day. This is important for us to begin to understand."

In the car, I continued explaining the book. "The hero comes North to go to college to become a lawyer. He falls in love with a white woman. He tells her it's too dangerous to get married. But she's sure they'll be ok. "

Woodie nodded. "He's right. It's a terrible risk to take with all the racism in this country." I'd seen a photograph of a black and white couple in *LIFE* Magazine surrounded by hateful white faces. On the cover of this book was a painting, like a Klimt, of a biracial couple with their arms around each other. I never imagined that in two years my first love and I would stand together the same way in front of a mirror, gazing at ourselves.

Dad was on his way to give a tour at The College of Nursing he had designed; it was next door to the Rec Center. I said, "Just park at the College. I'll walk over to the pool."

I didn't want to be seen getting out of this expensive car when I got dropped off at the Pool. Didn't want anyone to think I was a spoiled rich kid.

One day I pointed to the Nursing School across the field to Mr. Flannigan. "My dad designed that school."

"That's cool," he nodded.

"It is, I mean, really cool." I stumbled awkwardly to explain about the crushed white stones pressed into epoxy panels that reflected the sun. I pointed, "And those levers move to block the sun to keep it cool inside."

"Man, we could stand for some of those over here!" He laughed and then looked towards the campus. "But seriously, who ever thought to put that big ugly tower on campus? We're no New York City! It's like the Man hanging over us, casting a big shadow across our town." We turned towards campus, to see cranes on the top of the tower, hauling materials up to the top. "It keeps getting taller and taller, like the Tower of Babel. When will it stop?"

I stared into his handsome, serious face. I'd never thought people wouldn't like my dad's tower. I hadn't imagined how it affected people living next to it. In the beautiful painting at Woodie's office, the dorm was shown with trees and grass around it. It didn't show the crowded, nineteenth-century four-story apartments on Jefferson Street across the street.

I offered, "It must feel like a big intrusion on the neighborhood."

He added, bitterly, "What's left of it. Okay, back to swimming lessons."

———

MY JOURNAL FROM 1969 shows a culture in flux and the changes slowly seeping into our life at home. I planted fifty-four tomato plants, countless pachysandra to cover hillsides, weeded for days in ninety degrees, and spent all my babysitting money on fabric to sew mod outfits on my Singer sewing machine. My father got crazy over the groundhogs and put rags and gasoline down the hole to burn them out. My brothers were disgusted. They said he burned the babies to death and the mother ran out another hole. My best friend got tipsy on champagne at a neighbor's outdoor wedding while I got moody and sarcastic. We continued on my father's grand plan for landscaping around the house: "August 3rd. It's a relief when the weekends are over. We are presently building a little canal on the west and north sides of the house. Digging out earth, digging up rocks, and dumping them. Wow—my back has never hurt like this."

At thirteen, my brother Wood was growing his hair longer so he could tuck it behind his ears. He spent afternoons making gunpowder with his best friend. On a hill in our yard he was trying it out, blowing up his collection of car and ship models he'd spent years carefully gluing together. I complained to my mother. "Isn't using gunpowder against the law?"

"Oh, Elizabeth, it's just fine. Just as long as they don't blow off their fingers. And I made your brother swear he wouldn't." She laughed. "Relax. He can do what he chooses to do. It's fine." Our father would have forbidden it and yelled at him, but my mom had been developing a philosophy with us. She would say to us, "I trust your ability to make a decision. Just walk it through first. Once you make your decision, I completely support you, even if I don't agree with you."

That summer I became lonely without realizing it, hungering for a deeper connection. My best friend, Linda, adored my family and went with us everywhere, on vacations or swimming, or helped us garden. She knew some things were weird in our family. When my father sometimes answered the door stark naked except for *TIME* magazine in front of his groin, she'd say, "Hello, Mr. Garber, is Elizabeth home?" as if this was the most normal thing. She'd laugh it off. "Your dad is such a character." She sighed, "You have the best family." We conferred on clothes and sewed constantly. Our latest project had been the *Seventeen* Magazine Model Search. We made outfits, took black and white photos of each other posing on granite boulders in our gardens with my mother's Brownie camera.

But I had a secret side I didn't understand. I apologized in my journal about getting upset about things. Linda started leaving and waiting until I got over being grumpy. Intense moods came over me. I was consumed with feelings and wrote my first poem. One moment I'd been happy to show off a new outfit I'd sewn to my friends, and then in the next I couldn't stand chatting. I suddenly was aware we were standing on a planet spinning in a vast universe of planets and suns. How could people act like nothing was going on? I saw my life from a telescope and a microscope at the same time.

Everything changed, and writing in my journal seemed to be the only thing that helped.

After I sobbed over *Five Smooth Stones* when the grandfather was killed, I sat up late reading *The Autobiography of Malcolm X*. Spending two days a week all summer volunteering at the Corryville pool, the contrast between the inner city world and my village seemed so intense I could barely stand it. I couldn't talk to Linda about this or about my summer's crush on Mr. Flannigan, which I noted in tiny, almost invisible handwriting in my journal.

———·———

SOMETHING WAS HAPPENING to us in the glass house; something was happening to our life, to me. One summer evening after dinner, I felt antsy, strangely uncomfortable. I slid open the sliding door and called out, "I'm going for a walk. Back in a while." The muggy heat smothered me after the cool dry air in the house. I was sweating by the time I stepped off the deck and walked across the yard, crossed the stone slab bridge across the stone stream my father had sculpted out of the clay soil. I passed through the orchard we'd planted to the little hill my dad had made with his bulldozer, placing a rock slab on top. I wanted to look at our house, the gardens, our life. From a distance I hoped to gain some perspective. To try to see what was going on.

I didn't wander around the village at night looking at all the big houses lit up, like a lot of teenagers did. It was as if a leash held me to the borders of our property and all I could do was watch our life under glass, where my family passed under the spotlights in a blur of movement. We were so exposed living behind glass walls, but we also seemed invisible, buffered by this land around us. Who really knew what was going on in our house? I looked at my bedroom window when the desk light shown down on my books. I wondered if anyone watched me from the outside like this. I yearned for someone who would someday really see me, the real me, the secret me.

———

SUMMER WEEKENDS MEANT landscaping with Dad. He stood astride the bulldozer, shouting orders over the deafening roar as he leaned his head to avoid the plume of blue diesel smoke. Even though this was the 'little' bulldozer we called Peanut, it was slowly lowering a two-ton granite curbstone we had helped him wrap with heavy chains around the nine-foot blade. My brothers and I all wore leather work gloves too big for us, afraid of those chains holding onto the granite, afraid the hook of metal might give way, the chain might slip, the chains might crush our hands or arm or leg. I was fifteen, Wood was thirteen, and Hubbard was ten. The Ohio summer damp heat drenched us all in sweat.

Jo left early every Saturday for her first college class in twenty years. At forty, she was going back to school, taking a class called an Introduction to Corrections, at St. Xavier. She loved the class, even though Woodie got mad every Saturday morning. "We've got gardens to build! Why are you leaving?"

She answered calmly, "Remember you asked me to start

working part-time? I've got to go back to school first." She waved happily as she drove off.

Woodie roared at us, "Is the curb straight?"

Wood and I eyed the slab, adjusted the pry bars to press against it. I shouted back,

"It looks good."

"What?" Dad shouted, as the bulldozer's engine revved louder.

We each gestured with one hand, thumbs up.

Dad's reddened face and bald head nodded at us, sweat streaming down his neck through clay dust and grit. His bare chest was sunburned, dirt streaked, his khaki pants soaked with sweat around the waist. He held onto the knobs controlling the blade as he leaned forward to peer into the trench.

Hubbard stood ready with a shovel load of sand, to toss it in to stabilize the slab when we positioned it into place. At the end of the long covered porch, Wood and I held six-foot pry bars in the trench to guide the slab as Woodie lowered the unwieldy granite toward the trench we'd been digging for weeks in Ohio clay.

Clay hardpan: yellow, gravel-studded, and impenetrable. Woodie repeatedly slammed the bulldozer blade into it, trying to crack it open. If the blade slid, the hardpan smoothed hard as marble. But if he backed and filled and came in at an angle and hacked into it, it would crack. We stepped in with pick-ax and mattock, breaking and digging, shoveling out crumbling clay and gravel until we made a twelve-inch-deep, eight-inch-wide trench. We measured and dug to level, over and over, until the trench extended around the perimeter of the porches and the end of the house, over 150 feet of trench.

Now granite curbs weighing from six hundred pounds to two tons were fitting into place, like puzzle pieces in my father's grand plan.

We would spend five years transforming overgrown woods and fields tangled with grape vines and poison ivy into acres of Japanese-inspired gardens. My dad often bragged that it was fifteen years of his offspring's childhoods. The house would be bordered with granite, with rounded stones inside. There would be a stone slab bridge over a "stream" of white river stones edged with dwarf conifers. Granite boulders he found alongside farmers' fields in Prebble County, northern Ohio, dropped by the glaciers, would be set into the gardens. We would plant 1,500 pachysandra to create masses of ground cover, and a thousand hemlock seedlings on hillsides to create living privacy screens. After five years of work, expanses of lawn would lead to distant streams and stones. It was a "work in progress," or "design as you go," he explained to visitors. His stacks of legal pads were filled with notes and drawings, his books on Zen temple gardens were studded with book marks, and plant books and catalogues fell over in piles next to his bed.

Some of his inspiration came from being a great scavenger. The granite curbs were brought by dump trucks from urban renewal projects as they ripped up Upper Vine Street in Corryville. When my dad found out they were dumping the granite into the river, he talked to the foreman and paid to have the drivers bring the loads out here to dump on our land.

Dump trucks carried cobblestones from Third Street, downtown, so we could build a stone spiral patio thirty feet in diameter. Each stone was thirty-five pounds, and most were gummed with asphalt we had to chisel off before each stone was set into a leveled bed of seventeen tons of sand. Woodie announced this was Jo's project to do with us. "It's good for you to have your own project to feel proud of."

Later she growled to us kids, "Just what I need, one more project! He's trying to keep me home doing more work." But she was obedient, and even though we groaned and complained, we didn't mind working with her because we'd talk as we worked. We kept busy on her project steadily on hot summer days for three summers until we completed the spiral.

Dad got the village of Glendale to bring truckloads of oak leaves they picked up from raked piles along the streets, dumping down a hillside in our yard, forty tons of leaves a year for four years. When we were younger, the first year, we jumped in that pile of leaves and slid down the hill, not knowing that after it had compacted and broken down into rich leaf mulch, we'd be shoveling and hauling it out by the wheelbarrow load to plant evergreens in mulch to offset Ohio clay.

———·———

AS WOODIE LOWERED the slab into the trench, we were all feeling confident. This was slab number three. Four curbstones a day was our record and the job was almost done. Jo would soon be home from her summer school college class. Then we'd have lunch and a break in the air-conditioned house, before we would see our friends.

Over the rumble of the bulldozer, Wood glanced at me for a second. "I'm thinking about BLT's for lunch."

I kept peering down my crowbar, eyeing the slab as it edged lower. "Great idea! As soon as this gets into place, I'm making us some iced tea. We have to take a break!"

Hubbard groaned, "I'm so thirsty. How come you always make the tea? Why can't I make the tea?"

"Wood, stay focused!" Woodie shouted from his throne on the bulldozer above us.

My brother glanced up, looking mad, and shouted, "I am!" while he muttered under his breath, "God damn him!" He leaned hard against the pry bar to direct the curb stone into the bed of sand.

"Hub, start tossing in the sand!" Woodie directed. As the sand flew into the hole, he called out, "Atta boy!"

The curb settled down into the trench, inches from the bottom. We had to get the chains out. The bulldozer was left trembling in neutral, as Woodie clambered off, grabbed my pry bar, shouted directions to each of us, orchestrating the unhooking of chains. We each hauled out the heavy links as two tons of granite slid into place on the bed of sand. We stood back exhausted and relieved. We'd done it again.

But Woodie leaned over to measure and yelled, "Hell, it's off by half an inch at this end." He threw his whole weight against the bar, and then something happened. The butt of metal hit his forehead, and he began to fall back, in slow motion, like a huge tree going down. We stood, stunned, watching his big tall body forced by gravity to sit down on the edge of the porch. His hands went limp, let go of the bar, before his chest and head slumped sideways onto the wooden planks. Blood began to well up from the rip in his forehead.

Hubbard cried out, "Is he dead? Is Daddy dead?"

I took charge. "Daddy's not dead. He'll be okay. I need your help. Fast." I looked into their scared faces. "Hubbard, get a towel in the bathroom. Get it wet with cold water. Wood, turn off the bulldozer. Be careful the front loader doesn't jerk."

I climbed off the porch to move the pry bar out of the way, leapt back up to put a shirt under his head. He looked scary pale under his sunburn, sweat streaming across his face as blood seeped down over his forehead and past his eye. As soon as Hubbard brought me the towel, I knelt down and held it firmly over the wound. I somehow knew I had to stop the bleeding so it could clot. The bulldozer shuddered silent. A relief of silence billowed around us as we stared at our dad, his hulk sprawled over the porch.

"Hubbard, go look at the clock. How soon will Mommy be home?" He dashed off again.

Then Woodie groaned, opened his eyes and looked at me. "What happened, Sugar?" He tried to sit up.

"Daddy, take it easy. Let's slow down the blood first. You really banged your head."

I turned and whispered to Wood, "Get a glass of water."

I looked down into my father's pale face. "Dad, I think I should call an ambulance."

Even though his voice was weak, he shook his head. "Hell no! I'm a tough old goat. It'll take more than this little bump to stop me."

By the time Jo got home a half hour later, the bleeding had stopped. We'd helped Dad stagger into the house to lie down. We spread towels over his side of the bed and he lay there with a cold washcloth on his head.

He told Jo, "You'll be so proud of our daughter. She was calm, cool and collected. I'm impressed. The boys too. They did great." He looked at each of us standing in a ring around the bed. "Time for lunch, and . . ." he paused. "You can have the afternoon off. You deserve it."

———·———

MY MOTHER WAS busy that summer. She read about a government grant program in the newspaper and she decided to raise matching funds for a federal study to investigate the Cincinnati Workhouse. She built a team, ran meetings, and planned fundraising events. She found out about a radical play called *The Cage*, about life in prisons, that was traveling around the country and would be performed in Cincinnati at Playhouse in the Park that fall. The man who wrote the play and the actors had all been incarcerated in San Quentin. She arranged for them all to come to our house for a reception and to talk about prisons as a fundraiser for the grant. I went to see the play with my parents.

I sat in the dark in the front row at the little theatre in the round. On stage in a jail cell, black and white actors were guards and prisoners. They acted out strip searches, men getting raped, and guards beating them up. Under the spot lights, I watched sweat dripping down their naked chests. One man had a scar on his back, another on his face. The theatre went dark. As the audience clapped, I was shaking.

The next evening our house was ablaze with theatre spotlights streaking red, blue, and yellow shadows on the fireplace wall. We had helped Jo cook all day, stuffing and rolling hundreds of grape leaves with a filling of rice, lamb, and dill. We laid out platters of food, served glasses filled with wine, carried plates to and from the kitchen. We watched the actors as they shook hands with the guests and talked about the situation in American prisons.

Then one of the actors came up to me and asked if I had a record player in a quieter room. He had *Abbey Road,* the brand-new Beatles album none of us had seen yet, under his arm. I nodded, and tipped my head, *follow me.* My brothers and some of the actors slipped away from the crowd into my corner bedroom. Once we closed the doors, it was quiet and dark with only a desk lamp on. He set the record on the turntable with box speakers. There were eight of us, the black and white ex-cons settled around the room, on my twin beds, and on the desk. My brothers and I sat on the rug leaning against my closet, awed to be included, as we listened to *Abbey Road* for the first time. The music was strange and cool.

We all listened, our faces serious, nodding our heads with the music, trying to figure out the words and rhythms. In "Come Together," there were words I thought had to do with being black, shoe shine, and Muddy Waters. John's voice chanted, punctuating each word, "One thing I can tell you is you got to be free." We nodded our head with the beat. Then the chorus kept returning, "Come together—right now."

We could have been a play. The cultured voices from the party in the glass room, and three white children sitting at the feet of the ex-cons, listening together in the near dark. At the end of the song, one of the men said, "Damn, that was something else."

We all nodded. "Yeah." It was.

THE HIPPIE

The architects of the Modernist movement . . . wanted
their houses to speak of the future. . . . They wanted
their armchairs to evoke racing cars and planes,
they wanted their lamps to evoke the power of
industry and their coffee pots the dynamism
of high-speed trains.

—ALAIN DE BOTTON,
THE ARCHITECTURE OF HAPPINESS

A ROBIN'S-EGG-BLUE VW MICROBUS CHUGGED UP
our driveway on a late summer weekend in 1969, as my
brothers and I washed and polished Woodie's Jag, his new
BMW, and our green and white VW bus. We sprayed mud
off the tractor tires. We stopped and stared at a painting on
the front of the approaching VW, a larger than life portrait
of an Indian guru with a long white beard and hair flying
outwards, like the sun's rays. On the roof were a dozen very
long sapling poles. Even though it was the Sixties, in Glendale, Ohio, the only hippies we'd ever seen up close were in
the special Woodstock Edition of *LIFE* that summer. We
gazed with astonishment as a petite young man with a soft
mustache and a fuzzy brown ponytail got out of the bus. He
walked up to Dad, put out his hand, and said, "You must be
Woodie. I'm Chuck. Jo invited me to come visit."

Jo had told us about a C.O., a Conscientious Objector to the war in Vietnam, who worked with bishops and rabbis at an inter-faith coalition in the city. He helped her edit letters to judges and politicians about prison reform and was the fastest typist she'd ever seen. Twenty-year-old Chuck now looked at the car my dad was waxing and asked, "Is that the new BMW Bavaria? It's the six-cylinder, right?"

Dad lit up. "I don't usually go for a sedan but I have to ferry around a lot of clients these days to show them my buildings." He laughed, "But I'm not suffering. This baby could cruise at 120 mph all day if I had the Autobahn to drive on instead of these ridiculously low speed limits."

Chuck nodded, "I hear they are built for cruising in the Alps—great suspension."

My brothers and I glanced at each other and stared at his bell-bottom jeans, jean jacket, and tee shirt. Usually Dad made nasty comments about dirty lazy hippies.

Chuck looked up at our house and observed, "What an interesting American variation on the European International Style. Jo said you were an architect. Are you a student of Le Corbusier?"

My father was charmed. "Jo's at a class but please, join us for lunch." He led Chuck under the overhang and up the steps to the main level of the house.

Chuck didn't reveal that the house took his breath away, but he would later describe it as ascending into a glass pavilion surrounded by exquisite gardens. As a child of a typewriter repairman in Cleveland, Chuck had studied the Sunday paper's Modern 1950s house designs, drawing his own crude floor plans and elevations. He was ten when he read about the Guggenheim opening in New York, and bi-cycled to the library to learn more about Frank Lloyd Wright. After graduating from high school, there was no money for college and no thought that he could ever study architecture. He started working as a bank accountant until Selective Service ordered him, as a classified 1-O, to perform two years' alternative civilian service, which brought him to Cincinnati. His first year he worked as a hospital orderly carrying bedpans, making beds and taking bodies to the morgue. A series of events led Chuck to work as a secretary for a social action agency. My father was the first architect he'd ever met.

As he entered the great room, Chuck admired the indi-rect light from the clerestory windows. He added, "I love the design of Eero Saarinen's Womb chair."

Woodie nodded. "We've had that chair since before Elizabeth was born. She grew up in it. I had it recovered when we moved into the house."

I glanced at Chuck, somewhat unnerved. I was disap-pointed in myself. I hadn't known the designer of my favorite chair.

My father fired commands. "Elizabeth, get out the leg of lamb from the refrigerator. Hubbard, go out to the garden and pick some ripe tomatoes and a bunch of basil. Wood, go down to the wine cellar. Hmm. Let's see, which bottle?" He paused and assessed this young man wearing moccasins. "Do you enjoy a good bottle of wine?"

"Oh yes, I've just begun to learn about wine."

"Okay, then. Wood, get out a bottle of the 1961 Château Cantenac-Brown Merlot." He explained it was a Bordeaux in the Margaux family, which we drank for the best occasions, but he wanted something more affordable for a good luncheon wine. Chuck nodded with interest as our dad took him on a tour of the house. I carved slices of lamb, leaving a crackle of garlic and rosemary on the thin edge of fat. I set the table and added a dish of our mother's homemade mayonnaise and slices of whole wheat bread she'd baked that morning before class.

Over lunch Chuck turned to the boys. "What are you interested in?" Dad listened quietly as Hubbard and Woodie, at age ten and thirteen, told him about their car collection they arranged in an old glass case.

"Are they Matchbox cars?

"No," Hubbard explained, "No, they are Corgi cars, which are bigger, three or four inches long instead of two." He explained how they saved up money every year for when we went to Canada on a day trip from our Grandmother's farm outside of Buffalo.

Wood explained, "We buy one Corgi each. Sometimes our dad gets some bigger scale cars. I'll show you."

Chuck stood in Wood's room next to the case as the boys pointed out the Duisenberg, the Model T, and the Woody Ford.

Hubbard pointed proudly. "Our dad used to race these cars, an XK 140 Jag and Bugatti." Amazingly, our father didn't take over the story. There was something in Chuck's quiet intelligence and attention that allowed us all to shine.

I showed him my scrapbook of our trip to Mexico the previous summer. I pointed out a photograph of our family and our friends, nine of us, standing in front of a motor home with an orange stripe. I unfolded a map of Mexico and traced our route from Texas to Mexico City east to the Yucatan, and then west to Oaxaca on the Pacific Coast, and then back to Ohio. Six weeks on the road.

Chuck turned the pages. "You've done a great job combining your journal pages with photographs and postcards."

I blushed. "I just have a Brownie box camera."

He looked carefully at my black and white photographs of the new modern Museum of Anthropology and Pre-Columbian ruins. "You did well." I beamed.

He asked, "What ruins did you go to?"

I pointed to them on the map: Teotihuacan, Chichen Itza, Uxmal. "And these were our favorites, Palenque and Monte Alban."

Chuck commented, "Isn't it interesting how early and late Mayan architecture varies so much. The intimate little palaces at Palenque are so different from the vast complexes further out on the Yucatan."

Dad nodded, "They've both inspired me." They walked away talking.

My brothers and I stared after him, amazed. Was there anything he didn't know about? Years later, when I was exasperated, I asked him point blank, "How do you know *everything*?" He smiled like the Cheshire Cat. "I read *The Whole Earth Catalogue*, every page, every edition." In no way did his answer diminish my awe of his ability to converse at depth on any topic.

By the time he left, Jo still wasn't home from class, but my brothers and I clustered around him like he was a rock star. Wood asked, "Why do you have poles on the roof?

"I bought a fifteen foot-diameter canvas teepee in Eden Park at the Arts Fair. Two brothers harvested lodge pole pines in Colorado. Now they're going to Stephen Gaskin's Farm in Tennessee."

Wood and I looked at each other. "Wow." We read about how hippies from The Farm helped people on bad acid trips at Woodstock.

Dad clapped him on the back. "We'll have to have you out for dinner soon. We'll break open a true Chateau Margaux for you next time." We all wanted him to come back. We wanted to bask in his thoughtful attention.

We had no idea that this lunch we'd thrown together with leftovers had been the finest meal he'd ever had. That night he'd eat his usual dinner: an egg, tomato, and lettuce sandwich for $1.75 at the Tick Tock Shop Diner on McMillian Street, next to the university. He was as captivated by us as we were with him.

That fall, after I turned sixteen and got my license, I drove our VW bus into the city with my brother Wood to visit Chuck. He told us to meet him at The Falafel Shop on Calhoun Street, the cool hippie area overlooking the University. We had stared out the window of Dad's car when he took us into town a few times to show us Sander Hall under construction, but he never let us out of the car up here. Now we were on our own. After careful parallel parking, my brother and I got out of the car and stared. Up and down the street were people with long hair and bellbottoms, just like the Woodstock movie. We felt awkward, so lame, two suburban kids surrounded by hippies wearing leather fringed vests, moccasins, even ripped fur coats and leather hats. Posters to concerts plastered brick walls and telephone poles. "Kill Pigs" was spray-painted on some walls. We passed head shops with bongs and posters and strobe lights flashing, and creepy bars with open doors into dark rooms smelling of smoke and beer. We were relieved to see Chuck waiting for us at a table with chairs on the sidewalk. He looked cool here, like he fit in, but welcoming, familiar and waiting for us, like we were special.

"I ordered us three falafel specials in pita bread, with terrific garlicky cucumber tzatziki and Greek salad with extra feta and olives."

We stared at him. We hadn't heard of any of those things before. We sat and watched, nervously tucking our long bangs behind our ears. Hippies were everywhere, sitting on steps and leaning against doorways, laughing and talking loudly in a language we didn't know. "Man, that's so groovy!" "Bummer!" Groups of crew-cut college kids walked by, hooting at girls in very short dresses with lace-up leather boots or ankle-length granny dresses. I watched the girls carefully to see if they wore a bra or not. I'd tried going without a bra under a heavy sweater. I was so skinny and flat-chested that no one would notice except me. I felt naked and daring. I always wore a bra when I went to gym because we had to put on thin white blouses and red shorts. I didn't want to get sent home from school for "indecent exposure," like the wild-looking hippie girl who transferred to our school. We'd heard she didn't even wear underpants under her short dresses!

As I ate my pita sandwich, we watched Sander Hall under construction down the hill, a block behind a red brick church with two spires. There was a huge crane on the dorm roof. It was about fifteen stories so far, towering over everything around us where nothing was over four stories. I explained to Chuck how the forms were bolted into position and concrete was poured around a steel structure one floor at a time. The three of us stabbed at the bowl of salad, grabbing bites of feta and black olives. A friend of Chuck's with greasy long hair pulled up a chair. He lived down the hall from Chuck's room.

I didn't know what to say, so I said, "My dad is the architect of that dorm."

"You're kidding! That's terrible, man. People hate it!"

I was shocked. "Why is it terrible?"

"Can't you see? It's like a big prison. The University is going to force all the students to live in those concrete cells."

I glanced at Chuck for help.

He explained in his level, calm voice. "Students want to live off campus and hang out with their friends on the street." He gestured around him. "They don't want to be required to live in a dorm, let alone in a skyscraper."

His friend was getting amped up; his eyes looked glazed and out of focus.

"That dorm is The Machine! It's Big Brother hanging over us, a prison sentence waiting for us."

Chuck explained that it was going to have a dining hall where three thousand students would have to eat together, three meals a day.

Wood nodded. "That's how many people live in our town. Breakfast with everybody in Glendale. Shit, that's a lot of people."

I glanced at Wood, startled by his swearing.

Chuck's strange friend continued, his voice eerie and bizarre, "And there are going to be fires, man. People are going to die up there!"

Chuck shook his head. "People are so afraid of fire because of that fire up at Ohio State when those girls died. It's in the papers all the time."

I looked horrified. "It's a concrete building. How will it catch fire?" I spoke with authority, "My dad is making it really, really safe." I felt protective about Woodie and his design.

His friend stood up abruptly. "Catch you later!" He nodded to us. "Sorry about your old man. Gotta go."

As he wandered off, Chuck explained he was a pharmacy student and cooking up drugs in his room. Wood nodded like he understood, like this was cool.

But I was shocked and whispered, "He's making drugs? They're illegal!"

Chuck smiled and nodded, taking a pretend toke on a joint, sucking in air, and he spoke holding his breath, "Yup, they're all illegal." Wood laughed but I couldn't. All this started to scare me. Distracted by some guys walking by with ripped jeans showing their butts, I looked away immediately, embarrassed.

Chuck changed the subject. "Want to see where I live?"

"Yes." We both stood up, a little nervous about seeing how a real hippie lived. It seemed impossible that Chuck was only four years older than I was. We followed him down an alley to climb rickety wooden back steps up to the fourth floor where we faced a line of windows.

Chuck paused, out of breath. "It's so weird. People are

afraid of fire in Sander, when we all live in real firetraps!' He laughed. "If this went up in flames, we wouldn't have a chance!"

He yanked open a window and blocked it open with a ruler. "Climb in! Welcome to my palace!" He dived in head-first, stood up and held back the curtains for us. I put in one foot first gingerly, trying not to get peeling paint from the window frame all over my favorite pants and white sweater.

The little room was dominated by a mattress on the floor, an Indian print bedspread, and books lined up in wooden packing crates. I looked at a detailed poster on the wall of buildings in a desert. Chuck explained, "It's Arcosanti. A visionary new city in Arizona. I have to ask your dad what he thinks of Paolo Solari's work."

We looked around to figure out where to sit, and Chuck gestured us all to sit on his bed. He explained, "It's a sleeping room. A deal for $25 a month. All these buildings are full of them. They divided up apartments. We share a bathroom down the hall." He showed us his hot plate for making tea and heating up soup. He had a plate, bowl, mug and a spoon.

I wondered what would we talk about. "So what do you and our mom do?"

He switched his voice to a professional tone, "Every Tuesday she meets with a group of rabbis and bishops about the volunteer organization she started. You know, The Citizens Committee on Justice and Corrections. Right?"

We shrugged. She told us this stuff she was doing, but we really didn't get it.

"Jo started stopping at my desk. She told me how she was attempting to address some of the worst conditions of incarceration in the country. Her intention is to close the Cincinnati Workhouse. Is that righteous, or what?" We nodded. Chuck could slip from hippie talk to official language so easily.

He continued, "I've met lots of counterculture activists at protest rallies against the war, but she's the first 'mainstream' activist I've met. Do you have any idea how awesome your mom is?" We looked at each other and shook our heads. She was our mom. I had to give her advice on what to wear and not to wear. She was really insecure.

He spoke with respect. "She's educated, articulate, attractive, obviously connected, and trying to effect real change. A far cry from the hippies I normally hang with. And she has a plan."

He launched into a story. "One day Jo asked if I could do some typing for her. She had a letter she needed to send, asking the Mayor of Cincinnati for his intervention in some matter. She handed me her hand-written draft, and I was introduced to . . . dyslexia." He smiled and shook his head.

Wood nodded, "She can't spell."

I added, "Her handwriting is awful."

Chuck laughed, "I tried to make sense of her letter, but finally I asked her to come and sit with me: 'Maybe we can do this better together. Jo, I'm not really clear what it is you're trying to say to Mr. Gradison.' I put a fresh sheet of letterhead into the typewriter, and said, 'So what is it that you are trying to say?' She told me, and I listened and typed. Her thought structure was clear. Her request was simple and direct. The letter was half its previous length. I whipped out the letter and she read it. Her eyebrows went up slightly, a little smile passed across her face, and she said, 'Where's a pen?'"

He grinned. "We've been doing this together ever since!

"So, you guys, I'm your mom's secretary."

I stared at him, amazed. I thought just dads had secretaries, women in high heels with red lipstick, like Woodie's.

Listening to Chuck's story, I thought of my mother growing up thinking she was dumb because she struggled to read, barely passing her college classes when she first tried, yet here she was, fearless and taking action. In school I was one of the smart kids, and sometimes I felt embarrassed when my mother stumbled, mispronouncing words. But I didn't speak up like her. I was too shy and scared to ask questions. She was so much braver than I was.

Before Wood and I left, I tiptoed down the hall to the shared bathroom. Loud rock and roll from one door, loud classical from another. That must be the three ballet students. I wondered if that burnt smoky smell was marijuana. The bathroom was disgusting, everything greasy and stained, stinky pee in the toilet, and cockroaches slinking around the sink.

After I raced back to Chuck's room, I blurted out about the cockroaches.

He said, "You should see the rats at night down on the street, now those are gross!" He added gently, "You two are really just babes in the woods." His voice was kind, not like he was making fun of us, and strangely, I knew it was true.

While I waited for Wood to return from the bathroom, I stood at the window, looking up at Sander Hall with the crane towering over it. It was huge, overpowering the brick storefronts and shops, overshadowing the church steeples. Like a big city tower plopped into a village, a grid of gaping rooms waiting for students, like a hungry ghost.

Sander Hall, circa 1970s

INTENSIVE CARE

We are a landscape of all we have seen.

—ISAMU NOGUCHI

ONE EVENING OVER CHRISTMAS BREAK IN 1969, after the dinner I couldn't eat, I cried out as I lay down on my bed. My father came in and lectured me. "You have no tolerance for pain. You are making a big thing out of nothing." After he turned away impatiently, I lay on my side, eyes tearing. I tried to read *Out of Africa* by Isak Dinesen, but I couldn't slip into the sounds of the night on the Ngong Hills. I was caught in pain, trying to get through a long night.

I had been determined to get over my fear of sled riding. I was sixteen, hadn't pulled a sled over to Gunney Hill since I was a kid, but the rare powdery snow had enticed me. The Village policemen blocked off the road and set out a barrel with a fire for warming hands. I lay on my belly on the sled, my hands on the crossbows, my face just inches above the spray of snow, going fast. Sunlight glinted in the tracks worn smooth into the hill, making the track faster, slicker. I squinted. The sun and snow were dazzling. I steered around slower kids, when suddenly a train of boys holding ankles, four sleds in a row, started whipped back and forth across the hill like a snake as I slid towards them. To keep from crashing into them, I moved the bar quickly, steering sharply to my left, and plowed into a telephone pole. The sled shuddered, wood against wood, and my body was thrown forward, twisting sideways, my left hip and low back thudding against the tarred trunk. I lay there until I could breathe again, and slowly pushed myself up to stand.

One of the boys came up. "You okay? I'm really sorry."

I nodded. "I'm okay. Just the breath knocked out of me."

I took slow steps up the hill, warmed my hands at the barrel. I knew I couldn't walk home. I called from a neighbor's house, and my mother was irritated. "Are you sure you can't walk home?" She was put out when she came to pick me up.

I was in pain all night, and began peeing blood at dawn. A few hours later, I was hooked up to IVs in Intensive Care at Christ Hospital. My kidney was ruptured. We had to wait to see if it would stop bleeding internally. My mother drove in and out of the city to visit every day. She brought me pretty new pajamas. A cute guy, who called himself my vampire, took my blood every hour. Nurses took my bedpan and gave me shots. When I cried, they all went away so my mother could comfort me for a while, before she had to go home. I cried because I hurt, because I was scared, and because my father hadn't come to see me.

I cried. "Why won't Daddy come see me?"

She tried to soothe me. In her last years of trying to explain away his behavior, she murmured, "He can't take it when people are sick. Some men are like that. He still loves you. He just doesn't show it very well."

I held onto her hands, crying. "What would I do without you?"

I lay awake on New Year's Eve, the old woman in the bed beside me snoring, the nurses laughing down the hall. They'd turned off my movie halfway through and told me to go to sleep. I lay awake afraid. What if I didn't get better? What if I needed a kidney transplant? But I was sure no one loved me enough to give me a kidney. Not my father, he was too busy and important. Maybe my mom, but I couldn't take hers, too many people needed her. I went down the list, my brothers, my friends. No, no one. When would someone really love me? I stared at the curtains hanging around my bed. Is this how my life will be, lonely and isolated? I reread notes from my friends written with purple pens, filled with hearts and exclamation points: Love you!!! Get better soon!!!! But the notes didn't touch the chilled emptiness I felt.

Junior year continued after the January 1970 break, but my day was punctuated with tourniquets tightened around my arm, the prick and shove of the needle, blood filling more tubes. Now every four hours. Checking to see if my kidney was still seeping blood.

My mother called one morning. "Oh sweetie, I feel so bad. I can't make it today. I'm got two final exams before I have to race home for the boys."

"I'm okay, Mommy." In the hospital, I'd started calling her Mommy again, not Jo. "Do great on your exams. I'm so proud of you. I'm studying the college guide book you gave me. There are so many cool colleges."

"That's great. I'll see you in the morning and you can tell

me about them." Then she added, her voice hopeful, with a forced cheerfulness. "I think your dad will be able to come by after work today, if his meetings don't go too late."

All day I waited.

After lunch, my nurse helped me go for a walk. I shuffled in slippers, tried to hold onto the totally embarrassing jonnie, with my other arm connected to a stream of tubes on the IV pole she pushed along. My back ached where I'd hit the telephone pole, my stomach hurt from no food for days, and my legs were wobbly, but I was proud when we reached the window at the end of the hallway. I sat in a chair to rest. The hospital was on a hill. Below me, like a scale model of a mismatched toy city, was Mount Auburn, with beautiful old mansions turned into offices, streets of old brick row houses, and just beyond, the University of Cincinnati. My dad's high rise dorm was rising to tower twenty-seven stories over all of this. Someday it would be covered with mirror glass, and would look sleek and silvery like in the architectural rendering at Dad's office. But now it was a tower of empty spaces, a grid of empty rooms. Cranes on the top floor hauled up piles of materials and took them to different levels. They were under a deadline to be ready for students next year.

I showed my nurse, a stocky black woman. "My dad is the architect of that tower. If he's not too busy, he'll come visit today."

She nodded, "You must be proud of your dad. That's really something."

I studied the grid of streets, finding the curve in William Howard Taft Road where his office was upstairs in the brick house with the turret. I was pretty sure I could see the roof.

"All right honey, we've got to get you back to bed. Don't want to wear you out."

All that long afternoon I read about colleges. I found the ones my mother's parents and siblings had gone to. Like memorizing nursery rhymes, I had learned to recite their colleges and where they were professors. The names of colleges were like pearls in a fine necklace: Amherst, Oxford, Kenyon, NYU, Johns Hopkins, Stanford, with Harvard the diamond at the center. My aunts went to Swarthmore and Mt. Holyoke, but then they got married and that was it. Even my grandmother had a masters in Philosophy and English from the University of Michigan.

In that family, my mother was a disappointment. Her academic family was terribly upset with her leaving college. Years later, helping my youngest brother, Hubbard, learn to read, she discovered someone who struggled with reading the same way she had. The words flipped around the page for him like tiles falling off a Scrabble board. Meeting with his teachers year after year, she ignored the ones who said that he was lazy and lacked incentive, and found the ones who understood. Now there was a name for this. Dyslexia. They taught her how to tutor him. She sat with him every night at the kitchen table until he was able to read on his own. Her reading and writing improved, until she had felt brave enough to go back to college.

She went to village council meetings to practice taking notes, certain that she could learn to listen and write at the same time. At first she came home in tears, ready to give up.

She persevered, coming home exhausted, but she kept going until she could take notes. Now she was enrolled part-time at the University of Cincinnati, coming home with heavy books which she faced each night as we washed the dishes. Her typewriter clicked late into the night as we fell asleep. She asked us to listen to her papers, embarrassed at first to read out loud to us, faltering over the words on paper splattered with white correction blots.

At first Dad thought this was a good idea, finishing her degree. She could get a part-time job, help out with the family bills. But when she wasn't always there cooking meals and landscaping when he wanted her, when she wasn't at his beck and call, he grew impatient, demeaning, putting down her classes and dreams of a degree.

We were watching our mother grow up, her voice becoming more certain, impassioned with her studies in criminal justice. She would be the first woman in her family to have a career, to put her education to work. That was how important a college education was. I couldn't wait to start myself.

The winter dark came early. I heard the rattle of china and food trays, but I still wasn't allowed to eat. I glared at the IV tube. It sure didn't feel like it was giving me dinner. I glanced toward the door, dreading another blood draw, but there was my dad, wearing his Brooks Brothers suit with a yellow plaid bow tie.

My heart leapt and I started chattering with excitement. "Hi, Daddy, the doctor told me my kidney is getting better. I'm hardly peeing any blood now." I wanted his approval that I was doing a good job. I was getting better so I could go home, so he didn't have to worry about me. I wanted to please him but he didn't looked pleased.

"I watched Sander Hall from the window today. I can't believe how tall it is."

But he didn't respond by telling me about how construction on the tower was going, or his meetings at the office. Standing at the foot of my bed, his eyes were not kind behind his black glasses. He didn't sit down next to me, or take my hand. He glanced at the college guide on my lap.

I picked up the book to show him. "I've been reading about colleges all day."

He grimaced. "I'm sick of college students. I've been on campus all day. They are just filthy bums or women's libbers. Graffiti everywhere. That campus is a pig sty."

I tried again cheerfully. "I'm thinking about a small college. Have you heard of Bennington in Vermont, or Reed College in Oregon? I think I want to study Sociology or Psychology."

He scowled and almost spat his words. "Don't get any ideas about going to some liberal college where people waste their tuition on protest marches. I'm sending you to Katherine Gibbs Secretarial School in New York. Then you'll have a way to work your way through school, just like I did during the Depression."

Stunned, I stared down at my book, incredulous. Me, a secretary? Never. Did he think I wasn't worth going to college? Who did he think I was?

I had no idea the extent of the recession of the 1970s that was coming. I didn't know that architects felt how the economic winds were blowing sooner than most anyone else. If only he could have said, "we." As in, "we" need to start thinking about how we are going to pay for college tuition. If only he could have said a storm is coming and we have to figure out how we will get through. But "we" was not in his vocabulary; sharing information and working together was not in his training. So much pain could have been avoided if he could have let down his walls of control. But it was too late. A guerilla war was already underway, in our house and across the country. We were children in training to become snipers, getting ready to join the army of the young, preparing to bring down the old order. The conflict was inevitable, tragic, and essential.

When I looked up, he spoke sarcastically, "Your mother's so busy with college, she doesn't have any time for me and the boys. We're left to fend for ourselves."

Then he glowered down on me in the hospital bed as if he had just remembered why he had come. "But the worst is, I won't tolerate you turning your mother against me."

I was stunned, and cried, "What did I do, Daddy? What did I do?" I searched my mind trying to think. We sometimes complained about my dad, but didn't everybody?

He glared at me. "You had better stop it, young lady. I won't tolerate this!" Then he turned and left. I never found out what sin I had committed. Without knowing it I had become complicit with a revolution, but when he cross-examined me, I still felt like an innocent, meekly denying I had done anything wrong.

I stared at the empty doorway listening to his quick sharp footsteps fading down the hallway. What had I done? My body ached. I felt cold all over, and shivered. I pulled the college guide to my chest like a blanket to warm me. I would go to college, no matter what. He wouldn't stop me.

Elizabeth and Alvin, 1970

FIRST LOVE

Architecture is a matter of "harmonies,"
it is "a pure creation of the spirit."

—LE CORBUSIER,
TOWARDS A NEW ARCHITECTURE

A GYMNAST WITH MUSCULAR SHOULDERS AND A slender waist, chestnut-brown skin and a quick flashing smile, Alvin was pursued by boy-crazy white girls in angora sweaters who wore lots of makeup and frosted nail polish. They oohed and aahed over his body, whispering to each other. They passed him notes in class in their curlicue handwriting, pink ink on notebook paper. I read over his shoulder. "I'm lusting after your body. Want to meet after school?" Alvin blushed, crumpled them up and glanced at me, embarrassed.

I was the Twiggy skinny girl with no bra and tortoiseshell glasses, and one day in study hall, he gazed at me with relief, sighing, "I never thought I'd find anyone I could talk to about the Tibetan Book of the Dead." We fell in love talking.

We'd become friends in college-track English and Trig. We waved our hands in the air, answered questions, researched on note cards, and competed in reading races with each other. While our English classmates groaned after the teacher passed out 900-page copies of Drieser's *An American Tragedy*, Alvin and I raced each night to see how many pages we could read. One night I fell asleep happy, sure I was in the lead, but he stayed up late and woke up early. When the buses discharged crowds of students to surge through the entry hall, we found each other. I crowed, "I got to page 580."

He grinned. "Sorry kiddo, I'm at 614."

I pretended to glower. "I'll get you next time." Laughing, we raced off to our first class, comparing notes on the story. The novel's tragic twists of fate became our comedy as we predicted the plot and decried the despicable hero.

———·———

HIS SHORT AFRO glistened as the ceiling lights on our porch illuminated his ascent up the stone steps to our front door. Early evening in February after dinner, I'd sat at the round kitchen table near the glass wall waiting for Alvin to arrive. It seemed everyone else in my family was also watching for this young man who was coming over to study with me. At sixteen I'd never gone out on a date or had a boy come over. "We are just friends," I assured my parents at the dinner table. "We've been studying together in study hall."

Hubbard called out, "I'll get it," and ran to open the door. Alvin greeted Hubbard warmly, before my father walked up, blocking Alvin's way into the room and kept him standing in the open door. Dixieland jazz was playing on the huge sound system so loud he had to speak up to be heard.

Alvin put out his hand. "Hello Mr. Garber, I'm Alvin McClure. Elizabeth invited me over to study."

My father shook his hand, and didn't say his usual 'call me Woodie.' "I hear you are a gymnast. I used to do gymnastics when I went to Walnut Hills years ago." This was the best college prep high school in the Midwest, located in Cincinnati.

Alvin lit up. "I went to Walnut Hills too, my mom too. I was on the gymnastics team."

My father startled. "You went to Walnut Hills? Well," he faltered, "Well, did Elizabeth tell you my father designed the Walnut Hills campus in the thirties?"

"No! How cool. Such a classical design. I love the library the best, like Thomas Jefferson's Monticello."

Woodie opened the door wider, finally allowing Alvin to enter the house, closing out the damp cold air that had blown in as they talked. But he blocked him from entering the Great Room where I waited at the kitchen table over my books. The questioning resumed. "So what are your events?"

"I started gymnastics in third grade where they started us out in the old German style, probably how you learned, with hanging rings and rope climb. I like parallel bars and hanging rings best."

Woodie immediately launched into his best events. As he rattled off competitions and coaches, Alvin nodded at the right pauses, intensely aware at sixteen of holding his own power with this barrel-chested man who was competing to best him at every stroke, like a pissing contest. He observed this man was an authoritarian of the "old school," a know-it-all. He'd never had a white man take this stance with him before and he stood his ground.

Woodie ended, "I got us a set of parallel bars and a horse that we keep out on the side porch so my kids can get stronger. My son, Wood, is starting gymnastics but he's just not applying himself worth a damn."

Finally my father let him pass into the Great Room. After Alvin glanced around the brilliantly lit room at the floating sculptures, the huge circular orange and red woven rug, the mahogany grand piano, he turned and beamed a warm smile to my mother. "Wow, this room is way cool."

"I'm glad to meet you, Alvin. It's great you're helping Elizabeth with her trigonometry. I don't have a clue when it comes to math."

My father interrupted. "I've been too busy with work to help. Besides, I can't stand the way they teach New Math. Mumbo jumbo if you ask me. Why don't you both sit here at the kitchen table so you can get some work done." He shouted to Wood at the other end of the long room, who'd been buried in a book, oblivious to everything going on. "Wood, why don't you turn the music down so people can concentrate around here." My brother looked up confused, as if he'd been startled from another world, but jumped up immediately to obey. To Alvin, it was clear that this man was a bully who browbeat his children into submission.

My mother excused herself. "I've got homework too, for my class on Saturday," and she went into my parents' room.

Dad said, "I'll finish up the kitchen," which allowed him to hover across the open kitchen counter a few feet from where we tried to chart out sine and cosine waves on graph paper. He wiped down the stove and counters with excessive vigor while lecturing us on how we needed to learn how to clean better.

I finally asked, "Daddy, could you be a little quieter while we are trying to study?"

He finished cleaning, picked up the latest *Time* magazine

with The Band on the cover. He came over and asked, "So young man, are you into this kind of music?"

Alvin looked up at the cover of a group of long-haired musicians. He'd already seen the two ten-foot shelves of record albums next to the Eames chair. "The Band's doing some pretty interesting stuff, but seeing as you like jazz I think you'd really like Chicago, a cool new band with a strong jazz and Latin beat." He turned to me. "We really like their song 'Does Anybody Really Know What Time It Is?'"

I nodded. "I think you'd like it, Daddy. But we've got a test in the morning." I could see my dad was trying to show he was hip, but he wouldn't leave us for a moment. Finally he walked to the other side of the room, settled into his leather chair, feet up on the ottoman. His bald head gleamed, as his hand tapped and his head bobbed out the complex rhythms of Earl "Fatha" Hines on piano.

We tried to plot pencil lines on graph paper while the vast room spun around us, the bright lights bounced off the glass walls, the oiled walnut cabinets glowed and the jazz throbbed like a heartbeat in a New York club. Absorbed in his magazine, Dad would call out "Oh yeah" after particularly fine moments from the keyboard. Alvin and I slipped each other quick glances as we made an effort to work out the formulas we needed to know. At eight thirty, he glanced at his watch. "I better get home before my mom gets on my case."

I walked him to the door and we smiled shyly, saying, "See you at school tomorrow," before my father leapt to his feet, stumbling as he walked to the door.

He orchestrated a vigorous hand shaking "Thank you,

young man, for giving my daughter a hand at her homework. Here, I'll turn on the spot lights to light up the drive. Watch out on your bicycle, there are some deep ruts."

As Alvin started down the stairs, he called after him. "Maybe you could give Wood some pointers on the parallel bars if you come by another time?"

Alvin turned and looked up at him. "I'd really like to do that."

———

A FEW DAYS later at dinner, my father asked, "So what does Alvin's father do?"

I explained that his father had died when Alvin was five. His father had started out working for the post office. I looked at my mother. "You told me that the post office and being a porter on trains were the only professional jobs open to black men back then." Alvin's dad had worked full-time and went to college and law school at night. It took him sixteen years. He became the first black legislator in the State of Ohio.

My mother asked, "What was his name?"

"Alphonso Bruce McClure. What is so sad is that he died right before the election for his second term. He was even a delegate to the Republican National Convention in 1956 in California. Even though Alvin was only three, he remembers the long train ride out west and the crowds cheering Ike at the Cow Palace."

My father's face was impassive hearing about Alvin's father. He didn't comment or even show interest. He started complaining about construction on Sander Hall, how the contractors were behind schedule. But I wondered if he realized then he was up against more of a challenge than he'd thought. My father and Alvin, like boxers, were sizing each other up as they edged around the ring. When the fight finally began, it would be a battle of wits.

The similarities between our fathers was part of the unusual comfort Alvin and I discovered as we became friends in study hall. We were both the oldest children of accomplished older fathers who had married young wives. Alvin asked, "What's this thing about marrying younger women? I don't get it." We rolled our eyes, both agreeing that we wanted to be with someone who was our equal.

We had both accompanied our fathers and learned about their worlds in ways our younger siblings didn't share. Both fathers took their families on long unusual trips. He told me about how in 1955, when he was two, they had traveled on the Queen Elizabeth to Europe and returned home on the Queen Mary. "It was the first time our people had money to travel." In Italy everyone thought he was so cute. "But seriously, who would take their family with small children around Europe right after the war?"

We kept saying, "This is so weird."

I explained how my dad took us all over Mexico before the Olympics in '68. "We were there a couple months before the police used tanks to fire on student protestors. We were going to Guatemala until the guy at the Embassy who said it was safe to travel got killed." So weird. But we were both proud of our dads. His father took him by the hand when they walked around the neighborhood and everyone called out, "Hey, Bruce," and waved. I told him about walking on construction jobs and everyone saying, "You must be Woodie's daughter."

I'd found someone who had a similar class and family background. We felt so similar that, to us, being black and white didn't seem a big deal. We had no idea how serious a problem it would be for other people.

Alvin had grown up in a mixed neighborhood with white, black and Jewish professionals in Walnut Hills, near Woodburn Avenue. He started Walnut Hills College Prep in sixth grade. He had just started high school when the riots came. He joked, "You haven't lived until you've seen military jeeps with mounted loaded fifty-caliber machine guns cruising down your street." He and his friends spent days and nights watching from windows, smelling smoke, on lockdown by their mothers. But then his voice dropped, sober. "People burned out businesses in our own neighborhood." I heard the sadness, as he continued. "Ever hear of Redlining? No one could get insurance on their houses any more. Suddenly people were doing drugs, serious drugs. The neighborhood was never the same." Then his parents moved to suburbia.

After years of talking and joking with the smartest, coolest kids in the city, he felt trapped in a strange segregated wasteland at Princeton High School in suburbia. When he walked through the black neighborhood in Glendale, nobody talked to him, or guys at the corner murmured "Oreo" after he passed by. He hadn't made a good friend since he left Walnut Hills.

At school I found the smart kids boring, doing what the teachers said, and no one seemed to be saying anything real. I wrote an impassioned essay for English class about a storm building up into such a fury that the skies burst forth with freezing rain. Lightning split a towering oak, splintering its grasping arms, which fell, crushing a small child huddled below. The teacher commented in red ink: "Liz: There was one problem. I sense strong emotion; however, making analogies of your emotions to the natural landscape and elements is very hard to do." I growled to myself, hasn't she ever heard of *Wuthering Heights?*

Sometimes the only time I felt happy and understood was when I was reading. One lonely weekend a year before, I had found a faded old book, *I Capture the Castle*, in our bookcase. By the end of the first page, I was enraptured. The awkward, witty Cassandra wrote constantly in her journal about her eccentric family. She had a brilliant depressed father with a beautiful unusual young wife and they lived in a dilapidated old castle. Reading Cassandra was like finding another me. I kept the book next to my bed and didn't share it with anyone until I met Alvin. Perhaps I knew I was falling in love with him when I decided to loan him the book.

He took it home over a weekend and read it all. He biked over to return it. He handed me the book, nodding. "Cassandra is just like you." Someone finally knew me, the real me.

Alvin and I started going to a social action youth group and became friends with a private school student named Peter, whose house became the hangout for kids wanting to talk about politics, race, and the war in Vietnam. Peter, Alvin, and I began to call ourselves the Mod Squad, like the trio on television. I was growing my hair long. Peter was the mop-headed white guy and Alvin, the cool black guy.

Soon after Alvin's first study date at my house, my father set down rules. "Not that I'm racist, but . . ." Like a sermon he'd been practicing or a legal argument, he built his points about the dangers of inter-racial relationships. Yes, it was fine to be friends, but we had to know the dangers. He laid down the first rule. "I *never* want the two of you out as a couple, only in odd numbered groups. It's for your own safety."

When I told Alvin the next day at school, we rolled our eyes, thinking the same thing: I mean really, this is 1970! We continued as we had, doing homework together at my house after school before my dad got home or staying late at the library. We were still just friends.

When we biked over to his mom's two-story ranch at of the end of Annadale Lane, she said, "Call me Jewel." A handsome woman, she dressed more stylishly than my mother. When we drank a Coke at her kitchen table, Alvin softened his accent a little, from 'yes' to 'yeah,' but mostly he spoke like me. His mom spoke in a harsher black accent than the softer inflection of the black women I knew in Glendale.

She said, "Aren't you two so cute," fussing over us, making us blush, but then she turned on his little brother J-J. "Hold that lip in before I knock it in. Don't want anyone thinking you're a dumb nigger." J-J and Alvin instantly sucked in their full lips into a thin straight line.

Alvin said, "We're going down to the den to listen to music now."

I thanked Jewel for the Coke and followed him.

He whispered, "I learned to keep my lips tucked in." He explained that growing up black you tried to make yourself look and act white, even making your lips not look so different. I kept looking at his lips, so soft and textured, a little pink showing at the center. I touched my thin lips.

He was reading the liner notes on the record cover for *Wheels of Fire*, by his favorite band, Cream. As the song began, "In a white room with black curtains," I leaned back into the couch feeling breathless, watching Alvin as he read, running his tongue over his lips and tucking them in without thinking. What his mother said that really shocked me was the word 'Nigger.' I'd never known someone black would say that word.

———

THAT LATE WINTER in Cincinnati was dreary without a single day of sunshine, but at school we were all abuzz. On March 26, there was going to be a twelve-hour rock concert at the huge arena in town, The Cincinnati Gardens, where they had basketball games and the Ice Follies. Joe Cocker was coming, plus a lot of other bands. Everyone got the poster. We'd all seen the Woodstock movie, and now we had our chance for a concert, close to home, without mud. For twelve hours we could step into the outrageous world of rock and roll. It was too good to be true. We all calculated how to get our parents to let us go and how to pay for the $10 ticket.

Everyone counted up their savings, the lucky ones their allowance. I had my babysitting stash of coins and dollars. Amazingly enough, Alvin's mom said "Yes." Even more amazingly, my parents said "Yes" when I explained, "My youth group is going."

We were ecstatic, comparing notes on the bands. What

time should we get there? Secretly imagining being together all that time out of our parents' grasp. *Ten Years After* was lined up for 10 p.m., followed by Joe Cocker. Our transistor radios pounded out blues and rock every morning. It was hard to study or concentrate; all we could think about was twelve hours of rock and roll, together.

A few days before the concert, Jewel changed her mind. He couldn't go. Money was tight. If she wasn't giving him the money for a lock on his locker at school, then he couldn't expect her to buy a ticket to this concert. "Even if you had a ticket," she declared, "you can't go." Period. End of conversation. She'd made up her mind. We were devastated. Each day we hoped something would change. I called right before I got my ride and we almost cried. "I'm so sad you won't be there." He went back downstairs, put on his headphones and tried to bury himself in Eric Clapton and Jack Bruce. A few hours later she called downstairs, "You can go to that concert. Maybe you can still catch a ride with someone." He dashed out the door.

My sixteen-year-old-girl's excitement over the idea of a concert was quickly overwhelmed by miles of traffic backed up on the highway, and crowds billowing and surging around the entrance. Long hair, afros, tight leather pants, embroidered jeans, and more people than I'd ever seen. I was a naïve, scared girl staying close to friends caught in a crowd pushing forward. A band I didn't know filled the vast hall with pounding pressure in my ears; a haze of smoke swirled blue, red, yellow from spot lights overhead. I felt scared and small. We climbed up level after level of steep narrow steps, finding a row of empty seats. My friends went off to look around but I crouched on the edge of my fold-down seat, mesmerized by the jostling crowds. Rivers of hippies and rednecks streamed up and down the aisles. I felt impossibly young and lost. I guessed the smoky smell was pot.

There were white and black girls in lacey tops or tie-dyed tees or long dresses with their arms around guys with long blond hair, or wavy curls gone crazy, or with black guys in dashikis or tees with a raised fist. Couples hugging and kissing, bare-chested guys in leather vests, and bra-less breasts, poking out of shirts, nipples in tight tees. Bodies were wrapped around each other, arms crossed and stuck into back pockets, bodies in tight clothes, sweaty leaping dancing bodies all around me, couples making out. Blurs of long hair flashing, heads bobbing with the music, and bodies of all colors, dancing with arms stretched out into the smoky purple spot-lit sky under the metal roof. And I was alone and scared, perched on my seat. Friends came, sat, left. Hours passed watching the spotlit cube of erupting drummers and writhing guitarists. I was tired, reeling, wanting to go home, when a friend shouted about the din, "Somebody saw Alvin. He's here, somewhere. He's looking for you."

I leapt up, heart pounding, and raced down into the endless rumpled river of long hair and matted clothes, scanning in every direction, pushed along, until I pulled myself out of the current to stand a few steps above to look. Then I saw him emerge from the crowd, fresh, beautiful brown face, pink-edged full lips smiling, impossibly handsome, calling my name. No longer the shy kids who hadn't even held hands, we poured into each other's arms in a full body hug.

Nearly crying with relief, I kept saying, "I can't believe you are here."

He whispered in my ear, "I found you, I found you."

I led him back to my narrow shelf of seats above the mayhem. We sat holding hands and laughing, with tears on our cheeks. The music picked us up and carried our torsos swaying and turning in our seats, my head tilting and rolling across his shoulder. As *Ten Years After* chanted "Goin' home, with my baby," the guitar glinted and whirled on the writhing stage. "Gonna see my baby, see my baby fine." The drummer's arms hurtled and that smoky voice drove us all like a train down the track. "Take my baby, take my baby mine." Drum sticks hurtling. "*I'm* goin' home" repeated, pounded, chanted "home" for ever, and his arms were around me, "goin' home," and then it was just our lips, delicious soft lips dissolving into each other, our bodies filled with a roaring, chanting, cheering crowd, a driving guitar, and a smoking voice, "I'm goin' home, see my baby." Hazy electric air charged with dancing, and bodies wrapped around each other, and I was kissing the endless, impossible sweetness of his lips.

Everything got complicated after that. As I leaned on Alvin's shoulder, gazing into the crowd, people stared at us with harsh faces, frowns. We'd entered a new territory. We were the first and only interracial couple at our high school that year. Every day there were glances, double takes, people looking us up and down. Black girls I didn't know murmured "Stay away from our men" when I walked to the school bus. The people who knew us didn't give us any grief. We studied together, grinning as we competed to answer questions in class, passed longer and longer notes, and we tried to find places where we could keep kissing.

Alvin worked out three hours after school for gymnastics, going off to weekend tournaments. I worked on my father's endless landscaping projects on weekends, planting trees, digging trenches, placing granite stones in the spiral terrace we'd been building for years. We talked on the phone until our parents or siblings yelled at us to get off. If we were lucky we were able to sneak to my house after school when no one was home. We were good kids, no drinking, no pot, and no hands below the waist. We had no idea my father wouldn't give up until he'd separated us

Sander Hall's Solarban
mirror glass panels

MIRROR GLASS

Suppose the walls rise towards heaven
in such a way that I am moved.

—LE CORBUSIER,
TOWARDS A NEW ARCHITECTURE

"ABSOLUTELY EXTRAORDINARY." OUR DAD GLOWED
with enthusiasm, pointing to the mirrored wall rising to the
sky above us, reflecting the double church spires and wisps of
clouds slipping across the surface. The mirrored glass panels
were being set into place, floor by floor, working their way
to the top of the dormitory. "I've been waiting for this ever
since I first envisioned Sander Hall."

Late afternoon on a spring weekend in 1970, my brothers, mother and I, all in bell bottomed jeans, leaned against
the VW bus on a hill overlooking the muddy construction
site. The building loomed high above the campus while, in
the valley below and leading off into the distance, lush spring
green leaves glowed as they punctuated the campus and
neighborhoods and parks beyond.

A building this size lives in the architect's mind for years
before it finally stands on the landscape, open to everyone
else's comments. It was the vision of the building, a glass
tower reflecting the sky that my father waited for expec-
tantly, little knowing that the worst battle for Sander Hall

would come from the color of Cincinnati's atmosphere. He had researched and educated the board, "selling" them on the mirror glass panels, documenting their remarkable energy savings for heating and cooling. The reflective beauty allowed both incredible views and privacy for students.

Our father waited with excited anticipation for the panels to go up. The color of each city's sky is distinct. Boston's Hancock Tower would glow a crisp blue. Glass cubed buildings were lighting up the sky in L.A., Houston, and Louisville, each a distinctive shade, from deep blue to silvered grey. He wondered, what color would these panels reflect at the university on a hill above the city of Cincinnati? They wouldn't know until they were installed.

Barrel-chested and stocky, wearing a plaid shirt and khaki pants, Woodie stood in front of us, gazing up at his tower. "Look how the mirror glass reflects a golden rose. I've never seen anything like it in any other city."

We clustered close to our mother as we watched clouds float across the surface.

"You won't believe the sunset against this surface." As if he were describing a fantastic wine, or painting, he was radiant with enthusiasm. He paced back and forth, gazing up from different angles. "Simply sensational." His bald head and face glowed with the early evening light as he glanced at us to make sure we fully appreciated this moment.

We heard voices of students on a Saturday night on Calhoun Street behind us, the rhythmic thudding of a drum as a rock band started playing in one of the bars. The air cooled and the mirrored wall stretching high above us streaked orange and red with the sunset.

My brothers and I watched the sunset play across the twenty-seven story projection screen, looked at each other, raised our eyebrows, nodding. I said, "Yeah, it's outta sight, Woodie. I mean, it's really cool."

"You're damn right it's cool!" His big voice laughed. "That glass will keep them cool all summer." He had explained it before, but we were patient as he explained again. The glass panels were called SolarBan II, produced by Pittsburgh Plate Glass. Double glazed, they were constructed with two quarter-inch pieces of glass separated by a half-inch airspace.

He looked at us, and we nodded before he continued. "There's a coating on the inner surface that gives the building its reflective qualities. It will save thousands and thousands of dollars in heating and, more importantly, cooling costs over the lifetime of the building. And it will give the students privacy at night so you can't see right in. They won't need curtains."

He stopped lecturing to gaze up at the wall of glass as the sunset dulled and faded, enchanted by the reflection. "It's breathtaking."

We grew restless and still he stood there. We nudged our mother, hinting that maybe we could walk up to Calhoun, but she shook her head. We knew better than to disturb his reverie. We were a private audience to his triumph. The mirrored wall darkened to a midnight blue. The dew chilled us as we watched him become a dark shadow in front of his tower.

A few nights later he arrived at the dinner table in a rage. "Pink. This god-damned woman on the Board of the University says her mother made her wear pink when she was a girl, and she hates pink. She says this mirrored glass has to go." We were glad he was yelling about someone else and not us.

Countless meetings followed. He took board members on field trips to Columbus and Louisville to see how the same glass performed. He reported on the energy savings of this glass. But nothing would change this woman's mind. The contractors were furious. Delays held up the project, put them behind on the deadline for completion, costing the project thousands of dollars a day. Tempers flared on the job.

Someone noticed that one of the panes of glass had been installed the wrong way. The dean insisted that the color was better that way. He ordered three more panes on the completed northern facade to be turned in order to determine whether there was a noticeable difference. The contractors turned the panes. Woodie and his office team of architects, draftsmen, and co-op students gathered with the head contractor and the maintenance crew from the university and looked at the tower. Woodie paced, eyeing the building furiously. "Who can tell which panes have been changed?" Even though they scanned the building, trying to see if they could tell a difference, no one could say which were the reversed panels.

Woodie told us the daily news on every step of the project at dinner. That night he was relieved, no one could see the difference. They could stop this costly delay and get on with the building.

But after the Board meeting, he was trembling with rage again as he sat down at the table, staring past us through the glass walls of our living room to the gardens beyond. "The Dean insisted he could see the difference. He made it clear that the 'pink' panels were now a milder pink. They could live with them this way." His hands shook as he tried to cut his steak. "He demanded that all the glass panels on the whole goddamned building be turned around. Sheer stupidity!"

Woodie repeated to us what he had explained to the Board. "This change will halve the energy savings of the glass. The individual air conditioning units for every single dorm room will have to be replaced with more powerful units. Who will pay for all this?"

They had done calculations. If they turned all the windows on the North, East, and West sides it would cost $14,000. Then at least they would keep the windows the right way for the solar protection on the South wall. The other option the University wanted was turning all the glass in the tower and the dining hall. This would mean 280 dorm and 137 cafeteria mirror glass panels would be turned and re-installed. In addition, 290 air conditioning units would be removed and replaced. They did the math, adding in costs for delays, insurance, engineering, and modifications in installation. This came to $30,000. (In 2012 dollars and increased cost of labor, this would be equivalent to a quarter of a million dollars.) The Board would let them know in writing in a few days.

At dinner that night, after he mapped out these options, we kept our heads bowed, ate quietly and truly felt sorry for our dad.

Two nights later, when he told us about the letter from the dean of the University, his voice barely contained his fury. "They want all the glass turned. They see this as my error because the glass does not look like a sample we passed around at a meeting three years ago."

He looked dazed. "And they expect me to pick up the tab."

He stabbed at his chest with his strong stubby forefinger on every 'I.' "I have to pay for the changing of all the panels." Stab. "I have to pay the re-installation of the air conditioning units." Stab. "And I pay the bill? Forget it." Then he looked at us. "Do you know the value of that money?"

We shook our heads, looking down.

"Of course not. You have no idea about the value of money." We glanced up, scared that now we were in trouble too. "That's the equivalent of six years of college tuition and board thrown out the window. It's armed robbery."

At sixteen, I had no idea how much college cost, or how much my dad made. I made fifty cents an hour babysitting on weekends, saved up my crumpled dollars in a jar, and spent it all on fabric and patterns to sew my own clothes. Living in a house filled with art and sculpture, I assumed I'd apply to college and my dad would write a check. None of us could know that this dorm would be his last commission, that in a few years my father's total yearly income would tumble to less than $5,000 a year.

Construction resumed, every glass panel was turned, every air conditioning unit replaced, the wiring adapted, the heating and cooling systems adapted. Finally the work could resume. Under pressure, and behind on their deadlines, they were pushing for months to finish the dorm on time for the start of the school year.

As summer heated up, my father oversaw the final construction decisions while wrestling with legal action against the University over this bill. His lengthy deposition recounted every detail of the process, yet the University demanded his office pay $30,000 for what was called "a mistake on the architect's part." Despite Woodie's articulate explanations, it was decided that he had to pay the bill.

———

WHEN HE CAME home from battling with the University, seeing Alvin and me together became the match that lit my father's short fuse. We didn't wonder why he was home for dinner nearly every night and sometimes during the day. We didn't know there were no new jobs coming on the heels of the fiasco of his prized high-rise dorm. We didn't know that the recession we read about in the paper, like all recessions, hit architects first. No one builds in uncertain times. What we knew was that Woodie was a time bomb set to go off at dinnertime.

Anything could set him off. For years, we'd flinch as he verbally slashed away at our brother Wood who sometimes walked to school weeping. Now I had become the enemy.

"*You!* You have no work ethic. You never apply yourself." His lips thinned and he'd hit harder. "You have no integrity." His pointed finger hammered at us under the spotlights as he reached his final point. "You are never going to amount to anything."

My brothers, mother, and I learned the art of resistance, quick glances with our down-turned eyes as we were interrogated in his glass cage. Over the years, we each fought back, saboteurs, secretly carrying on with our own lives behind the lines. But when we got caught in open fire, when we argued and defended ourselves, he pounded our defense relentlessly. We never knew when the next assault would begin.

One night at dinner, I recounted how funny it was teaching Alvin to shift gears on our VW bus.

"Now I understand how patient you had to be with me when I was learning." I laughed. "The bus jolted and shook and stalled out over and over as he tried to drive up the hill." My mother and brothers nodded, smiling.

My mother agreed. "But then he finally got the hang of it, after all. Good job, Elizabeth."

My father's words lashed out like a slap at my mother. "You coddle these kids." He glowered at her. "They've got to face up to the facts of the real world. Your daughter is playing with fire and it has got to stop." Sweat beaded on his bald head. He wiped his face with a folded white handkerchief from the stacks I ironed every week.

His furious mind turned on me. "For your own safety, I have laid down rules and you have defied me at every turn."

"We followed your rules," I protested. "We only go out in odd-numbered groups." In fact, we did follow his rules when we were in public. When we were alone at my home or his, it was our secret.

"I made it very clear to Alvin and to you that you were to end this."

"At school we are in classes all day together. This summer we are studying for SATs together. He helps me. He's the best friend I ever had. I won't stop seeing him."

"You disobey me and I won't stand for this." He repeated what I said, twisted it, and threw it back at me. He'd roar, "Answer me. What did you say?" I tried to repeat what I'd said, but eventually after his distortions and roaring words back in my face, I couldn't remember anything.

Sometimes he paused, mid-assault, as if admiring his work, saying, "I should have been a lawyer. I've had to fight so many battles in my day." He found pleasure in the chase of an argument, building a relentless attack, and creating strategies to get to an admission.

Then he turned on me. "I told you this relationship had to end. Why do you defy me?"

One night he slid open one of the glass doors, gestured me outside onto the porch with the gardens spreading out beyond us. He nearly choked with rage. "Where is he touching you? Has he touched your breasts?"

"No," I'd glare back. "No."

"You have no morals." Spitting the words. "Have you touched his penis?"

Shocked, I turned on him. "No, of course not. No." Despising him. This father who hated me because someone else was touching his possession, my body. Did he hate me because a black man now stroked my back? Was this a battle over who owned me? Becoming his enemy had miraculously saved me from my father's evening visits for "back rubs." Now my body was my own, no longer having to submit to my father's touch. My only comfort now was knowing I could tell Alvin everything the next day. He would listen and hug me. Soon we'd be laughing and happy again.

One summer evening my mother invited Alvin for dinner. We shucked corn and set the table. He helped Wood and Hubbard on the parallel bars on the porch, and talked music with my dad. Afterwards my father took him aside, "I need to speak to you."

He had set up two folding chairs on the stone spiral in

the garden. He launched into his lecture, building his case. Because high school and college are a time to study and not to be distracted with relationships, because I was young for my age and immature, because, and because, always coming back to and "because of the issues of safety for blacks and whites, I don't want you to see my daughter again." He wanted Alvin to know he was a sensible, thoughtful father making a sensible, thoughtful, and logical case.

Alvin listened and did not engage in discussion. He did not answer yes or no. He was a student of Aikido. He did not fight, he did not engage in discussion, he did not take the bait. He listened until my father finished speaking. He nodded to simply acknowledge the speaking. As they walked away, my father was certain his will would be done.

Alvin knew we would do nothing of the kind. We loved each other. We were not going to be ordered around. My father never raised his voice against the broad-shouldered black athlete standing in front of him, who did not call him sir, who did not provoke, who did not obey. With Alvin, he was cautious, but he walked back into the house, turning his fury on his wife and children.

UNDER SIEGE

A daughter who does not obey is not a daughter;
she's an enemy.

—FREDERICO GARCIA LORCA,
THE HOUSE OF BERNARDA ALBA

ALVIN AND OUR FRIEND PETER FROM YOUTH GROUP
lay belly-down in the snow on the little hill behind the orchard, passing binoculars back and forth, watching our house.
Beyond the blue shadows of trees, the series of sliding doors
blazed with light, the crushed glass panels glinted. They heard
my father's voice attack. "Jo, you allowed this to go on!"
Phrases biting with rage. "Over my dead body!" They could
see Jo and the boys hunched in chairs at the dining room table.

"Can you find her?" Alvin and Peter asked each other,
scanning my room and the rest of the living room until they
made out my profile in the orange Womb chair, head down,
arms crossed, knees pulled up tight against my father's rant-
ing. "You will obey me or you will never leave this house!"

Nearly two weeks before, I had made my last phone call
to Alvin, the first day of Christmas break. I whispered, "I'm
grounded." My father had said I couldn't leave the house until
I stopped seeing Alvin. "Can't talk anymore. I love you."

THAT FIRST SATURDAY of Christmas vacation, my father announced his coup. He had no choice but to put me under house arrest. He mapped out the terms. You are forbidden to leave the house for the two weeks of vacation. Because you have refused to obey me, you will never return to Princeton High School. "You will be sent to a military boarding school in January where you will be taught the meaning of obedience, once and for all."

Our house was locked down, our family sucked into a war zone, the language of Vietnam seeping in under the door. I spent days staring at the floor, shrinking from the onslaught of words, furiously glaring at my captor when his back was turned.

He raged, "You have no morals." Cross-examining me with impossible questions that were unanswerable. He'd demand "Answer me!" over and over, until he broke me down, until I couldn't think how to answer any more. Then he turned on Wood, on my mother. We argued and defended ourselves, while he turned and twisted everything we said, used it against us. He roared, "Answer me! What did you say?" We tried to repeat what we'd said, but couldn't remember our own words after a while.

He picked us off one by one, breaking us, snapping our minds like dry kindling before starting a fire, until silence, enduring, and hating was all that was left, until we shuffled away, finally dismissed.

Alvin and Peter hid out in the dark, watching the house from the demilitarized zone. Peter came to the house to visit, pretending to be neutral, and my father was instantly polite and friendly, shaking his hand, inviting him to a meal. Before leaving, Peter secretly handed me love notes from Alvin.

My mother didn't know what to do. Finally, at the end of

the second week, she went to the Episcopal minister. The word had spread through the village that something was going on in the glass house where the lights were left on all night as my father paced and lectured. Somehow my mother convinced him to let the minister come and speak with us. She spoke quietly, "We can't keep going on this way. School is about to begin. We have to get through this."

On a grey winter afternoon with rain-stained trees hovering outside the transparent walls of the house, a soft-spoken, middle-aged minister asked my family to sit around the low Eames coffee table. He looked at each of our weary, drawn faces. At seventeen, with straight hair reaching below my shoulders, I slumped in the Womb chair and flashed glances at my father, glaring and defiant. Wood and Hubbard, now fourteen and eleven, looked confused. How had they gotten trapped in this nightmare for two weeks? Couldn't they just leave? My forty-one-year-old mother sat upright, her face serious and hopeful. Sixty-year-old Woodie filled his yellow legal pad with furious notes. He rotated a modern metal and leather sling chair back and forth, ready to begin the proceedings.

The minister spoke kindly and carefully. "I want to hear each person's point of view." He set up a structure where we would each speak and listen with strict time limits.

My father spoke first. "Elizabeth trapped me in a terrible position until I had no option but to act. Here I'm worried sick about her safety being in this relationship with a black man yet she flagrantly disobeys me."

The minister asked me to reflect back what he said. I stared at the floor and muttered, "It isn't worth saying anything to my father."

The minister said, "Everyone will be heard around this circle."

He asked me again if I could reflect back what my father had said. I tried to do that without zinging it full of sarcasm. "He said he's worried about my safety."

He asked my father, "Did she hear you correctly?" He waited until my father clarified, "She doesn't understand the dangers of being in an interracial couple."

I reflected back again on what I'd heard.

My father nodded, "Yes, she heard what I said." He started to add, "If she'd only . . .," but the minister stopped him.

"No comments, please. We are concentrating on speaking and listening."

Then the minister asked me to speak and my father to reflect back. He spent hours with us. Hard work to listen and respond carefully. Then he said, "This is enough for today. I don't want any more talk about this tonight. I want you to eat together and go to bed early."

He came back the next day. The room was more sober, calmer, less like a war zone. He commented to my father, "Woodie, it seems that you need to shoot cannons to make yourself heard."

He spoke directly to me. ""You are fighting guerilla warfare, shooting arrows from behind trees, firing sarcastic quick remarks."

This quiet man negotiated a ceasefire. I was allowed to go back to school. I was allowed to see Alvin. I would see him in odd-numbered groups. My father was to stop shooting cannons. I was to stop shooting arrows. A peace treaty. We all agreed. He brought a spell of sanity into our home.

THE FIRST DAY back at school, Alvin and I were ecstatic. We had won. We couldn't stop hugging at our lockers, holding hands as we walked to class, gazing into each other's eyes. We'd almost lost each other. But we had won. My father had not separated us.

After school, when we were finally alone, we flew into each other's arms with a new passion that was unstoppable. We held each other as waves of desire washed over us. We gazed at each other and stroked each other's faces with deepened tenderness. We arranged an elaborate ruse, where we would each sleep over at a friend's house when, in fact, we went to another friend's house whose parents were out of town so we could have a night to be together. We held each other all night. I woke up to the reassurance of his arms, his body wrapped around me, and slept again. Yet I was terrified and trembled uncontrollably when our touch inched below the waist.

A few years before, my mother had advised me about sexuality. You should save your virginity until you meet the love of your life who you will marry. She daringly hinted that it could be okay before marriage, since she had broken that rule herself.

I agonized over my decision. I bored my friend Billie Jean with endless discussions of my dilemma as I studied *The Harrad Experiment* like a new Bible of sexuality. Alvin and I lost our virginity in February of our senior year and vowed to always love each other.

Yet within the month my father orchestrated our separation.

Garber house exterior

GRADUATION

A great building must begin with the unmeasurable,
must go through measurable means when it is being
designed and in the end must be unmeasurable.

LOUIS KAHN

A MONTH AFTER OUR FAMILY COUNSELING SESSIONS, Woodie glowered at me at dinner. "I was tricked and coerced by that minister. You got everything you wanted. I completely lost."

I shrugged. He no longer had the upper hand. He wasn't able to restart the war. I smiled and jumped up from the table. "Gotta go." I dashed out the door. Senior year and graduation seemed to have a momentum he couldn't stop.

Then, he saw an article in *The New York Times* about an experimental high school on a square-rigged sailing ship. It was his dream to sail around the world and the school captured his imagination as the place to send his "problem" son. After Alvin and I had slipped out of his grasp, he had turned on my brother again, hammering him about his grades, his attitude, his lengthening hair, and his black friends at the Corner. When he spoke to the director of the school in Manhattan, he also mentioned his "problem" daughter.

A week later, my brother and I, at fourteen and seventeen, were sent to New York City on our own, our first flight, for interviews with Stephanie Gallagher, the director of the Oceanics School. My father planned our removal from home, and my mother had no say in the matter. My brother was accepted as a student, and I was hired to begin that summer as the Director's assistant and for the year as librarian for the school of forty students. I would work for room and board, instead of going to college. The four-masted barque, called *The Antarna*, would set sail from Miami, motor through the Panama Canal to the Galapagos Islands and then return through the canal, following the northern coast of South America before crossing to the Ivory Coast and north to Europe. This was an unimaginable escape for my brother, whose favorite books were the eleven volumes of C. S. Forester's *Horatio Hornblower* series about life at sea during the Napoleonic wars. When I got home from New York, Alvin and I knew my father had finally succeeded in separating us after graduation. But we were certain he couldn't keep us from loving each other.

In the spring, protest rallies against the Vietnam war spilled out in downtown Cincinnati around Fountain Square. Alvin and I held on to each other in a crowd edged with police in riot gear. Peter and I were part of a group that started an underground newspaper, writing articles and anti-war cartoons. The first edition had a clenched fist on the cover. We loaded up boxes of papers and headed into the city, selling to crowds of college students in front of the Esquire theatre and head shops on Ludlow Avenue near the university. Back at school our copies were confiscated from our lockers and we were held in the office until our parents picked us up.

Towards the end of the year, a pall began to settle over me that pulled me away from Alvin and my other friends. I thought it was the restlessness we all felt, on the verge of leaving home. We walked down the polished linoleum hallways dreaming of exciting lives. But like dew invisibly soaking a meadow overnight, a depression was slowly descending, gathering me into a subdued unhappiness. The moodiness of my teens, the rumbling anger and frustration I'd focused into finely honed sarcasm, was now turned on myself. I cross-examined myself in my journal or as I fell asleep. What was wrong with me? How could I make a difference with my life? I became distant, observing through a chill remove, watching high school vanish like a dream.

I started going home after school and falling asleep, just wanting to escape, not wanting to get up. I was worn out, weary, and flattened by a sadness that would subdue me for the next nine years. I read Sylvia Plath's *The Bell Jar* and felt closer to her than to Alvin or anyone else. Until now Alvin and I had been inseparable, equally compelled to fall into each other's arms and words. Now I began to drift into a distance and he clung to me, trying to call me back. I felt smothered and wondered if I loved him.

I was like the boy in the fairy tale of the Ice Queen: a sliver of ice had fallen into my eye, and I saw the world coldly. There would be no photographs of me laughing for the next nine years. I would stare out of photographs with a sad weariness behind a series of glasses: round tortoise-shell like Le Corbusier, wide aviator frames like Gloria Steinem, small wire-rimmed circles like John Lennon. I would explain, "I don't laugh, I smile." A small crooked sad smile that took effort. Numerous times over the years, strangers would come up to me on the street: "Life isn't all that bad, you know." The demons that sent my father to bed for months now breathed in my ear.

Graduation grew closer. In the fall, Alvin was going to University of Michigan at Ann Arbor, Billie Jean to Oberlin, Linda to Kenyon, and Peter would wander until he became a Baha'i. Because my father had decided I was too young and immature to go to college, I was being sent to the ship. Even though it sounded cool, a chance of a lifetime, underneath was the knowing that my father had succeeded in mapping my future, in continuing to control my life. I had no say in the matter.

MEANWHILE MY FATHER had a big event coming. The Literary Club of Cincinnati always had an end of the year gala meeting for all members and their wives before the summer break. My father had invited them years before, but our gardens took years longer to finish than he had imagined. The date was postponed until this spring, when it was going to be held in our house and garden.

He had ordered special cases of wine years before to age to perfection. He and my mother planned the menu, hired rental chairs and tables. Rena organized a crew, including my brothers and me, to set up and serve. Woodie was on us relentlessly to get the final touches done on the gardens. He had followed a timetable of jobs for the last year. We finished the granite spiral of stones, creating a thirty-foot-diameter terrace that would last as long as a Mexican ruin. After years of cover crops, grass had been planted. Ground covers filled in. Azaleas and magnolias bloomed in the Japanese gardens where crushed white stone was poured into place and raked in patterns. The orchard was established and an acre of vegetable gardens was well cared for. The work of every weekend for the last five years of our childhoods was ready to reflect our father's magnificent plan.

———·———

BUT WHAT HUNG over my father was the paper he had to deliver that night. Every time he wrote one of his Literary Club papers, he felt intimidated by the intellectual wordsmiths in the club, the lawyers, theologians, and professors, whose distinguished papers left him feeling humbled and unworthy. He stuck with what he knew, knowing he brought an unusual flair to his Literary Papers over the years as he delivered talks addressing his passions: "Auto-Biographical" about this love affair with cars, "Bugattism" for his passion for the finest Italian racing car.

In 1967, he had delivered "You Make Your Nest," describing the process of building our house. Now was the follow-up, "And Then You Feather It," on the landscaping of the grounds. A spring paper was shorter and livelier, and suitable for the ladies. But as he dreaded and agonized over writing the paper, his project took over the Eames coffee table, piled with yellow-lined legal pads filled with his illegible script. He leaned back in his leather chair scribbling furiously as lit cigarettes sent up spirals of smoke. We could hear the furious slashing of his pencil across the page, the crumpling of paper thrown to the ground, his rifling through the thesaurus and dictionary and his spine-crushed copy of Strunk and White's *Elements of Style*. We tiptoed out of his way. Being an architect dealing with design and engineering problems all day, he felt woefully inadequate as a writer. Now that his architectural work was drying up, he felt even more insecure. Years later, he told me that as he wrestled with his papers for the Literary Club, he built up to a point of such anguish that he considered suicide.

As I wrote my last research papers that year, I too stayed up late, sometimes all night, in my room under a spotlight, stroking my eyebrows and lashes over and over, until the hairs fell out and I stuck them into a glob of white glue to collect them. I tried to force my mind into designing a thesis sentence, organizing an argument, crafting a conclusion. Under the pressure of the deadline, I too felt weighed down by a feeling of failure. Sometimes I was blessed. Sometimes this alchemy of pressure brought leaps of inspiration, startling my teachers who praised the insights, but wished I was more solid with arguments based on research.

But other nights, in the long dry hours stretching though the darkness outside my long window, an intensity built up that brought me to the place where suicide became the only solution. I doubted I could complete the paper, which meant I wouldn't pass, which meant I couldn't get into a good school, and so on, until I felt my life balanced on the success or failure of this paper. The anguished thinking of my father had flowed into my mind unannounced. When suicidal dreams live in a house, even unspoken and unfulfilled, the veil between life and death is torn, leaving a hidden wound in the psyche of the family, a sickness seeping tastelessly like a gas, a poison enveloping children as they sleep.

At school I'd gotten a list of graduation requirements for seniors: when to pick up the gown, when to practice marching, when to show up at the football stadium for the ceremony on June 14, 1971. I stared at the date. The same night as the Literary Club dinner.

My mother sounded calm as she told him at dinner that night. "It's really not a problem, Woodie. I'll get the dinner ready to serve, and Rena is here. I can just duck over to the ceremony for an hour and be back. Easy. No one will notice I'm gone."

He raged, "You aren't going anywhere."

He turned on me, spitting the words. "You know your high school graduation means nothing, absolutely nothing!" This was a supreme inconvenience that I wouldn't be there to help serve his dinner. But no one else would leave. "This dinner has been planned for years. Nothing is going to interfere with it." Eventually he allowed my brother Wood to go to my graduation for just an hour.

Gazing up at the bleachers filled with parents, as I sat in a sea of six hundred blue-gowned figures on folding chairs filling the football field, I could see Woodie's point. It was boring and endless. In the bleachers, my brother Wood recognized me by my long striding walk, saw me cross the stage as they reeled off names and diplomas as fast as popcorn popping in a pan. Then he biked home.

Maybe it did mean nothing, even though I had worked hard for my honors. I stood near Linda's parents as they took photos and she told me about the car they had given her. I didn't say what I got was twenty-five dollars so I could pick out my own Mexican necklace at my father's favorite store in New York.

I pushed through the crowds of families and waited while Alvin's family congratulated him. Then Alvin and I went to a party in Glendale. Kids were getting stoned or drunk, saying stupid things. Some parents were flirting with kids. I had nothing to say. Alvin's best friend from Walnut Hills was visiting. I hugged Alvin good night. "I'm tired. I'm going home." I walked up the line of darkened mansions on Sharon Avenue, and turned down Lake Street. There was our house, sparkling with luminaries around the gardens, the stone circle, and down the drive.

I followed a little path around the hill covered in hemlock trees and could see the lights in the house were turned down. The sliding glass doors were open, and I could hear a Getz/Gilberto samba playing on the stereo. My parents were cleaning up in the kitchen. Everyone was gone, the tables and chairs taken down. I walked through the yard, keeping in the shadows, past the empty cases of wine, a different variety for each course, and some bottles still floating in galvanized tubs of melting ice. I didn't want to go in. In the dark off to my right, I heard giggles. I walked through the orchard, sparkling with fireflies, to the little hill where Alvin had hidden in the snow watching the house last December. I heard my brother Wood talking with his friend Tom. I called up to them. "What are you doing?"

More giggles. "Taking our pay. Come on up."

I took off my sandals and climbed up the rough slope. On

top, lying on a wide slab of limestone, were two fourteen-year-old boys looking at the sky. I sat down and asked wearily, "How did the evening go?"

My brother Wood sat up. "That motherfucker bragged about how we had happily planted six thousand bloody plants." In our father's paper, he had counted up the numbers. "We shoveled seventeen tons of sand for the terrace. The happy family!" My brother's voice continued in quiet fury. "What was really disgusting was when he described Jo like he was a fucking slave owner, how her shoulders got bigger and her hips narrower from all the work. That fucker."

He shook his head. "But damn," he lifted a bottle in the dark, "this wine is amazing. Take a sip."

I put a long narrow-necked bottle to my lips and took a sip. It was not like wine, it was thick, intensely sweet. I put it down instantly and hissed. "Wood, this is one of those priceless bottles of Trockenbeerenauslese. What are you doing with it?"

He laughed. "I'm taking my pay. He never gave us a bloody cent for all the work we've done, so I take it in wine." He leaned towards me, clearly tipsy, "Now, doesn't that taste amazing? We've been up here trying to figure all the ways to describe it, haven't we, Tom?" Tom nodded.

Wood patted the stone next to him. "Relax. You've had a hard day. Just look at the stars for a while."

Elizabeth on board the Antarna, 1971

THE SHIP

Architecture is the will of an epoch
translated into space.

—LUDWIG MIES VAN DER ROHE

SEPTEMBER 1971, TWO WEEKS BEFORE WOODIE
sent his "problem children" to the school on a sail training
ship, Sander Hall dorm was due to open. The night before
the opening, Woodie was pleased. "I can truly say I've done
something fine for these students. I've given them a place to
live and thrive." At 61, he was a man at the pinnacle of his
career.

The pressure had been relentless, finishing every detail in
a building so big. Full speed ahead, down to the wire. The
landscaping would be finished later. My father was on the
site every day those last few weeks, and personally oversaw
the installation of the modern furniture in the large ground-
floor lounges. Each night at home, at the dinner table inside
glass walls overlooking the gardens, we listened to his day-
by-day reports. We drove by the construction site countless
times. This was it, the tower was finally done.

The front door clicked shut. He slumped into a chair at
the dinner table. His face drawn. "It was like a line of ants. I
saw it from my office and went down to see what was happening. I thought it was students moving in." But off-campus

students and residents from the tenements in Corryville and Calhoun Street next to campus were carrying off the sleek steel and leather furniture my father had picked out and placed. "The campus police didn't do anything!" By the end of the week, the lounges were stripped bare. And that was only the beginning.

1971. 1300 students. 27 stories. One supervising adult per sixty freshmen from cities, small towns, and farms all over Ohio assigned to live in a high-rise tower.

Students complained about not being able to open their windows. They felt trapped in a glass box. The rooms were too small. Too high. Too scary. Quickly dubbing it "The Zoo," neighbors watching the dorm said it was mayhem. Students left the bars and kept partying, the mirror glass walls in each room lit up in chaotic patterns over the face of the tower. All night long.

———.———

A DAY BEFORE we left for the ship, Woodie waited until the sunlight poured in from the west porch and from the clerestory windows above. He moved the dining room table out of the way of the walnut cabinet wall that separated the kitchen sink from the living room. The Polaroid camera was ready. He called to Wood and me, "The light's just right. Let's get these photos done. Wood first." I waited in my underwear with a towel around me in my room waiting until he called me.

My fifteen-year-old brother walked out of his room in his underpants and stood in front of the wall. Dad said, "For crying out loud, take off your underpants. This is to see how your body changes with puberty and how your muscles develop from a year of good hard work." Wood pulled off his underwear and stood at the wall, exposed on both sides by glass walls, his face staring at the floor as our father barked, "First shot, forward. Second shot, profile right. Back view. Left profile. Okay, you're done."

Living in a glass house, forbidden to close doors or use curtains, we were visible to anyone coming up the stairs or approaching across the lawn. We lived an over-exposed life, and now this, our naked bodies, photographed and documented, to be studied. We were living in an era of pulling down the barriers. Glass-walled houses allowed the private world to be made visible to the outside. We lived overexposed, in a life designed by an architect determined to break the tyranny of Victorian modesty. How many architects became tyrants, designing the lives their clients or families would live?

Our father wasn't the only parent in the 70s photographing his children nude. His modernist-inspired nudism had merged with the sexual revolution of the 60s. An era of over-exposure, exploitation and violation in the name of freedom and liberation. Woodie gave himself full license over his children's bodies, since he considered our bodies his property until we were twenty-one.

The camera flashed and whirred, spitting out white glossy cardboard squares with black squares. "Hub, help me with these photos." Hubbard, at twelve, took each photo as they came out of the camera, lined them up like cards on the table, turning his head down, looking away. I watched our mother who was in the kitchen, staring down at the counter as if she was paralyzed, her jaw tight, looking down. My brother raced to his room and slammed the door.

Woodie shouted, "Elizabeth, out here, your turn."

"Do I have to take off my underwear?"

"You shouldn't have to ask that question. The body is a beautiful thing. There's nothing to be ashamed of. Haven't I been telling you that your whole lives?"

I came out with a towel around me, seventeen years old, and unwound the towel and set it on the table before I stood with my back to the wall. Hubbard turned so his back was to me and kept his head down. He was not going to the ship, so he didn't have to have photos taken.

My father barked at me, "Stop hunching over. Stand up straight. Be proud of your body. You are a beautiful young woman. All right, forward shot."

I stared across the room at the Bertoia sculpture hanging in front of the stone wall. "Turn, profile." I will freeze my body. "Turn. Back view." I will feel nothing. "Profile. Done." The camera whirred and spat black-squared photos.

He said, "Now that wasn't that bad, was it?" I grabbed my towel and ran back to my room. He called out to both of us, "When you get home next spring, we'll take a second round to compare."

My brother was dressed and standing in his doorway next to mine. We stared at each other. Wood growled, "Over my dead body, will he ever do this again."

I nodded, and we whispered the same words to each other. "That bastard. I hate him. I hate him."

———·———

WOOD AND I flew to Miami. Our taxi pulled off the causeway onto a dock, maneuvered through a maze of stacked shipping containers before parking in front of a stained white-hulled, three-hundred-and-eighty-foot, four-masted barque, once christened the *Sea Cloud*, now called the *Antarna*. The ship had been built as a luxury yacht for Marjorie Merriweather Post when her husband Admiral Davies was US Ambassador to Russia, and now sailed under the Panamanian flag. As we climbed out of the taxi, what we saw when we looked up at the ship were long-haired hippie kids in ripped jeans on deck, in the rigging, and on the gangplank coming down to welcome us aboard.

These were American high school students, age fourteen to nineteen, thirty boys and five girls. Some had been kicked out of the best prep schools, others out of local high schools—a seventeen-year-old pathological liar who convinced us he'd served a tour of duty in Vietnam, sons of famous TV and theater actresses, wealthy corporate kids, naïve Midwestern kids, serious druggy kids, and scholarship kids. I was the school librarian along with six American teachers, a crew of Norwegian mates, a Swedish captain, an American radio officer, and Mexican cooks and engineers.

This was the Oceanics School, offering an education of a lifetime aboard a sail training ship, where our father had sent us away to shape up and be worked hard. My mother had been suspicious and questioning of the school from the very start, but she had had no word in the decision. Standing on the dock, my brother and I looked at each other and practiced our hippie expletives: "Fuckin' amazing!"

———

WHEN MY BROTHER climbed the steep gangway onto the ship, he was shown to a steep metal ship's ladder. With his duffle strapped to his back, he descended into the bow bulkhead, a steamy room where thirty teenaged boys slept in bunks that climbed the painted metal walls. They each had a clanking metal locker for stowing gear. Some already had posters on the wall, and others had put up Indian bedspreads like curtains for privacy.

My brother had long been a realist. Subjected to our father's continual criticism, he had found refuge in the talk at the Corner. He developed an X-ray vision that saw through the white lie of Glendale. He was a young man who remembered what he'd lived through. He found the boys on the ship who would compare notes on how bad their old man was, and soon they could laugh about how much they hated them, the old bastards. He set out to erase the pain. He joined the boys who discovered the Coast Guard bar on the next dock, smoky and dark with pounding music, pool, and cheap beer on tap. The bartender never carded the young kids that paraded in from the sailing ship and left hours later, tripping and giggling as they swayed up the gangplank, holding onto the strung ropes.

As school librarian, I joined the five girl students, and was ushered to the carpeted maid's quarters at the stern of the ship. Besides working in the rigging and being students, it was planned that we would wait on wealthy visitors who would stay in the staterooms, fitted out with elaborate wood paneling, chandeliers and gold-plated bathroom fixtures. It was our Director's vision that donors would see up close what an opportunity this was for kids and contribute to the school, once we got the school up and running and the boat shipshape.

The Captain called all the students to attention with a silver boatswain's whistle. We had to get the boat in order before we could head for sea. For now, classes were temporarily suspended. Once at sea, classes would resume. We were all ordered to wear blue jeans, with blue shirts tucked in, our hair tied back. We started the day scrubbing the teak decks with brooms and salt water while learning Norwegian sea chanteys. We rubbed the brass until we could see our reflections. We served dinner in the mess halls. We stood watch, signing everyone in and out at the gang plank.

On deck we all learned to use marlin spikes to splice ratlines with tar-soaked jute lines. We memorized the names of every mast, yardarm and sail, quizzing each other constantly.

"Which is the foretopgallant yard?"

"Good. Okay, name the running rigging."

"Halyard, sheets, and braces."

"Which line is made fast to this belaying pin?"

"Shit, man, I have no idea."

"Don't freak out. Just think about it." We helped each other follow the lines up the yards to where the sails would one day be attached.

My brother Wood joined the small troupe of students who volunteered to descend the clanking metal steps into the engine room. With its three-story maze of walkways, it was like a drawing by Escher. There were tangles of electrical lines, water lines, tanks, and bilges surrounding a 3,000 horsepower engine. Joining the Mexican engineers, they wore their blue jumpsuits proudly, becoming known as the "grease monkeys," who served their chief with unswerving loyalty.

On a dock off the MacArthur Causeway, between the towers of Miami and Miami Beach, an abandoned square-rigged ship started coming back to life under the strong direction of our fine captain and first mate. Living on the ship was strangely similar to the glass-walled house I'd left, with the oiled walnut cabinets. On the ship with varnished teak cabins, we lived and slept on deck, open to the weather, exposed and visible to anyone watching from the darkened shore. Here was another glowing white Olympus, floating above the mundane world. I felt completely at home on the ship, a place so beautiful I couldn't stop watching the curve of the hull, the bow sprint stretching far over the water, the masts rising gracefully above us.

———.———

AS I JOINED the crowd of students and teachers on the fantail to tell stories about our lives, amnesia took me by surprise. I became the shy girl who lost her voice and watched the others. When everyone began to share about where they were from, my recollections were like a child's. "I live in a beautiful old village in Ohio. We live in a really awesome glass house my dad designed. We grow our own food and my mom makes bread."

The young girl I re-inhabited was Daddy's girl. Amnesia wiped the slate clean of the terrible memories from the last few years, for a while. I entered as Woodie's daughter talking about art and architecture. On the fantail deck of the square-rigged sailing ship, I told about my dad driving me in the Jag with the top down after a snowfall. Or the Kandinsky lithographs he'd bought when he was poor and living in New York. When I was a baby, he raced cars on weekends, rally-racing on dirt roads across country. I said we had photograph of him airborne on a curve in a XK 140 Jag. "That's my dad."

"Wow," they said. "He's so cool."

When I called home from the pay phone on the dock, my mother was worried about us and the school, but my dad was excited. After a month on the ship, I told him, "We don't have any shelves or places to put the library," and he was inspired.

"I can pack up the VW with my saw and tools. I can make you all the shelves and storage places you need. I can't wait."

"Me, too, Daddy. That will be so great. I can't wait to see you." I really was excited, completely hopeful I would get the dad of my childhood, completely forgetting the dad of my teens. Certain I would get the father I hoped for.

"Me too, Lilibet," his voice warm and loving, as he called me my girlhood name.

When I told my brother, he looked at me like I was crazy and walked away, shaking his head.

———

AFTER HOURS OF splicing lines and scrubbing decks, I was still loyal to my job as school librarian, organizing boxes in the crowded storage area where they were stacked and pulling out books for students to read. I welcomed my dad's offer to build shelves for the library. After my first month away from home, I was suddenly homesick. When I saw the familiar green and white VW bus drive up to the dock and my father behind the wheel, I felt a surge of love and happiness. This was Home. This was Dad.

He called out, "Hey, Sugar. Show me the ropes on this ship."

I hugged him and gave him the tour from one end of the ship to the other, while my brother watched warily and kept his distance. My father instantly felt needed. He had a job to do and a crew of volunteers who were quick learners. We had assessed where bookshelves could be built up the bulkhead wall in the mess hall. He calculated the curve of the wall and how much of a lip the shelves needed so the books wouldn't crash down in high seas. Soon the saw was whining through fresh pine boards at his impromptu shop on the dock to the left of the gangway.

My brother disappeared into the engine room. From the rigging I observed the progress of the carpentry crew. My dad was at his best, teaching enthusiastic students, and a new friend, Pogo, lingered long after the day's work to talk about architecture. The library was a success, with fresh pine shelves holding the books I'd labeled and classified all summer. Students lingered in the mess hall after meals, pulling down books and passing them around. In the hot afternoons on break, before dinner, before bed, above and below decks, students were reading: *Moby Dick, Heart of Darkness, Call of the Wild.* Older students and teachers devoured books by Alan Watt on Buddhism, Frankl's *Man's Search for Meaning,* and Hesse's novels: *Siddhartha, Demian, Steppenwolf,* and my new favorite, *Narcissus and Goldmund.* My new friends Kimble, Pogo, Brendan, and Ted pondered whether we should be like the pure monk Narcissus or follow the path of Goldmund, going out into the world of sex and experience. We asked each other, "Who ultimately lived a better life?"

My father discovered more projects, bunks to build. When the dynamic young school director, Stephanie Gallagher, thanked him profusely, she added casually, "We could keep you busy for a while!" He took this for a full invitation. He was growing more demanding with my brother and me, ordering us out to dinner with him. There he launched into his old lectures on our behavior, our attitudes and our work habits. In the busy dining room he kept his voice low but we knew he was accelerating, the pressure was building.

A few days later, he told us to meet him on the starboard deck on the bench outside the radio operator's door. When we reluctantly slouched onto the bench, he faced us on a chair he'd brought on deck. He was strangely elated as he gazed at the series of lines knotted around the rail of belaying pins, out to the harbor traffic and the sea in the distance. He set the stage to his speech. "You know, I've wanted to spend a year at sea my whole life." He turned and his eyes insisted we nod in agreement. Yes, we nodded warily, yes, we knew.

He built his case. "When I saw the article about this school, I thought, I could give this gift to my children." His tone sounded so magnanimous, as if he were the kindest man in the world to have given his children this gift. We looked down, murmuring, "Yes, this is great to be on the ship," but we glanced at each other. We also knew we were here because he deemed my brother such a failure he had to be sent away to learn a thing or two and I had to be kept away from Alvin. Our father noticed our slouching, and his voice amped up. "Sit up straight when I'm talking to you! Don't you appreciate going to this school? This is a chance of a lifetime and you bloody well better appreciate it."

We sat up straighter, immediately saying, "Of course we do. We love it on the ship." But we were bracing for something. Other students strolled by, glancing at us, raising their eyebrows when they passed behind our dad's head—mouthing to us silently, "Are you okay?" When our dad looked away for a moment, we raised our eyes and shrugged, before our dad turned back to continue delivering his speech.

He announced with pride, "I've decided I will stay on board for the rest of the year. I think Stephanie's made it pretty clear that I have a lot to offer to the school."

His words stunned us. My brother and I both sat bolt upright, leaning against each other. We were instantly absolutely clear and spoke with one voice. "You can't stay. This is our school year. You can not stay. You have to leave."

Now it was our father's turn to be stunned. "What do you mean, you ungrateful children. Don't you know I've done everything in my life for you and your mother? This is what I want to do more than anything in my life. You mean to deny me this?" His face got red and he started to spit as he lashed out at us.

My brother and I were fearless and clear, repeating the simple words. "You cannot stay. We will leave if you stay."

Our father repeated his attack. "I've sacrificed my whole life for you and you deny me this trip of a lifetime? You are spoiled rotten kids. I'm ashamed to be your father." He glowered at us, as if he despised the sight of us. We watched as a thought struck him.

Inspired, he leapt up, roaring at us. "You are no children of mine. As of this moment, I disown you both. I will have nothing to do with you for the rest of your lives. You won't ever get another red cent from me." He paced in front of us, peppering us with his final lines. "Don't think you can *ever* come home again. You have no home!" He stalked off down the deck, turning toward the gangway.

We sat there, stunned, looking at the thicket of lines, made fast, wrapped and orderly in front of us. Students who had been hovering in earshot yet hidden from view came up to us. "You guys okay?"

Wood and I looked at each other. We were fifteen and eighteen. Our father had just disowned us and told us we could never come home. We looked at each other, wondering, "Are we okay?"

Then we grinned. The year ahead gleamed with promise. We were liberated.

Wood said to me, "I think this deserves a celebration. And you haven't had a drink yet to celebrate your birthday."

Our father left without another word to us, but said good-bye with great warmth, hugs, and claps on the backs of his "favorites" who had worked with him. He packed up the VW and was gone in a few hours, leaving only tracings of sawdust on the dock for a few weeks, until rains washed them away.

I went with my brother that night over to the Coast Guard bar with a group of friends who toasted us. After one beer, I felt wobbly, sobered and tired. I leaned over to Wood, "Oh, no. I just remembered. I've got to call Jo and warn her."

He nodded grimly, "Good idea," and then turned back to laugh with his friends. In the solitary light of a pay phone looking up at the gleaming white ship, I felt like I was standing on a stage set.

While our father had spent less than a month on the ship, we had no idea what life at home was like when Hubbard and Jo were not locked into roles under our father's tight rein. Every day after school, they starting going places and doing fun things. "The most amazing thing," Hubbard told us the next summer, "We weren't scared all the time. We broke the rules!" Our father had forbidden us to ever to have junk food. Hubbard bragged that they went to McDonald's to try it out. They were not impressed with the burgers, but liked the milkshakes and fries and laughed all the way home. Hubbard began to pray his father would never come home. He'd say over and over as he fell asleep, "Don't come back. Don't ever come back."

My call warned them. Paradise was over. Once I got off the phone and was caught up with life on the ship, I forgot to imagine his homecoming and how my mother and brother would have to hear lectures about us. But those weeks with Woodie away had changed everything at home. Our mother, seeing what life could be like, began to make a plan to save herself and her children.

Wood and I thought we were free of our father's heavy hand, but we were still living an extension of our father's dream. He had chosen a risky, poorly organized school on an unseaworthy ship, fueled on inflated visions, much like something he would imagine.

With the naïveté of the young, we didn't worry about being disowned at all. We occasionally wondered how we were going to support ourselves when we left the ship. But we didn't think about life after the ship. We knew our mother would always welcome us home, and that home was wherever she was.

When the rigging was completed, the boat shipshape, the huge engine started and we left Miami for the Bahamas, and then motored towards Vera Cruz, Mexico, for the hull to be scraped and painted in dry dock. Everyone had to leave the ship while the work of sandblasting and toxic painting was underway. The students and teachers were given $2.50 a day to explore Mexico and told to come back in three weeks. Our instructions for returning were to look for the masts, so we could find where the ship would be moored.

As we left the ship, Stephanie said, "Don't do any drugs. We can't get you out of jail."

My group of friends divided up, one girl per team, for a hitchhiking race to Mexico City, meeting at a particular cheap hotel in the next few days. My hitchhiking partner, the patrician Brendan, with windswept blond hair, was one of the Exeter students, kicked out for having beer in his room the week before graduation. I wore a skirt, he a white button-down shirt. In minutes we got a ride with a German industrialist who had just picked up a new Mercedes off the dock. We arrived at our hotel faster than we calculated was humanly possible to get to Mexico City.

My brother Wood and another long-haired fifteen-year-old were left without a girl to help with hitching rides. They rode in the back of an oily truck through the mountains.

Later their packs were ransacked, their cameras stolen. Left on the side of the road in the mountains, cold wind slicing through their clothes, they walked down the road toward the only light they saw. When they reached a peasant family's home, they were welcomed, put in front of the fire, fed spicy soup and tortillas, and invited to sleep on their floor in front of the fire. It took them three days to reach Mexico City. I was terrified something might have happened to my little brother. When he regaled us with their escapades, I stopped worrying about him. Our adventures continued for three weeks.

Back on the ship, we motored out into the fresh breezes of the Gulf as we hauled, hand over hand, the heavy canvas sails into the rigging and lashed them to the yardarms. Mainsail, lower and upper topsail, topgallant, royal, and one skysail. From the foremast to the mizzen mast, sail by sail, we hauled them up to the yards, and finally to the stern, the jigger mast, rigged fore and aft, with staysails between the masts. A few days out of Vera Cruz, we had twenty-seven out of the thirty sails lashed into place.

We sailed around the Yucatan, passing the misty blue shores of Cuba off to port, where fishermen in wooden boats waved hello. We rounded the mountainous emerald island of Jamaica before setting sail for Panama. Out of sight of land, I began to doubt the existence of earth, thinking maybe there was only this gentle riding of swells, with sails unfurled. I loved this life, falling asleep at night under the filled sails high above, waking on deck with the dawn. We traveled in a dream of wind—white canvas whipping overhead, lines hauled around brass capstans—in a dream of ships, in a dream of silvery water as we lay on the bow deck watching dolphins leap endlessly in the swells off the hull. We climbed the bow-sprit, far out beyond the ship, and watched her sail towards us. We watched every sunset for the green flash as the sun was extinguished in the waves, and we awakened in time for sunrise to turn the sails pink with dawn. We cheered when the west horizon grew solid, increasing into a shoreline of harbors as we re-entered the world of shipping lanes and harbor masters.

But we had sailed into a trap. Our Captain called us up on deck to stand at attention. He informed us that Panamanian officials had contacted the ship that they would be conduct-ing a search of the vessel. He begged all the students, teachers, and crew to please get rid of anything illegal they might have.

"Please," the Swedish captain implored us, "this is serious."

The Panamanian harbor and military officers arrived on a PT boat. Everyone from the ship stood on deck, nervously watched as every nook and cranny of the four-masted barque was searched.

We sighed with relief when they acted friendly and told the Captain that they didn't find anything. Stephanie, the school director, and her assistant went ashore with the offi-cials, but the next day we heard they were being held in jail. The PT boat came back, and our ship was ordered to anchor in a backwater bay of Cristobel harbor. The PT boat and offi-cers didn't leave. They anchored alongside us, the machine gun uncovered and pointed at the ship. Rumors and wild speculation raced from teenagers to crew to teachers around the ship, but we couldn't have imagined what eventually turned out to be the truth.

The ship's owner had originally leased the *Antarna* to the Oceanics School without informing the school of the extent of the rotten rigging or of daily mechanical fires in the engine room. Stephanie had signed the contract, interviewed students, hired crew and gotten the school underway. When the bills started mounting, she kept convincing donors to support the school through the thousands of dollars in bills to get the ship seaworthy, including going through dry dock in Vera Cruz. As we sailed to Panama, Stephanie was certain the ship's problems were over and now wealthy passengers could come aboard to sail for a week at a time to experience and support this remarkable school at sea.

What we didn't know as we sailed into Panama was that the owner of the ship had flown in early to convince Panamanian officials to make a drug raid on the ship. He was certain that his bribes would work to kick off the hippie school, and that they would hand the now-gleaming, re-rigged, seaworthy *Antarna* back to him. Little did he imagine that the Panamanians, after searching the ship, would decide to take control of the ship for Panama, which they could do because the ship was registered under the Panamanian flag. They would hold the American students and teachers, and the international crew members, hostage. Stephanie, our director, was put in jail so we wouldn't try to escape with the ship.

Stephanie, always a smart fast talker, had gotten out of jail in a few days. Early on, we'd been scared, exchanging rumors like trading cards as we grasped onto any news of our fate. We heard the jail was full of Americans, sailors and hippie travelers. We heard the American Embassy wasn't answering calls from Americans in trouble because they didn't want to disrupt the Panama Canal negotiations.

At first a harbor taxi arrived regularly with Stephanie, always looking unflustered with her smooth black hair and Jones of New York suits as she talked with the Panamanian officials. Stephanie met with the students to let us know she was hard at work making what would cost $6,000 in phone calls to everyone she knew in the states to get us out of here. She was letting our parents know. Not to worry. We watched and waited. We wondered which kid's parent would have the most political pull to help us. One kid's mom was a famous actress with her own show on TV, and a couple dads were CEO's of big companies. We wondered whose calls to senators would have the biggest clout to release American kids being held hostage in Panama. Our bets were on the TV actress.

The trade winds had stopped and there was no breeze in Colon Harbor. All over the ship, students camped out under lifeboats or under canvas strung up for shade at the fantail or lay sweating on their bunks with headphones on, listening to the Grateful Dead. We hadn't seen the Captain or First Mate for days. They didn't come out of their quarters. Some days we watched the parade of container ships steaming towards the canal. It started to feel like we had been living here forever. We passed the binoculars around, trying to make out what flag they were flying under.

We turned our binoculars on the Panamanian Navy PT boat at anchor a few hundred feet from our ship. At the bow, the machine gun was still pointed towards our ship. Under cover, the crew had their feet up, hats down, and looked asleep to us. One of us would nudge another: "Maybe we could make a run for it and get out of here before they wake up."

"Yeah, sure." We rolled on our backs, put a pillow under our heads and went back to reading. All over the ship we lived on books, working our way through all the novels by Herman Hesse, *Lord of the Rings*, the *Dune* trilogy, and Carlos Castaneda books.

We waited and waited as our stores of food and water ran down, waited until Stephanie's negotiations—and who knows how much money—were successful in freeing us. The Panamanian officials told us we were lucky and allowed to leave. We packed up the school books and supplies, the library, and our gear, filling an endless costly trail of little boats to a dock, loaded and unloaded onto trucks, then loaded onto a train, and carried across Panama to a privately charted plane to Puerto Rico. The ship would remain in a back bay for years, the sails and rigging rotting in the relentless sun.

In Puerto Rico, we were loaded onto school buses, put up in a Catholic boarding school overnight, until buses carried us up and over narrow twisting mountain dirt roads to deposit the students and remaining teachers in front of a tiny one-room concrete block building overlooking pastures where cows with long horns grazed. Stephanie had arranged it all by phone from New York, finding a parent with a "farm" where we could stay until she found us another ship. Ever the magician, she had one almost lined up, she assured us.

We swam in the breakers, read in hammocks, slept in clusters in a meadow with weary friends, too lost in dreams to talk much, until I woke up one morning. A young Puerto Rican man was reaching his hand inside my shorts. I sat up, looked at him and whispered, "What are you doing?"

He smiled. "Don't you want me?"

"No!" I pulled my sleeping bag up to my chin. I lied, "I have a boyfriend," and gestured to my collection of friends nearby.

"Then why isn't he sleeping next to you?" he asked persistently.

I said firmly, "Go away." Finally he did.

That day, my brother and I decided it was time to go home. We hitchhiked to a little hamlet where there was a pay phone. We called collect. Our mother answered. She was fierce and crying at the same time. "Get to the airport. I will have plane tickets waiting for you. Come home."

She snuck into the bedroom while our father napped, took his wallet, found his credit card, stretched the phone cord into my room, and made her calls.

The summer after the ship: Wood,
Hubbard, Elizabeth, 1972

PRESSURE COOKER

1972

I have the capacity in me for every crime.

—RALPH WALDO EMERSON

I HAVE NO MEMORY HOW OUR FATHER RESPONDED when we returned from the ship. But that summer it seemed our family disappeared behind a wall of thorns that grew up around the house, impenetrable, encasing us. It seemed we saw no one, and no one came to the glass house. Our father was home too much with little work. Our mother slipped out to work at the Probation Department in the city. The garden grew, we cooked meals, yet for me the summer remains only in fragments, scraps of nightmares, torrents of words yelled at all hours of night, as we were broken down, our minds battered like prisoners, separated from life.

OUR MOTHER GRADUATED from college on a broiling hot day in June, with Honors in Criminal Justice. Woodie drove our family into the city for the ceremony. He passed dangerously, cutting in front of traffic. People slammed on brakes and honked at him. We braced ourselves in our seats, held on to the door handles, glancing wide-eyed to each other. He was furious. We were hungry and he wouldn't stop for food. On campus, we climbed up into the football stadium finding empty seats, and sat under a broiling sun, watching hundreds of gowned figures cross a stage far below, for hours.

I watched clouds float by, reflected in the silver mirrored dorm towering twenty-seven stories over us. I asked Woodie, "How's it going at Sander Hall?"

His face grimaced. He spat the words, "The students are animals." He looked away furiously at the crowds of families and students watching the graduation.

OUR FRIEND CHUCK told me later what happened at Sander Hall. The first winter had been bad: thefts, robberies, rape. Then arson. Someone tossed a firecracker down a trash chute. Smoke rose, fire alarms rang. The fire department came. 1300 students filed down the center staircase in the wee hours of the night to wait in the first-floor lounges until All Clear. Over the years, students started setting off fire alarms daily. Students descended with the alarms until many ignored them to try to sleep. Students lit paper stuffed in garbage cans. Others lit paper shoved in around the fire alarm. Two freshmen girls, good students from good families, were sentenced for arson. Sander Hall was called "The Firehouse."

We looked for our mother, who was down there in the crowds of students in black gowns. She was safe, away from Woodie. Afterwards, when we found her in the crowd, she was radiant, wearing her father's gown, her short curly hair under her mother's cap, waving her diploma. She kept repeating, "I did it! After all these years, I did it!"

He growled at her, "What do you think you'll do with that?" and stalked off.

We followed him obediently. Tangled in a web, we began to dream desperate ways to escape.

———

ON A DAY when no one was home, my sixteen-year-old brother, Wood, took the .22 from the back of our father's closet in their bedroom. He loaded it and lay down on his father's side of the bed, and put the gun to his head.

The house was quiet. He heard the refrigerator humming, a lawn mower started up in the distance. The room was in shadow from the poplars on the east side of the house. He hated the smell of his father's sweat in the mashed feather pillow under his head. He'd show that bastard. His eyes scanned the room and stopped on his mother's bookshelf next to the window. The books she worked so hard to read, on prisons, concentration camps, and the history of Russia.

He remembered sitting at the kitchen table with his mother, how she made spelling lists fun. How she pulled him towards her for a hug. How he felt getting home from the ship when he threw his arms around her at the airport. He relaxed his finger on the trigger. He looked at her side of the bed. He couldn't do this to her. He heard the crunch of gravel of a car in the driveway. He jumped up quickly and put the .22 back in the closet.

ON THE HIGHWAY between Cincinnati and the suburbs, in Loveland, there was a section where concrete walls lined the four lanes, a deep trough for heavily loaded trucks and commuters to roar through, three stories below the street above. Every time I drove home from the city through Loveland, I had to restrain myself from driving our old VW bus into the concrete walls. I went to sleep imaging how quickly I would vanish, hitting the wall at sixty miles an hour.

MY BROTHER WOOD borrowed our mother's car, a two-door 2002 BMW. Late one night in town near the Art Museum, he came down a hill so fast that when he hit a set of railroad tracks he was lifted airborne, and bent the chassis when he landed. He laughed when he told us his calculation for highway exits. "Take the speed limit, multiply by two and add ten." My mother stared at him grimly. "I'll kill you, if you kill yourself."

ONE DAY, AFTER hours of yelling, my mother left the house crying, got in her BMW and left. Not sure where she was going. Just to get away. Our dad ran down the stairs, got into his more powerful BMW and chased after her. She headed out of the village on a narrow two-lane road. He passed cars, honking as he raced to catch up. He overtook her in the opposing lane, and yelled, "Pull over. I have to talk to you!"

Approaching traffic honked and screeched brakes before he pulled in behind her. He followed her onto the highway in his white luxury four-door BMW, pursuing her in her battered small grey BMW. Our father pursued her down the four-lane highway, quickly changing lanes with inches to spare at seventy miles an hour, with a crazed precision from his years as a racing car driver, trying to force her off the road. He would defend his actions later, saying, "I was trying to talk to her, and she refused." He claimed he was the victim of her moods.

She didn't know where to go as she drove farther into the city, until she thought of her old friend, a lawyer. She'd be safe there, if she could make it. She followed parkways and back roads through neighborhoods, Woodie gunning his engine behind her. She pulled into their driveway, my father's tires screaming to a halt behind her. He leapt out his door to chase after her, his voice roaring, "You will obey me!" Her friend appeared in time to throw open the heavy oak doorway for my mother, then to slam shut and lock, leaving my father to pace like a caged tiger on the road in front of the ivy-covered half-timber house. Hours later, he drove home. When she eventually returned, the yelling went on all night.

———·———

ONE DAY, WHILE weeding alone in the garden, my steady heart jolted and stopped. I felt a strange absence in my chest. Then my heart began to race. I could hardly breathe. I couldn't stand up. I sank down and lay on my back in the grass.

Everything went still inside me. I felt strangely calm. I had watched my dad's heart pound hard in his chest too hard and too fast as long as I could remember. When I was a kid, his heart would sometimes go too fast, they called it fibrillating, and it pounded so hard his whole body shook. He'd go to the hospital sometimes for weeks when they tried to slow it down. He almost died when I was seven. But he didn't. He was okay, but they told him they couldn't fix his heart. It would always be fast and irregular. He'd have to get used to it. But sometimes, when it went way too fast, he sank to the floor gasping for breath and had to be helped to bed.

As I lay on the warm earth, my ribs felt like a delicate bamboo bird cage and my heart kept leaping and banging against the sides. I looked up into the elm branches arching high above me. There was no one I could call. The afternoon echoed around me. Another big jolt in my chest, a long silence, and then my familiar heartbeat came back like footsteps on a path covered with pine needles. I lay in the grass a long time, cradling my chest, before I slowly sat up. I was a girl who'd discovered she had her father's heart.

OUR HIPPIE FRIEND Chuck, who had become Jo's best friend, sat with her at the round kitchen table when no one else was home. She was trying to figure out what to do. She felt stuck, stymied, unable to do anything. To get divorced was unthinkable for her generation. She kept trying, every day, struggling to get us through. But she was hopeless. "I'm just trying to save my family," she said.

He looked at her a long time. "What family?" He felt cruel and heartless.

She looked at him, stunned. "You're right."

———

HUBBARD, AT THIRTEEN, woke up nights, soaking with sweat, sobbing. He would dream for years of his father's funeral. But he was sure it was all his fault. Lying in the dark, hearing his father's occasional snore, the shifting of covers as his parents moved in the bedroom beyond his door, he felt sick with guilt. "What if imagining his funeral kills him?" He thought he was the worst person in the world.

Hubbard knew what was coming, better than any of us. He knew our mother was leaving. Our father hated his son Wood, so Wood, of course, would go with Jo. Hubbard was a child but he knew what he had to do. He knew his father would stop at nothing. The only way to keep Woodie from killing our mother was to stay with his father. His father had to have a trophy, something he could hold over Jo. Hubbard knew what his sacrifice had to be.

———

JO MET WITH Woodie's psychiatrist a few times. But she felt like Phil Piker was trying to put her back together so she would keep the family and my father together. The last time she went, she told him, "Woodie's always riding me and telling me what to do. He keeps throwing shit at me, and I have to catch it."

Phil asked, "Why do you have to catch it?"

That night, our father was cooking furiously. Throwing out orders, he told Jo, "Get down the chafing dish." She turned to him and said, "No."

My brothers and I stood, stunned.

———•———

THAT'S WHEN THE yelling never stopped, no longer focused on us, it was all a barrage aimed at our mother. Her crimes were endless. She'd stolen his wallet to bring us home. She had changed. She wasn't the girl he'd married. She was out to destroy our lives. She had to be stopped. He wouldn't stand for this. His voice lashed out at all of us. Sometimes we stepped into the path of his fury to defend her. He turned his wrath on us, taking anything we said to use it against her, hurting her more. He'd roar at her, "Answer me! Confess! You are destroying our lives!" There was nothing anyone could do to stop the wall of words, the attacks. We tried to repeat what we'd said, but we couldn't remember our words or our own thoughts after a while. His voice poisoned us and left us limp and hopeless. His voice rampaged through the glass-walled house every night and we couldn't get away.

One night, to escape the yelling, I snuck outside with my sleeping bag to the long porch overlooking the gardens. I was awakened when I heard the glass door slide open, and my parents entered the porch, not seeing me in the dark. Hour after hour of that long night, he lectured, browbeat, badgered; and she sat, mostly silently in a chair, as he paced back and forth or stopped, sputtering in rage. His voice rose and challenged, her soft voice dropped away to nothing.

My hatred concentrated that long night. I had to do something. To end this. Someone had to do something. He went on until dawn lit the mist rising off the fine landscaped gardens we'd toiled over for years. They never saw me. He rolled back the sliding glass doors and motioned my mother back into the house, and she followed, crumpled and obedient.

———

IT WAS A house of pain we stepped in and out of, sometimes finding relief when we left the house, sometimes forgetting. I found a strange comfort reading the books on Jo's bookshelf on the Holocaust, the rise of Hitler, and his insidious takeover of the minds of a population. Those books helped me. The Jews in Germany had lived in a country gone mad. My home was overtaken by madness, but I was fortunate, I could leave my house and the craziness stayed inside.

One morning, I woke up to the sound of someone quietly breathing in my bedroom. I lay under my covers curled on my side, afraid to open my eyes. Someone was in the other twin bed. I lifted up my head. A figure was sleeping on its side, its back away from me, with short dark hair showing above the covers. My mother. She'd come in during the night. She would sleep in my room the rest of that summer. Later that day I saw the phone cord pulled from the kitchen into my room, the door nearly shut. I heard her whisper "rape" as I tiptoed by.

August sweltered outside the air-conditioned glass. We

were held captive inside by the heat and our father's nightly yelling. It seemed we never left the house. No one visited us.

One morning, I woke up and knew what I had to do. It was so simple. All I had to do was kill my father. Then the yelling would stop. Then we would be free. I felt clear and calm as I calculated my plan. In the kitchen, as I put dishes and silverware away after breakfast, I lingered over the drawer of my father's collection of well-sharpened German and Japanese cooking knives. I examined their blades and handles. All I had to do was stab him in the heart. Nothing else could save us. All I wanted was to stop his voice, stop the threats, the lectures, the cross-examining. We'd be out of pain. Just take a knife. I looked them over. I fingered one of the carving knives he'd taught me to use, slicing precisely. I didn't know where I'd stab, didn't know the hardness of bone. I imagined only silence and freedom.

There had been a murder case in Cincinnati. The papers ventured that the teenage daughter had killed her well-to-do parents in a comfortable neighborhood on the other side of town. People wondered how a normal, quiet high school student could do that. The papers would say we looked like a perfect family. Except our neighbors who heard his voice yelling at night from the glass house. I thought about prison and made lists of books I'd want to take. I was resigned to my fate.

———

THE MURDER WOULD occur in the galley kitchen, between the oiled walnut banks of cabinets and below the steel rack of hanging copper cooking pots and lids. I chose the spot where my father normally chopped onions with a fine Japanese blade at the counter in the center point of the kitchen, where he commanded our lives in the Great Room. Rolling open the three-foot-wide drawer crowded with his cooking knife collection, his booming voice always demanded our full attention to his instruction.

His voice filled the house, down to the farthest reaches of the high-ceilinged room where Wood hid behind a book. His voice followed our mother where she folded laundry, out of sight, in one of the covey of bedrooms whose doors opened on either side of the kitchen. Hubbard slid open a glass door and vanished on his bike all day.

THE DAY CAME. We all stood in the long open aisle kitchen at the end of the Great Room lined with glass doors. The oiled walnut cabinets became a stage. My father stood in the middle in front of the closed drawer of knives. My mother and I stood on one side, my brothers on the other side. Time slowed down. Actors in position, playing our parts. I was poised. This was the time to step forward, open the drawer and grab the sharpest blade. But I couldn't move. His rage surrounded us like the Chinese red panel that circled the Great Room. We were mired in an erupting lava flow of sound.

Yet I grew stronger and clear. My intention was as sharp as a knife blade. The roaring wall of our father's voice went silent. Something powerful had also built up in my brothers and my mother, a calm of a unified hatred. We all turned our faces towards him. We didn't cower submissively.

Like the day a revolution sparks and a suppressed people all rise with a single-minded purpose and fill the streets, demanding freedom, we each turned our faces towards him. Silently and steadily, we channeled our fury into our eyes. We turned to face the barrel-chested man who had devoured our lives.

I never had to touch a knife. Something happened. We turned our eyes on him and he cried out like a stabbed bull. He crashed to the ground, his hands grabbed his fibrillating heart. Crying out, he was small and pitiful, like a statue of a dictator pulled down by peasants.

We didn't move. We stood there silently. We looked down on him on the white vinyl kitchen floor. His chest heaving, his face red, sweat slick on his face, sweat seeping through his shirt. He was fumbling on the ground, trying to sit up. No one knelt down to help. Not the ones who usually came to his side, not my mother, nor me. One at a time, my brother Wood, then Jo, then I turned and walked away. He lay there panting, gasping for breath until my youngest brother Hubbard helped him to bed and got him his heart pills.

I slid open the glass door and entered the damp heat of August, dazed. Disoriented. Free. I didn't have to kill him. I didn't have to sacrifice my life to free us. We had acted as one. We had liberated ourselves. We didn't know what would come next, but we knew we would save our lives.

———

ABOUT A WEEK after my father's collapse in the kitchen, he walked into my bedroom before breakfast and sat down on the desk chair to face me. My mother and I were sitting up against the pillows in the twin beds, drinking coffee, when he came in. The moment she saw him, I could feel her tense with fear, but curiously I didn't. In three weeks, I had plans to fly to France to study for a year and somehow that now gave me a sense of safety.

He was excited, and talking fast. "I just remembered. When I was about to leave for college, my great aunt Ada, the matriarch of the family, gave me an unimaginable gift. Her car."

I imagined it was a Dusenberg from the 1920s, something priceless, regal, and astonishing. He continued, "This was during the Depression. My father had lost everything. I was eighteen, and had no money for tuition. I never even imagined owning a car." She gave him the choice; he could sell the car for his college tuition payment to start at Cornell or keep it and not go to school. He beamed. "I loved that car, and it broke my heart to sell it."

My mother and I stared at him. He was oddly elated, caught up in an excitement we couldn't understand. He was acting like nothing was wrong, as if there was nothing strange about his wife sleeping in my room. He looked at me and continued, "So I have decided to give you my Jaguar."

I was stunned. His white convertible XKE Jaguar that he'd never let me drive? Give it to me? Oh my god, to own that car! To drive it! I felt I could leap out of my skin with excitement. All caution vanished.

He explained, "The choice is yours. Keep the car and not go to France. Or you can sell it to pay for your year away." He calculated I could get about $2,500 for it. I was to clean and wax it, run an ad in the paper, and sell it. "This is how you'll learn the value of money."

My mother remained silent but in the clenched muscles of her jaw, I could sense her warning. "It's a trick. He's crazy."

He reached into his pocket, and pulled out the key. "So what are you going to do?" He held out the key.

I looked at my mother cowering under the covers. I looked at the key and his strangely animated face. I took it. My ticket out the door.

TWO DAYS LATER, with a small bag packed and my stash of babysitting cash, I backed that long white lion of a car out of the garage. The top was down. I slid into the red leather bucket seat behind the wood and metal steering wheel. The engine revved and purred as my foot played the accelerator. I was eighteen years old. My mother's face was grim and scared, my brothers laughing and envious. My father, no longer manic, sternly admonished me, "You have to sell it before you leave for France."

I waved. "I know, I know. I'll be back in a week." I gave the car an extra series of revs as I steered down the drive across the creek and waved goodbye. I followed the narrow road past the old farm edging the village, before I headed to the highway and accelerated like a rocket out of the magnetic pull of their misery.

I drove east from Cincinnati, my hair whipping around my face, on the first solo long-distance drive of my life. I kept the top down in good weather. When it looked like rain I'd stop, unfold the roof like an accordion, fasten the black cover on snaps along the top of the windshield. It didn't bother me that it leaked in the rain. I double-clutched down, the way he'd taught me racing car drivers would shift gears. I studied the map, refueled, and checked the oil.

I visited friends from the ship. Near New Hope, Pennsylvania, Kimble photographed me in a meadow, my long hair golden in the sunset. I sat inside the open driver's door, the long white Jag gleaming rose. My eyes laughing behind wire-framed glasses, wearing my favorite Mexican embroidered peasant shirt and bell-bottoms. Cruising across New Jersey with three friends from the ship squeezed into the Jag, we sang "We All Live in a Yellow Submarine" as I drove down the Garden State Parkway.

As I turned west a week later, a toll booth attendant in the middle of Pennsylvania asked, "How fast can she go?"

"I don't know."

"Go find out. No one's come by here in a while."

The Jag accelerated to 120 miles an hour, effortlessly. It probably could have gone faster, but I didn't want to push it. I didn't need to. I was a girl who could drive a Jag, go to France, and leave home.

Villa Savoye, 1973

LE CORBUSIER

1973

*In this house, one will find a truly architectural
promenade which offers constantly varying aspects,
unexpected, sometimes astonishing.*

—LE CORBUSIER,

ON VILLA SAVOYE IN POISSY

AS THE TRAIN RUMBLED AND SHUDDERED ALL NIGHT
from Paris south to Grenoble, with students and baggage
clogging every aisle and squeezed into every seat, I leaned
against the cold black glass, my heart racing out of rhythm. I
had no idea that my mother was also sitting awake at night,
afraid of what lay ahead of her.

Within weeks of my leaving in September, my mother
informed my father she was moving out the following
Wednesday. On Tuesday, when she got home from work, the
locks had been changed. He never let her into the glass house
again. He informed her that anything she thought was hers
had to be written down on a piece of paper and he would
choose what he gave her. Desperate, she went to Sears that
night, bought a nightgown, clothes for work the next day,
two mattresses, sheets and pillows, a few plates, pots and pans,
and a vacuum cleaner. The next day he cancelled her credit
cards. This is what happened if a woman dared to leave.

The war of belongings would continue for years. My brothers, at sixteen and thirteen, were divided between them, Wood leaving with my mother, my younger brother Hubbard choosing to stay with his father.

My mother's letters to me were upbeat, taking ten days to cross the ocean to my rented room four stories above the narrow streets of old Grenoble in the French Alps. She never let me know how terrified she was. At forty-three, she was supporting herself for the first time. Fortunately, my father had told her a few years before, "Your volunteering is fine, but for my taxes it would be better if you got a part-time job." She had graduated from college, but when she started a full-time job as a probation officer, our father had not been happy. This was not good for his taxes. He had no idea she'd bought her ticket to freedom.

In her letters to me, she wrote, "Things were really hard at first when we moved to our apartment, but life is settling in. I made meatloaf and mashed potatoes last night. We thought of you."

In the letters from home, no one told me my father was haunting the parking lot of the dingy Kenilworth Court Apartments, where my mother and brother Wood slept on mattresses on the floor. No one told me my father slashed the tires of her car, or tapped her phone, or let the phone ring at all hours of the night, followed by heavy breathing or growled threats before my mother slammed down the receiver. The phone was wired to the wall and couldn't be disconnected, so they wrapped it in blankets in a drawer to muffle the sound. No one told me these things until I came home, when they were hauled out like war stories: how Hubbard found the tapes from the private investigator hidden in my dad's desk, how they just said any crazy thing, because they knew the phone was bugged.

One of my mother's clients on probation asked her why she looked so stressed. When my mother explained, her client lectured her. "You watch for when he leaves, then you pull up a van, pick the lock, and take what you want. Honey, it's yours!" When my mother said she couldn't do that, her client shrugged. "I just don't know what it is with you white ladies. Scared of your own shadow."

My father spent a fortune on postage for his twenty-page letters to me, his huge handwriting scrawling fury about how my mother had destroyed his life, page after page on his office stationary with his logo, a large orange stylized G in the bottom right corner. He never encouraged me, never offered sympathy for my loneliness, like my mother did in her letters.

His letters pounded me with lectures, including the need to keep precise accounts for every franc I spent and to send them promptly for his inspection, which I did:

Week of Oct 16-22 (in French Francs): food 28.90, transportation 5.40, birthday present 52.60 (rapidiograph pen, Modigliani poster for my room and little cake) for a week total of 86.90 FF or $15.40 US

I wrote in my journal. I filled thin blue aerogrammes to my mother and brother Wood in the apartment where through the walls they heard neighbors yelling and smashing plates. I wrote to my father and Hubbard in the modern house where the lights were left on all night, like an ocean liner sailing through acres of darkness. Postage was a weekly expense, sometimes nearly half of what I spent in food. I needed to write and I needed someone to hear me. The only connective line between my parents was the exchange of xeroxed copies of my aerogrammes so everyone had a copy of my tiny handwriting running over every flap describing my tentative life.

My brother Wood flunked half his classes, dropped acid on weekends, and paid half their rent from greasy night shifts frying burgers and eggs at Country Kitchen. Hubbard left home at dawn for swim practice. My father had no work. After bringing us up with the strict rule that television was only allowed on Saturday night, and only after all homework was done, he bought a large television the week my mother left. He set it down into the middle of the Great Room and left it on for hours every night to disguise the silent crater of an absent family. Hubbard came home late, stoned out of his mind, to find his father crying over "The Waltons," or snarling profanity before driving off in the Jag for hours in the middle of the night. Before I left for France, he had decided he didn't want me to sell the Jag. He wanted to keep it a while longer.

I was desperate for their voices, and flooded my family with accounts of my classes, books I read, jazz clubs I discovered, and colleges I was applying to (Bard, Reed, Radcliffe). I told my father I needed the Parent Confidential Form filled out by mid-December, never dreaming he wouldn't comply. On a tight budget, I boiled cabbage on a tiny camping gas stove and seasoned it with butter and pepper. I slathered torn chunks of baguettes with apricot preserves. I squeezed my life onto pale blue paper while I waited for word from home.

As I grew more confident with my French and traveling, I scoured my Michelin map and planned journeys to Le Corbusier buildings in Paris, the Cathedral in Ronchamps, and most important, Villa Savoye, my favorite house design since childhood.

———·———

AT NINETEEN, IN February 1973, I knew I was embarking on a pilgrimage when I woke in a hostel to the red haze of dawn over Paris. I walked fast over freshly washed stone streets, stepped into the smoky rush and rumble of trains at Gare St. Lazare, to purchase my ticket to Poissy. The train jolted staccato as street lights ticked by shuttered apartment windows. Men in grey work smocks scurried along sidewalks. Deux Chevaux, like armored beetles, and Velo scooters crammed the narrow dark streets. I was heading to the Mecca of Pure Design, the Taj Mahal of Modern, a miniature Chartres for devotees of abstract: Le Corbusier's Machine for Living In, his Villa Savoye à Poissy. I was going to kneel at the feet of the god of my father. I was ripe with the meaning of the day, ready to etch my journey onto a thin blue aerogramme in cramped italic penmanship.

The evening after my trip to Poissy in February 1973, I filled two aerogrammes, titled them Part 1 and Part 2. I addressed them to both my brothers, and mailed them to the glass house as if my family continued to live there intact. "Some people go on religious pilgrimages," I began. "I went on an architectural one."

It was clearly a letter to my father from the daughter who

was a devotee, who wrote in such particular detail about Le Corbusier's design that I can't imagine anyone but my father would have bothered to decipher the cramped lines. What I didn't know was that, with the recession of the early 1970s, his office echoed without work. No one gathered in the conference room to talk specifications, there were no new blueprints, no one pulling down books in his library. In spite of everything that had happened, he and I still shared architecture. I had become his sole student, writing home descriptions to the only person I could share them with, writing what mattered so much to me because it would mean so much to him.

I arrived on an empty train in Poissy as commuters left for the city and passed harsh concrete apartment blocks shadowing narrow old roads. I felt invisible, and suddenly foolish, a dilettante. Who was I to go searching after modern buildings? I wasn't an architecture student. I was a girl who wrote in a journal, who was lost and confused about how to proceed with my life. I walked up a long curving hill, past the humming Simca car factory and a concrete-walled prison. The road curved until it crowned the hill. Overlooking the smoggy, densely built Seine Valley, my heart beat rapidly, from the effort of the hill, from anticipation, and with an urgency for my life to mean something. I believed, strangely, that writing to my father about the house would leave a trace that I had lived, more than simply existing.

I followed a long metal fence to a gate, where I read a tarnished brass plaque: Les Heures Claires (Villa Savoye), visiting hours, a button to push. After the elderly caretaker unlocked the gate, she and her friendly German Shepherd escorted me through an old forest. We followed the overgrown drive toward a distant image, which at first looked like a grainy black and white photograph, a compact, age-stained concrete structure, dwarfed by a long multi-story high school which blocked the view towards Paris. Once I focused on just the little building, it changed, becoming the sculpture I knew by heart.

I was walking over the drive I'd cut out of sandpaper when my father and I made the model for French class six years before. The house was unexpectedly small. The grid of white slender columns, *pilotis*, carried the weight. Walls like white ribbon wrapped around the house and the windows—cutouts of dark and light. The house watched us as we drew near, our footsteps crunching on gravel. I remembered the ground floor walls we'd cut and glued into place, and the curve, the perfect turning radius, for a car to be driven into the garage.

The Shepherd ran ahead. The grandmotherly caretaker, holding her worn sweater at the neck against the chill, let me know I had the house to myself. We walked under the over-hang following the curve of the glass wall, narrow slices of glass edged with metal, until we reached the wide black door. She unlocked it. "Et voilà, Mademoiselle," and left me alone.

I thought I knew this house. I'd learned to read plans on this house. I'd put my eyes to the cardboard windows and doorways. I knew how a person would walk through the space. I had imagined walking on the roof, with its curving walls and no ceiling. I was sure I knew what it would be like to enter those familiar rooms.

As I entered the ground floor, the entryway was dishev-eled and smelled of raw plaster, construction debris littering the floor. As I proceeded up the ramp to reach La Salle, the living/dining room, I was stunned by sadness. At first glance the walls were bare, stained, forlorn, a home without a family. I'd read that the Nazis and later the Allies stabled cows here, storing hay and feed in these rooms. I shuddered. Were there bullet holes in the walls? I walked around the abandoned rooms; the edges where dirty glass windows met the wall felt harsh and unforgiving. Loneliness crept into me like the chilled winter air.

Exterior ramp at Villa Savoye, 1973

Disappointed, I opened a glass door and walked across the terrace to one end and looked up. Suddenly, the design from the outside—the curving walls on the roof, the grid of interior and exterior spaces, and a glowing whiteness—blossomed into a thrill in my mind. Every view became exquisite. Even though the sky was a heavy grey, threatening rain, the house glowed with light.

I was no longer an observer walking through a building. I was in connection with the house as I walked up the ramp to the roof, pausing with each step to look in each direction, studying how the lines of the white walls and the proportions changed. The faded winter meadow was framed by each curve of shimmering white walls. The sensual white walls in the rooftop garden carved the sky. A cutout window framed a view of open space beyond. To be in this terrace room with walls and no ceiling was to have weight and shadow lifted from me. I thought of desert people who build terrace gardens, where they gather for meals, or pray under the vast sky. Corbusier had written, "Suppose that walls (in a house) rise towards heaven in such a way that I am moved." I was. On this terrace I felt alive.

When I opened the door to proceed down the twirling spiral staircase, I became part of a sculpture, a black and white composition that changed with every turn. A child of modernism, I felt transformed in the white spiral heart of the house. I was bringing the house alive. I entered the imagination of the man who had envisioned pleasure in the way the spiral stair met the hallway. He was guiding my eyes. I was seeing what he had wanted to be seen. I was a girl who had studied Corbu since childhood, who had turned the pages of photographs and plans like a fairy tale. This was My Corbu.

I explored the house, in communion with its creator. I felt the rhythm of white horizontal lines ridging the triangle windows of glass. A tiny sky-blue wall below a skylight drew my eye to the heavens. A deep blue wall led to the bedrooms. I wrote: "A divine orange wall in the living room." Entering the master bedroom, small shimmering blue tiles were set in a Roman bath drenched with diffused winter light. A bather could recline here, like a Modigliani nude, waiting to be admired.

I didn't know that the initial roof had leaked so badly that rain poured down the spiral stairs and skylights, until the family abandoned the house, threatening lawsuits until it was made livable. I was captivated by a cold white passion, a romanticized love for Early Modern, a trained awe for efficiently engineered steamships and motorcars. I was an enraptured girl, yet unaware of the slow chill in an ice palace of pure design.

Immersed in the play of Corbu's mind, I realized he eclipsed my father. I was no longer going to my father, a devoted priest, but praying directly to his paternal god. I took communion from the curving white walls. Descending the spiral was the beginning of freedom from being enthralled by my father. Maybe this is what leaving home is for. I was actually entering my own true life, not the life I imagined as a girl when I read Corbu's white books of plans.

I discovered, on that grey February morning west of Paris, on a spiral stair, the vastness of my own enthusiasm. As I wrote furiously into my aerogrammes, I felt thrilled with the idea of a life I was creating. My own separate life.

In going to my father's Mecca that he never succeeded in visiting, I discovered that my life could go beyond my father's. I didn't have to stay the child, waiting and yearning for his attention to bring me alive.

I now knew I could be the author of my own life, not knowing how long that would take.

JAGUAR

1973-75

Heaven and hell are within us, and all the gods are
within us . . . They are magnified dreams.

—JOSEPH CAMPBELL, THE POWER OF MYTH

BEFORE I LEFT HOME FOR FRANCE, MY FATHER AND
I stood in the driveway of the glass house, gazing with mu-
tual appreciation at his white gleaming XKE Jaguar. In 1972,
this 1967 E Type was already a classic; the sexy angled glass
over the headlights had been replaced in the newer models
with a more economical, practical vertical headlight. A Jaguar
was synonymous with Modern, with the black leather and
walnut Eames chair, with a man who knew wine, who was
cultured. And this car had been mine. I'd returned from my
jaunt to the East Coast. I'd vacuumed, scrubbed, waxed, and
polished every inch of that car to keep my end of the bargain,
to sell the car for $2,500 to pay for my year in France. In the
end he wouldn't sell her yet, she was too beautiful. He
planned to take one last trip in the Jag.

"But I still want to teach you about the value of money!"
His voice boomed, filling this valley below the house and the
steep slope leading to the gardens. "Look at this car. Now
imagine what your college tuition will be."

I couldn't. Tuition was a vague concept, a bill I'd send to my father. I had gathered up an array of college applications so I could apply from France. I'd been a good student, I'd write a fascinating essay justifying my two years of adventures before starting college, he'd fill out the financial aid forms, and then he'd cover the rest. That's all I thought there was to it. I was a privileged girl growing up in a wealthy village inside the most magnificent house I'd ever seen. I had no idea that my father had no work, that he would never design a major building again. None of us knew that. He was a robust bull of a man at fifty-nine, who could manhandle mammoth granite curbstones into place with his bulldozer and pry bars. He was my dad, and we could stand talking about Jags in the driveway, and the craziness of what had happened inside the glass house would vanish. I'd forget the rage that curled in my belly like a cornered animal.

He said, "Look at this car." My eyes lingered over the engineered sweep of the hood, remembering the ten days she'd been mine. Remembering my left hand on the polished wooden steering wheel, my right on the stick shift, a fine-tuned team of precision as I negotiated winding roads, wheels gripping the road as precisely as a Swiss train held to tight curves through the Alps. I was my father's daughter; he'd brought me up in his own image.

With his hands on his hips, he cocked his head and his grey eyes bore into mine. "Imagine twenty Jaguars."

I laughed. A crazy thing, but they populated my mind and I saw them. Filling the parking area where we stood, one after another, shining bumper to bumper, all tops down, all convertibles, red leather seats glowing like embers, long lean white bodies lining the drive, down the hill, across the creek, extending along the drive up to our neighbors. Gleaming. White. Jags.

"That's what your college tuition would cost me."

His arms flew upward like falcons lifting off and flying in different directions, he looked me square in the face and shrugged in a way that implied it was obvious. He strode away. I didn't understand. I was left looking at the single Jaguar, confused, not knowing the lesson he'd meant me to understand. Not knowing that the $2,500 he would give me to manage on a tight budget for my year in France would be the last money he would pay for my college education. Not knowing yet what he really meant by flinging up his strong hands in the late summer light.

———

WHEN I APPLIED to colleges from France in 1973, most architects were caught without work in a recession, but my father didn't want anyone to know. He was paranoid, didn't trust the forms were confidential. He was finishing up his last design jobs for the University of Cincinnati. He didn't want them to know he had no other work. In the spring, when I returned home, I'd been accepted to colleges but was awarded no financial aid. Only then, when I asked my father, did he tell me he hadn't filled out the forms. I couldn't go. I sank, defeated. I couldn't go to college? And that's all I wanted to do.

In my parents' divorce decree he'd agreed to pay the equivalent of University of Cincinnati tuition. I was determined. Okay, if I couldn't go away to school, I'd start that summer, even if it was in my own town, even if it had to be UC. I rolled my eyes; that was where just 'anybody' could go. But I would go. I would put in a year, and then transfer. I'd get good grades so I could get financial aid. When the $350 bill came for summer school tuition, my father refused to pay. He could have said, I don't have the money. He could have said, let's figure this out together. He was living in the glass house valued in the hundreds of thousands on acres of gardens in a wealthy village, but he couldn't say he didn't have the money to pay his own bills. My father was an enraged bull when I sent him the tuition bill, screaming at me, "You can't tell me what to do. *No one ever* tells *me* what to do," before slamming down the phone.

MY MOTHER GEARED up for battle. On her $10,000 a year job as a probation officer, she hired her lawyer again to take my father to court. Years later, after my father died, as we cleared through his old tax statements, we found that he made $6,000 that year—and spent $4,000 of it on lawyers to fight paying my year's tuition as a U.C. off-campus student. We lost in court. The judge stated, "You can't enforce a divorce decree for children over eighteen. Those promises depend on the good will of the parents."

My mother figured out how to squeeze my tuition out of her tight budget. I lived with her and my brother Woodie in a one-bedroom apartment across from campus. I slept on a daybed in the small dining room, squeezed my desk in the front hallway. My mom slept on the unheated porch. My brother Woodie had the tiny dark bedroom and stashed his pot and acid in the upright freezer that dominated his room, where my mom kept farm produce we froze in the summer. She joked that she'd get fired if anyone found out, either because they'd think she was stupid not to know that he was using drugs or because she did know and didn't stop him.

My mother knew my brother was hanging by a thread, knew that the best thing was that he felt safe, had a home where he was loved and where his friends could come. My brother calculated how many classes he could flunk and still graduate from high school, even though his SAT scores soared above mine. He came home, hands and clothes greasy, from his job at a garage down the street, and sat with his friends, stoned and laughing around my mother's dinner table. I hunched over my desk in the front hall reading Virginia Woolf.

The night before my first Introduction to Psychology class, I lay awake. No one knew my secret terror that I wasn't smart. What if I couldn't make it in college, like my aunts and uncles with their Phi Beta Kappas and PhDs? Walking to class that hot summer, I'd double over with a spasm of pain in my belly that grabbed so hard I couldn't stand up. I'd crouch down in the grass, trying to look fascinated with a flower or my book, disguising my shame, until I could calm my breathing, relax my belly, and walk again. Eventually I saw a doctor who said I had a spastic colon because I was an overly sensitive young woman.

Freshman classes were big and uninspiring. Nothing I thought or wrote stood out. Maybe I was a boring thinker. Maybe my mind was middle-of-the-road. My fear increased.

If I couldn't make it here, where could I? Maybe I wasn't whom I'd always thought I was. One day as I sat on a bench on campus, an older man peered into my face before he spoke encouragingly. "Can't you smile? It's not all that bad." Embarrassed, I tried, but it didn't last.

I read Joseph Campbell's *Hero With a Thousand Faces*, and wondered how my life would fit in the hero's journey. When the fall semester's list of classes included a graduate seminar in Mythology, I appealed to the dean and gained permission to join four grad students. In a little room on the top floor overlooking the campus, a young red-bearded professor, who had just completed his PhD in Celtic Studies from Harvard, pulled back a veil like a magician, showing us patterns in the stories of ancient cultures. In the library, I discovered folklore concordances where I could trace details from fairy tales—three brothers, youngest sisters, wicked stepmothers, poisoned apples—in variations around the world. I read theories pointing out that a tripartite system of class (king/priests, warriors, and farmers) in Indo-European society was echoed in myths. We studied parallels between Greek and Nordic mythology: Zeus and Odin were the highest-ranking sovereign leaders, Poseidon and Thor were warriors, and Demeter and Freyr were connected to the fecundity of the land. I'd never known the heady pleasure of losing myself in study, hours vanishing into ideas.

My first paper argued that a tripartite system existing in Nordic mythology could be found in Icelandic sagas. My professor wrote, "This was as good a paper as I've ever read, either here or at Harvard." Harvard! From that moment I was filled with certainty; I knew the map of my journey. I would go to

Harvard to become a Professor of Mythology and Folklore. But how was I to get there? I had no idea. All I knew was that I had to transfer out of Ohio and leave home. My father couldn't stop me anymore. I was my mother's daughter now, and as her dependent I qualified for financial aid. Naïve, I had no idea how my father's legacy would continue to haunt me.

From my professor's glowing recommendation, the next fall I entered the white-trimmed brick quad at Johns Hopkins in Baltimore's sticky heat. Dominated by pre-meds, the small group of Humanities students were welcoming, with friendly professors' doors open to us at all hours of the day. My first class was a seminar on the Odyssey, a handful of students around a table; the young professor with curling hair and a profile like a Greek hero stood at the board, writing a word first in Greek characters and then English, *menos.* I was worried.

He explained, "*Menos* is usually translated as confidence or strength, particularly strength that is breathed in. Athena could breathe *menos* into a hero. In the beginning of *The Odyssey,* when she disguised herself to help Telemachos discover the fate of his father, she called herself Mentes. She is encouraging him to become the man he is meant to be." Professor Nagy (pronounced nadj) continued scrawling words across the board, as he switched effortlessly from English to Greek, Hittite to Indic. His enthusiasm warmed us as we followed his leaps of connection effortlessly.

He continued, "But *menos* isn't for heroes only. This breathing strength of mind flows in the sun, in fire, moist winds and rivers." Dr. Nagy kept going back in time, tracing *menos* to *manas* from Indic poetry where it meant not only the strength that made the sun rise and the wind to come but was also the power of the poet, the strength that was breathed in from the cosmos. Professor Nagy paused; the delight in his eyes made them more penetrating. "What is the strength that is latent in you that has to be breathed in by the gods?"

I left the class trembling, as if I'd been a torch soaked in oil and the lecture was the match. All I wanted to do was study *The Odyssey* and find the underpinnings of earlier mythic stories. With boundless enthusiasm, Dr. Nagy encouraged me. "You've got to learn Homeric Greek. I'll tutor you. Keep at it all summer and you'll be up to speed by fall so we can continue working together."

But that spring, I overheard Professor Nagy had been awarded a full professorship at Harvard, starting in the fall. Barely thirty, he was referred to as a "wunderkind." He was leaving and I was devastated. School looked like a wasteland without his classes. My fatherly counselor, in his office overlooking glossy magnolias in bloom, asked, "Why not try to transfer to Harvard?"

ODYSSEUS'S DAUGHTER

1975-76

*The verb odussomai means "hate," so Odysseus's name
could be One who is wrathful and hates or is hated.*

—DR. EMILY VERMEULE,
HARVARD LECTURE NOTES, 1975

IN THE NARROW SHADOWY ROOM ON THE THIRD
floor, overlooking the snow-covered Radcliffe Commons, the
dull sameness of the brick dorms weighed on me like the failing of my mind. I studied Greek all Sunday, writing pages of
vocab lists and verb endings, repeating, saying aloud the
words again and again, writing columns of the same word,
trying to lock them into my mind. It was my Sunday ritual as
I began second semester. I'd moved into South House, thinking this would help with finding friends. I was lonelier than
ever. I watched out my window, the snow-drifted quad, the
plowed paths, watching girls in princess coats and flats bringing home their dry cleaning, while the rest of us slumped
over armloads of books wearing blue jeans and parkas in a
decade of crumpled clothes.

On Mondays, in my Homeric Greek class, words I'd
stitched through my mind all weekend vanished without a
trace, vanished as if I'd never heard them. This was what
stunned me. I'd always been able to do whatever I'd set out to

do. I knew I'd had trouble with foreign languages, but I was determined. I'd spent four years in labs learning French in high school, and three years of Spanish. When I got to France, I couldn't speak a word, but I persevered and lived months without English, speaking with humor and enthusiasm, even though it was never grammatically perfect. I'd studied a year of German because professors of classics had to read German. I was enthralled with classicists who delved into the linguistic layers of Homer. I planned after Greek to learn Latin, Hittite and probably Old Norse at some point, since I had a soft spot for medieval Icelandic sagas. But my mind was failing me, killing off the dream of my life, to be a professor. Greek was evaporating out of my mind.

I began to yearn to die. The pressure had built up so long and hard that now all I wanted was to disappear, to be done. I couldn't keep going any more. All I had to do was find how to die. I went searching for an easy dying. I hoped falling in the snow and slush in front of bus could do it. I hoped it wouldn't be too painful.

As I walked to class across the Harvard Commons, I imagined a mushroom cloud erupting across the Charles. How was I living my last moments on earth? Was my life meaningful? Had I found happiness before this brief life vanished? Had I done anything to make a difference? No, I had failed. I was so weary. I couldn't keep fighting any more. I was my father's daughter, sliding under a crushing sea of failure. My mind had betrayed me. Sheer will and determination had driven me here, to prove myself to my father and my professor uncles, but now all I wanted was to disappear, to be done.

I was sinking, but my mother's voice long distance from

Ohio wouldn't let me go. She was unswerving. I'd say, "Mommy, I don't think I can make it. I can't do this."

She was fierce, loving. "I know you can get through today. I'll talk to you tonight."

I cried, shaking. "I can't. I can't do it."

From her apartment in Cincinnati, as she dressed for another day as a probation officer, she said with determination, "I will speak to you tonight." Day after day, she offered me the lifeline of her knowing. When I had no idea how I could live through that day, she knew without a doubt that I could and would.

I kept my appointment for a weekly talk with my counselor, a kind man whose handshake was large and soft like his caring face. Even though I didn't tell him much, I felt him studying my drooped posture as I slumped into the Harvard chair. *Veritas*, painted in gold, pressed into my back like the pattern of needles in Kafka's story "In the Penal Colony." My fingers ran up and down the smooth maple spindles, circling where they met the dark wooden carved seat. I couldn't meet his eyes when he questioned me. My gaze was caught by a water stain under the heavy radiator, hissing on a raw February afternoon. I was sinking and he must have seen it.

"Wait a minute." He returned with the university psychiatrist, an intense little man in a three-piece suit, who spoke each word precisely.

"Do you ever think about *death?*"

I wanted to laugh. "Yes, I think about death all the time."

When he asked, "Would you like to stay here a few days in the infirmary?" I met his gaze. "Yes," I answered, "yes," certain for the first time in weeks.

AT HARVARD'S WELCOMING reception for transfer students, we had been assured we were the cream, beating higher odds than freshmen to be accepted. They expected great things from us. A white-coated waiter carved a massive half-side of roasted beef. As he piled slabs of bloody meat on my plate, I thought of Odysseus feasting after offerings had been made to the gods. I wandered back through the labyrinth of Cambridge streets that night, warmed and hopeful.

When I'd transferred into Harvard as a junior I was sure I'd find happiness. I found tastes of my imagined life of happiness in a darkened lecture hall, looking at slides of Greek vases, on a late September day in 1975. I was taking careful notes as Dr. Emily Vermeule's commanding voice led us behind the scenes to understand the myths. A mythic figure herself, as a young woman she had discovered a Mycenaean city.

"Odysseus is the least heroic of the Greek heroes. He is always the deceitful, malicious liar but also the most mature and eloquent of speakers." She showed an image of the large-chested hero. "He was a series of contrasts. He arranged that the Trojan War should be fought but then he tried to get out of it by feigning madness." I imagined him, the young father who tried to escape his destiny. If he left for war, it was foretold he wouldn't return for twenty years, and then as a beggar. "He stole statues from temples, tricked heroes, but he made the Trojan Horse, and so his wit finally won the battle of Troy."

I was captivated by Odysseus, this larger-than-life hero, a

tyrant who was humbled as he barely survived his journey home. I wasn't attracted to him, like the naïve Princess Nausicaa on the beach waiting for a fine husband—no, he was an older man, old enough to be my father. I didn't identify with the enduring Penelope, holding off the suitors with her grief and wit as best she could. I wasn't the young Telemachus who sailed off to other island kingdoms to listen for word of his father. I wasn't Athena watching out for him, steering him as best she could through the Gordian knot of fate so he could be released from the curses of Poseidon for having blinded his son, the Cyclops. No, I loved him like a proud warrior daughter, who would have stood waiting for his return without a doubt, ready to take the spear to vanquish his enemies.

I knew him because I read him, over and over, in English and, as I struggled to learn, in Greek. I had no idea then that I had found in Odysseus a man of my father's stature and moral complexity, but in a story with a happy ending. He succeeded in returning to his loving Penelope. Ever since I'd been a girl, I'd merged with characters in books. In high school I became Cassandra in *I Capture the Castle*. As I read the *Odyssey*, I loved him like a daughter, not realizing he was the father I yearned for. In reading, I could see his rage and despair, and they didn't hurt me. He would triumph in the end, he would conquer death, find his way home, destroy the suitors, return to his wife's loving arms.

As a child, I had been my father's companion, accompanying him on his jobs, seeing houses, colleges, and towers emerge from his drawings. In the *Odyssey*, I was a quiet companion, privy to his grieving on the beach, his longing to return home. I sat up late, a reading light shining over the page, and wept when the old nurse found the scar on his leg and recognized him. In disguise, when Odysseus saw his adult son for the first time, he was overcome with love and pride. That was the father I still hoped for, who would adore his sons, who would weep with love for them, and with grief for having missed their childhoods.

Reading Homer, I returned to Ithaca before him, knew the goatherd who was still loyal to his beloved master. I knew who was the most despicable of the suitors and waited excitedly for Odysseus's revenge. After the palace had been cleansed and Penelope had tested him for the last time, after they retired to their bed and the gods held back the night long enough so he could tell her his entire journey home, I wasn't jealous. I loved him like a loyal daughter who stood sentry over the palace in Ithaca all night. Who else knew him, loved him better than I? I was the daughter who still loved her broken father after no one else remained.

After the seminar was over, the lights switched on, notebooks were shuffled into packs, footsteps clattering over the scuffed wooden floors. As if the magic show was over, and daily life reeled dully before me. I wanted to stay, breathing in the excited air of her class, but I didn't know how to do that on my own. I knew there were years of study ahead of me before I could make brilliant connections like these Classics professors. Researching in the library, I explored Greek concordances for the origins of words, but I didn't have the background in languages that was needed, yet. But I was determined, taking notes on index cards on every article I read, creating my own library of quotes and ideas to carry with me into an academic life.

LEAVING GREEK MYTHOLOGY class, I watched a flock of pigeons rise up through the ancient trees of the quad, their wings as illuminated as my mind. But crowds of students poured out of the lecture rooms and no one lingered to talk. I began slipping into my old loneliness and yearned for a shared passion. Other students went off to cafés to gossip about skiing, or flying to Egypt for the weekend with their roommate who was a prince, or how many kegs they had for the next party in one of the houses along the river. There were other silent students, the ones who asked if they didn't have to speak in my Anthropology section for their grade. A few students confessed they were afraid people wouldn't think they were smart enough to be here. Like me, they went back to their rooms alone to study.

I loved my work-study job Saturdays in the shadowy Poetry Room in the Lamont undergraduate library. Being there meant I didn't have to figure out what to do on Saturdays when people with friends already seemed to know what to do. Being there meant I could listen to recordings of poets on reel-to-reel tapes under thick-padded headphones. Of course the first I played was Sylvia Path, but that trembling proud fevered voice disturbed me and I quickly filed her away.

I sat at my wooden desk in the Finnish-style modern library room, designed by one of my father's favorite early modernists, Alvar Aalto. There was a serene uniformity in the wooden desks, arched leg stools, chairs, and cupboards. The windows were screened so no direct light would damage the tapes and books. I studied in muted comfort, mostly alone. The librarian, a slight Greek man, would arrive with a kind smile to work a few hours in the afternoon. He invited me into his office where sunlight poured onto his desk, stacked with papers and books. He asked me questions about my classes and told me about the manuscript he was working on. A poet with books printed in Greek, he was now finishing his first collection in English.

As the fall continued, each time he arrived he said he could feel my emotions filling the little library. I liked writing out his name, Stratis, in Greek characters. He was about forty and I was twenty-two, my parents' ages when they got married. I thought he was the perfect age; a few grey hairs made him more handsome. I liked watching how his neatly trimmed mustache expanded with his smile. I liked glancing into his office as I put tapes away, his classic Greek profile focused on revising his poems. I didn't have a crush on him; instead, I was grateful for how he listened to me with quiet attention.

The Saturday I limped in on crutches after breaking my foot, he listened with sympathy to my failure at my first ballet class since fifth grade, which I could now make comical. I could tell him about the huge lecture hall doors I couldn't pry open and how students poured by and almost no one helped me. It was getting dark by five when I got up to leave. He said, "Let me take you to dinner."

I swung along on crutches beside him, passing the orderly eighteenth-century brick buildings and stately trees of Harvard Yard. We left through a cast-iron gateway into the whirling neon and lights of bookshops and cafés, rapid chatter of late shoppers and students, traffic pummeling and subway thudding towards Harvard Square. He took my elbow protectively as we hurried across the street and he steered us into a quiet bistro with candles already lit on the tables.

With a sip of wine, I answered his questions about my life. "My father is a famous architect. I sometimes think he's like Odysseus, because he's crafty, the smartest of the Achaeans, and can figure out any puzzle." I paused and felt encouraged by his warm dark eyes to explain.

"As I read *The Odyssey*, I have this weird idea that I'm Odysseus's daughter, even though, of course, he didn't have a daughter." After reading the book three times, I felt I was part of their lives. "I think his teenaged son, Telemachos, is kind of a wimp, and after a while his long-suffering wife Penelope gets annoying. I wish she didn't just mope around. But I'm his daughter and I know he's coming home!" I paused for another sip of wine, I could feel my cheeks flushing with excitement. "I grew up in a modern glass house, sort of like a little palace in a little valley all to itself. It was all lit up and glowed at night. We lived in an old wealthy village and we were kind of like aristocrats."

It was that word "aristocrats" that burned my cheeks with shame after Stratis began to speak, his eyes solemn as he spoke of the Nazis coming to his island when he was a little boy. He remembered them rounding up the men, his father, uncles and neighbors, the sight of their boat leaving the harbor, never to see them again. His stories merged with his poems, blood staining the stones in the village square, the swish of women in black dresses, the taste of honey and lemon.

I don't know if I corrected my story after he spoke. Did I say that my father went mad and drove us all away, living like a blinded Cyclops in his cave with just my youngest brother caring for him? Did I say my impoverished mother kept getting evicted from apartments because neighbors complained about my long-haired brother and his friends playing loud music as they worked on their cars on the street?

I couldn't have said what I didn't know, that I was building my life here like a precarious house of cards. When I told him my plans to become a Classics professor, he toasted me with his wineglass. After dinner, I felt blessed when he kissed me on both cheeks before he caught the bus home to his girlfriend. I carefully placed my crutches, step by step, on uneven sidewalks, heaved and shattered by tree roots, heading towards my beautiful room miles away. Even then I was beginning to sink, without knowing it.

The spasms in my belly returned, grabbing me on my way to class, forcing me to sit on a stone bench clutching my side until I could breathe. My first paper for mythology class was decimated in red ink. Dr. Nagy's brilliant lectures were reserved for grad students. I was left to plod unsuccessfully through Greek. I made short calls to my mother, who was worn out from moving again. The sharp pain in my abdomen began to come every day. Desperate, I took down a poster off a telephone pole that promised release from stress. A class in TM, for the princely fee of $60, enough for food for two weeks. I paid for the mantra. I began to sit for twenty minutes twice a day, repeating my mantra, breathing into the terror in my belly, calming the cramping pain. But the loneliness didn't abate.

I WAS SINKING. A month later I was escorted to the infirmary. Soon I was lying in bed in a hospital jonnie, my clothes and books stashed in a closet. From my bedroom window, I could see a concrete building facing Harvard Square, where a clock flashed the time and temperature in red. 3:47 pm. 27 degrees Fahrenheit. An hour before I'd crossed Harvard Square calculating how to get hit by a bus. Relief spread through my trembling body. Now it was so obvious. I whispered to the empty room. "I don't have to die to leave Harvard! I can just drop out!" When the nurse entered a minute later, she caught my first smile in weeks.

"You don't look depressed," the nurse said critically as she took my vitals. I wanted to feel shocked, incredulous that she doubted me—I was an undergrad on suicide watch. But she was right. Something was different, already. I called my mother from my bed in the health center. "You were right. I didn't have to die. I can just drop out!" I was elated. She answered, "Just come home. We can't wait to see you."

In a few days I packed and closed my accounts. I was given extensive tests in the language center. A voice on a tape recorder listed unusual sounds that I had to say back in order and move around like chess pieces to make phrases, but the sounds vanished as quickly as Greek. The evaluator told me I had such a severe short-term memory deficit that I would be excused from any foreign language requirements. When I stopped to say good-bye at the Poetry Library, Stratis gave me a copy of his poetry manuscript as a gift.

I steered a drive-away car across the Charles River early

in the spring of 1976, the back seat piled to the ceiling with books, quilts, posters, and clothes. I sang along with Dylan's new album, *Desire*, on the radio, happy to be alive, singing, "One more cup of coffee for the road, to the valley below." On the turnpike driving west, I wondered if the quirks of my mind had saved me for another life.

PARKER STREET

1976

*The urge for good design is the same as
the urge to go on living.*

—HARRY BERTOIA

"IMAGINE MIDNIGHT IN A RUN-DOWN NEIGHBOR-
hood." My brother, Wood, set the scene. "The police show up
in front of a three-story wreck of a house at the dead-end of
Parker Street. Someone had called. The drug dealers were
acting up again. They pound on the door with their guns
drawn." Wood pretended to open the door. "Here are Jo's
friends from Glendale. Marilyn, in a long evening dress," he
gestures and emphasizes, "with *jewels, and furs,* with her husband Dick, in tails, who have dropped by Jo's new apartment
after the Opera." Wood's voice raised into falsetto. "Is there a
problem, officers?"

He pantomimed the officers instantly slipping their guns
back into their belts, awkwardly stepping back and saying,
"Er, uhm . . . excuse us, ma'am, we had a report of excessively
loud music. There doesn't seem to be a problem now. Sorry
to disturb you. Good night." Wood slapped his thigh. "What
a great moment!"

This was my mother's apartment, where I came home on

Christmas break from Harvard in 1975. Jo had been evicted twice in the last six months. The landlords didn't like my brother's long hair, his black friends working with him on cars in the driveway, the loud music, or his penchant for running upstairs on all fours barking loudly. She'd finally told my brother, "You find us a place," and this was it. When they moved in the heat had been turned off, the water heater was broken, and snow drifted in under the windows. She called the landlord again and again; his secretary said they'd send someone over, but never did. They heated the kitchen with the open burners on the gas stove. My mom said, "This is what I used to see when I interviewed mothers on welfare in the projects."

Two days after they moved in, I arrived home for Christmas. When I saw a dumpster piled high in front of the house, I asked, "What's all that?" My mother sighed, "That's the junk we had to take out of the house before we could move in." I stood shivering with my hands over the stove looking around the kitchen. Layers of grime, grease, and dried lumps of food caked the grey linoleum. I said, "How about I clean the kitchen floor?" I went to work in a corner with a bucket of hot soapy water I'd heated on the stove and a scrub brush. Half an hour later, I called my mother to look at one linoleum square. "It's white with some cute little turquoise specks. Nice!"

We set up the record player to keep playing as we worked. Wood argued for The Who, Iron Butterfly, and Led Zeppelin. I wanted Joni Mitchell and Carole King. My mom groaned. "I can't take any more Carole King." We traded off every other record and I filled in my side with the Beatles.

For the floor, I figured out a system, a spatula to dig off the first layer, then a hard brush, then a sponge. Jo, Wood, and friends filled holes in the plaster, pulled down filthy wood paneling. They taped plastic over the windows and hung blankets for curtains. All Christmas week, I worked on that kitchen floor. When Chuck came to visit, he scrubbed with me and told me about the gay bar scene in the city. He'd come out the night Nixon resigned.

Wood, at nineteen, had been let go from the garage. He came home nights blackened with soot, his face grey. The winter was so cold, train cars arriving to unload at the coal-fired electrical plant would open their bottom doors but the load of coal was frozen solid. Wood had been hired to climb into coal cars with a sledge hammer to loosen up the lumps of ore. The grate was open to a butane burner below. He had to get the coal to drop through and not fall in himself. When he came home at night, he couldn't get warm.

Our father allowed our youngest brother, Hubbard, to visit for one lunch that week, and timed my brother's visit to the minute, as he had for years, before he returned in a rage to confiscate Hubbard from Jo's reach. Hubbard often arrived pent-up and restless, unable to sit or talk. Jo created a ritual. As soon as he arrived they loaded up the car and drove to the recycling center where there were huge dumpsters for cans and glass. Jo gave Hubbard the month's worth of wine and beer bottles in bags and boxes. He set to work with a vengeance smashing them into the dumpster. Six foot five since he was fourteen, he was tall enough to climb down inside. He slipped precariously, grabbing more bottles and smashing them against the thick rusted metal walls around him. When

he finally climbed out, he was grinning. "I'm hungry!" Jo
would bring him home and they'd have a great visit, until our
father pulled up in front in his BMW and sat on the horn.
Hubbard dashed down the stairs.

Jo got a call from a woman who screamed at her, "I'm
freezing!" Jo calmed her down and figured out she was another tenant trying to reach the same landlord. They realized
he was giving out his tenants' numbers so they'd yell at each
other instead of him. This lady didn't have heat or hot water
either. My mother got mad. She called the landlord with her
telephone book in front of her and said, "I'm a probation officer. If my heat isn't working in the next twenty-four hours, I
am going to call city hall and report you to . . ." She started
listing off every social agency she could think of. The furnace
was repaired that day and they delivered a new water heater
the next. My mother was the first person in her family to get
a divorce or live in an apartment. When she talks about that
time now, she says, "We had been very privileged. Parker
Street was when we all hit bottom. We didn't know about
poverty or surviving. We had to learn."

After I dropped out of Harvard in March, I carried my
books and clothes up to the unheated third floor room in my
mother's apartment with a view to the city far below. I
painted everything white, walls and floors. I found a white
coverlet, lined up my books but then I didn't know what to
do. My brief elation from leaving school was over. Now what
would I do with my life? I was lost, floating around the
house, looking out the windows.

Wood had a group of friends, mechanics, guys who rode
up on their motorcycles and girls who spilled out of an old

Toyota. Wood and his friends partied, the bathtub filled with ice and beer, loud rock and roll, pot passed around, and Wood telling stories that left everyone doubled over laughing. I didn't fit into that world. I hid in my attic room. I read under the covers until three in the morning to finish Doris Lessing's *The Golden Notebook*, making comments in the margins on favorite passages. Sundays I took *The New York Times Book Review* up to my room. I didn't know what else to do but read.

I helped around the house and made meals, but I was having a hard time with Jo. She worked hard, fixed up the house, and was angry. Her women's support group from Glendale was invited to have dinner at her new apartment. She cooked all weekend. At the last minute, one of her friends called, awkwardly saying she had a conflict and couldn't come, but wanted Jo to know none of the others were coming either. She said, "They're too scared."

My mother was furious. "Scared of what?"

"Well, your lifestyle. You know, being divorced, and, well, working, and . . ." her voice trailed off. "Sorry, I've got to go."

After my mother hung up, she threw her coffee cup at the wall so hard it shattered. Wood was impressed. "Hey Jo, you vaporized that cup! There's just a light dust hanging in the air."

But Jo was furious, slamming pans on the stove. "They aren't comfortable coming in here because I'm fucking poor. I'm actually making a damn living and not living in some nice big house." Her voice was sarcastic. "They're too scared to come! Poor babies! How scared do they think I am every goddamned day?" She picked up a plate. "I've never liked this plate." She smashed it against the floor. "Where is another?"

She started going through the mismatched pile of plates she'd been buying at a used furniture store up the street. She smashed another and another.

She growled, "When you live in Glendale that long you get all la-ti-da!"

Wood brought in a bottle of gin and another of vermouth. "How about a martini, Jo?"

"Good idea." She smashed another plate.

I'd never known my mother to get drunk, but she was drinking more and getting madder. I leaned in the doorway and watched my mother yell and swear. I knew she was breaking out of being so good, but I was scared. She turned to me, looking irritated. "Do you want a drink, too?"

I was a little scared to shake my head no. I said, hopefully, "How about we eat some of that good dinner?"

She said, "I'm not hungry, but you guys go ahead." I served Wood and Chuck, who'd just arrived.

"Fuck 'em!" Chuck said cheerfully about Jo's friends. "What great lamb curry they are missing out on. And I'll join you for a drink." He also reached over and took my hand, saying quietly, "You okay, sista?"

I nodded, adding, "I'd really like to go for a walk after dinner."

By the end of dinner and after several drinks, the conversation was off Jo's friends to the topic it always circled back to, my father. Sometimes I hated him as much as they did. But I still tried, having dinner at his house, or meeting for lunch in town. Sometimes I had such a great time with him, I would almost forget how bad it had gotten before we fled the glass house.

One time my father had called to say I must come and try out his latest, "real" French bread. When I drove up the drive, the transparent house blazed with light at the crest of the hill. He threw open the door, sweat rolling down his face as he handed me a wine glass sparkling with a new Spätlese he was nuts about. His voice boomed, "Sugar, you have to excuse the heat! The bread is rising! I've been up with it since six this morning." He had special-ordered French bricks for the oven, and the best stone-ground flour. He conferred with the recipe and the temperature gauge in the oven like a mad chemist.

"You won't believe this Julia Child recipe. It goes on for two days. It's a tyrant, but it's worth it!" My father cooked like he was sailing into a typhoon on his racing catamaran. "My rush now is in timing this last rising with dinner." The sink was filled with a mound of asparagus from the garden. He had standing rib roast to go in one oven and bread in the other. "Don't mind me, I'll do my figuring. I'll yell when I need help." He pulled out his yellow legal pad and began shooting words and numbers across the lines. I headed for the calm of the orange womb chair across the room and watched the life I'd once lived. He was a blur under the line of copper pans, vats, skillets, and lids gleaming red in the spotlights.

Of course, I still loved him. When he was like this he was the most alive person I'd ever known. Daily life paled in comparison to this luminous house blazing with Dave Brubeck's piano and Gerry Mulligan's sax playing "Blue Rondo à la Turk." The theme song of my childhood, the comfort of familiarity, my father calling me by my old names.

"Lilibet, I need you!" He flung open the oven door and I was prepared to slide a heated axe head into a pan of cold water. The bread had to be engulfed in steam at that precise moment of cooking. But in the balancing act, the axe slipped out of my grasp and crashed to the white kitchen floor, melting a harsh brown burn in the plastic. "No problem!" my father reassured me. Grabbing the axe, he hurtled it into the oven. Steam exploded and he slammed the oven door shut. We grinned at each other and toasted with our wine glasses.

He had been steadier since the return of his first daughter, Linda, whose mother had taken her away when she was eight. In her thirties, only after she had children of her own did she realize what it must have meant for my father to have lost a child. When he received a letter from her with photographs of his grandchildren he was delirious with joy. He had celebrated her return with a magnificent dinner party with family and friends for his prodigal daughter. Ten years older than me and having grown up in the South, she and I were from different worlds when we smiled at each other awkwardly. He called her regularly and reported to me all about her. Mostly I was relieved: another daughter helped lighten a responsibility I still felt to support his happiness.

Over dinner, he told me his plans to sell the house. "It's become a dead weight on my shoulders." He couldn't keep up the gardens. It was time to move on. He was going to do what he'd always wanted, to sail around the world. He was researching his options. Should he buy a boat and hire a captain to teach him? Should he sign on with someone else's boat as crew? He was in his mid-sixties, strong and healthy. "I'm going to have the time of my life," he predicted. He slathered butter onto slices of a heavy tough-crusted bread. I never told him it wasn't anything like "real" French bread.

Back in my chilly white room in the attic of my mother's apartment, above my brother's booming rock and roll, I imagined my life after he sold the glass house. I couldn't imagine it not being ours, but when I closed my eyes, the house was there. I could walk through every room and see it in all seasons. It would live in my mind's eye as it had been, at its best, for the rest of my life. The way it had looked as he baked bread that night or the way it looked when I sat with my model of Villa Savoye on the dining room table and watched our family mirrored in the glass walls. We didn't have to own it. The glass house would live on in me, untainted.

Sometimes I was lonely and called him, but he could turn on me with a barrage of fury against my mother and brother, trapping me to the black receiver. I couldn't say a word. Sometimes at my mother's kitchen table when she and my brother raged on and on about what a monster he was, I felt they were attacking me too. I almost wanted to defend him. Looking back at myself living in my mother's apartment, even though I knew she'd saved my life, at the same time I was still my father's daughter. I cleared the table and washed the dishes as they lambasted him. My brother cursing, "That son of a bitch."

I think only Chuck understood the pull I felt between worlds. The night my mother's support group dumped her, he asked me, "Hey, how about that walk?" I grabbed my jacket and was ready to walk down the stairs. My mother was drying off the white enamel coffee pot as she said angrily to me, as if I was somehow to blame, "If your father was Jewish, he'd at least have paid your tuition." Her words slapped me.

In that moment, my old sarcastic mind leapt into action. As I started down the stairs, I tossed back at her, "Well, if you were a Jewish mother, you'd at least ask me what I studied." The coffee pot whizzed down the stairs after me and slammed against the wall in the hallway. I was stunned.

My mother stood at the top of the stairs, my brother glaring down at me. She screamed at me. "Who sued your father and took him to court to pay your tuition? And I lost! That judge said, he couldn't believe a father wouldn't sell everything he had to put their daughter through Harvard. I sold my god-damned diamond ring for your tuition!"

She was breathing hard, and starting to cry. Wood comforted her. "I don't understand anything about Greek and Homer. I feel dumb and stupid when you talk about school. But I've done everything, do you understand me? Everything. To support you. Don't you get that?" Now she was sobbing. She walked back into the kitchen and sat down at the kitchen table.

Chuck sternly took me by the hand and said, "Let's take our walk. You need to wake up, girl." He took me down the steps and we walked for an hour, past one paint-peeling, broken-down house after another, junk cars parked in driveways, cars driving by blasting a heavy bass. We walked around the university. He gave me a good talking-to. But I didn't hear a lot of it. I knew what my mother had done for all of us.

What I realized that night was that I had to give up sarcastic retorts. I had been cruel and hurtful to the person who had saved us. I couldn't let myself hurt her or anyone that way again. I had developed my sarcasm, like a child whittling a stick. It was a tool I sharpened every day to stab out at my father, to show I was cool at high school, to make myself different and better than other people. I grew up in a place that lived on being better. Now I was humbled. I'd failed at Harvard. I'd dropped out. I didn't know where I was going or who I was anymore. But what I discovered that night was that I was someone who would not be cruel or hurt people. I had to go off sarcasm, cold turkey. No snide remarks, nothing said to harm other people.

I went home that night, crying as I apologized to my mother. "I'm so sorry, Mommy. I never meant to hurt you. I won't do it again." We hugged and cried before I went to sleep. But I was scared. Without that sharpness I was sure I would be as boring and dull as oatmeal.

My brother Wood decided to take charge, telling me, "You have to get out of your rut. It's time you got yourself a car." I had a house-sitting job that summer in Maine. "How will you get there?" He looked at me sternly. "Think about it."

My mother had divided her divorce settlement of $40,000 equally between the three of us kids and herself, so we would have money for school. We invested our money with an old family friend. We all wanted to save it until we really needed it. What we wouldn't know for a few years was that our friend lost our money and his children's hard-earned savings in the stock market. A few years later, he would die from a rapid illness, sick at heart, unable to tell anyone. When my brother Wood heard our money was gone, he said, "Good riddance. It was cursed money. We'll be just fine on our own." We let go of it. It was just money. What meant the most to us was that our mother had divided everything she had between us. She taught us generosity.

There was much discussion at the kitchen table about what I should do. My brother advised me to spend a chunk of my invested money on a sensible, sturdy car. But I only took out $600 for a black 1963 MGB sports car I couldn't resist. I drove home with the top down and pulled up in front of Jo's house. My brother stood on the curb, took one look and shook his head. "It's a piece of junk." He pointed out the cheap bodywork already cracking away from extensive rust, and the garish red carpet that had been stuck down to cover the floorboards. But I loved it, the rev of the engine, the comforting rumble, the leather seats, and driving close to the ground. I had bought my first car on my own. But it needed work. The accelerator was sticky. The engine had already begun to chug and sputter climbing Clifton Avenue hill and almost didn't make it to Parker Street.

Wood said, "Don't look at me to fix it for you. I'm not going to help until you can ask me an intelligent question." He walked back in the house.

Fortunately he had a steady stream of friends coming by after work and on weekends, who took one look at his sister standing over the engine of the MGB roadster and then looked under the hood as well. "Hey, what's happening?" The simple four-cylinder engine was irresistible. They assured me it was something a non-mechanic could learn to work on. I tried to find anything familiar. Deep on one side I found the dipstick. Cool. I could check the oil. Wiped it off with a rag, put it in, pulled it out. Ugh. Really low and dirty. Okay, I needed to learn how to change the oil and the oil filter.

I'd left memorizing Greek and now I was faced with a new vocabulary to study, and a steady stream of guys who all seemed to know something about cars. They'd say, "Let's hear the engine." I started her up. They listened and poked around. "Okay, you can shut her off." They looked for leaks, cracks, wondered out loud, and asked each other. "Do you think her carburetor is set too rich?" "I wonder about the timing advance?" "Hmm . . . at some point, I think you'll need to change the valve cover gasket." They'd walk around, "Tires okay, hey, I like the wire spokes." "What year is this? '63. Hmm." It was like listening to wine connoisseurs contemplating a sip. "Hmmm. That's the second year they made the MGB. Pretty good year." But they all agreed, "The person who did this body work didn't know shit." "But it's a cool car anyway." Then they'd walk up to the house to find Wood.

I decided to ask the next guy a simple question. "How do I adjust the accelerator? It sticks."

He answered, "Have you checked the accelerator cable?"

"Oh, wow. A cable! Brilliant. Thanks." I opened the driver's door, knelt down on the pavement, leaned inside as far as I could reach, moved the worn metal pedal and reached my hand underneath. There was a little cable. Now I had to discover where it went. I looked down into the engine in approximately the place where I thought the cable might come through and there was a little cable! Eureka! This was as good as making connections between patterns in fairy tales, like researching the repetition of poisoned apples in the multivolume concordance on folkloric patterns. I traced the cable to where it connected next. I'm sure Wood was amused, glancing out the window occasionally, like my Zen master, waiting until I would show up with an intelligent question.

I tried moving the cable back and forth, but it was sticky and didn't move smoothly. Now what? I polled the next guys, they all agreed. WD-40. I'd heard those strange syllables before but was clueless about what it was. One pulled a can out of his car, sprayed it on the cable, and voila! It moved with ease. Amazing! One challenge down, now a trickier one.

I explained that the engine was beginning to chug and sputter. I quoted someone who said it had a rough idle. His friends said, "You should check the distributor and the spark plugs." I nodded, looking serious, acting like I knew what they were talking about, but looking "smart" wasn't going to help me here at all. I had to risk looking stupid. So I asked, "Where's the distributor and what does it do?" They were pleased to point out a little box with wires coming off it, and whipped off the cover to reveal the innards.

"You got to check the wires where they connect to the spark plugs." They pointed to the wire leading to the ignition coil. I had to make sure the wires were good, no cracks in the distributor cap or the rotor. They pointed out carbon buildup and how I could see the bad shape the plugs were in. I had to make sure the plugs were set at the right gap. "You need a feeler gauge for that."

"A what? Feeler gauge?"

"Wood will have one."

I walked upstairs, found my brother, and calmly asked if I could borrow his feeler gauge. "Sure," said Wood with a dry smile. "Would you like me to show you how to use one?"

"Yes."

"And where are we going to use it?"

"To check the gap on the spark plugs."

"Nice. Good start."

After an extended lesson, leaning over the engine, checking things over, Wood took me on the back of his motorcycle for my first shopping trip to the local foreign car parts place. First on my list was WD40. I ordered the MGB handbook with photos and diagrams for any repair job. I would grow as attached to that grease-stained book as to my well-studied copy of *Our Bodies, Ourselves*. I got my own set of feeler gauges, set of spark plugs and wires, new distributor cap and rotor, basic metric tools, and a tin of white goo to clean the grease off my soft hands. I loaded them all in my backpack for the ride home. I was on my way.

I did everything he explained for me to do, on my own. If I ran into trouble, I'd ask the next guy for advice until I could ask my brother another well-informed question. Then I got my lesson. Adjusting the carburetor. I'd never seen the delicate interior before, where the blending of air and fuel takes place to make an internal combustion engine go. Every few days, we moved over the car with new topics and assignments. Set the timing. Replace brakes and change tires. Check and repack bearings. Change the oil and filter.

My brother explained to me the physics and mathematics involved in fine-tuning the engine. I learned vacuum advance, manifold, capacitor, timing advance, valves. He was a rigorous and empowering teacher. I gained confidence. The guys at the car parts place got friendly, asked: was I getting the hang of adjusting the carburetor? Did my brother think I needed a rebuilt one? They smiled when they handed over the oil filter. "See how you do with this." I thought changing oil filters was no big deal, people talked about doing that all the time. Why were they amused?

I sat on the curb, studied my manual, and peered into the engine as I built up my courage to begin each next step. Wood's friends dropped by and checked on my progress. His old friend from Glendale, Big George, watched me the day I lay halfway under the car learning how to change the oil filter. It took hours, like open heart surgery, reaching my arm up into the depths, while oil poured down my arm as I loosened the nut. Wood's new girlfriend, Anita, in silky shorts and a lace top, watched me emerge from under the car, using rags to wipe up the oil. She shook her head, "You are the dirtiest I've ever seen a girl get," before she headed upstairs to see my brother. But George brought over a folding chair and hung out a while, telling me about a bulletproof vest he'd designed and was trying to get patented. After a while, when he got up to go, I asked if he had any good jokes. He paused. "I'm so poor you can read the newspaper through my underwear." Later I told Wood his joke. He looked sad. "It's probably true."

⸻

I WAS GETTING closer to my departure day, giving myself two days to drive to Maine to watch over my Johns Hopkins professor's farm while she did a month of research at Oxford. My weekly visits to the foreign car parts place were coming to a close. I had a car that was running fairly smoothly. I had confidence and enthusiasm. At my last visit with the car parts guys, they came out to listen to the engine and wished me a good trip. I stocked up on rear shock absorbers to install once I got to Maine. Back at my mom's apartment, I ran up the stairs and into the kitchen waving the MG shocks that looked like a solid lump of machined metal. I announced to my mother, "They gave me the mechanic's discount!" At that moment, my mom later said, she knew I was going to be all right. I was returning to finish my senior year at Johns Hopkins that fall, and after that, who knows? It was okay not to know.

We stayed up late the last night. The upper two stories of my mother's house were ablaze with light as Wood spent hours trying to get the MG tuned smoothly before I headed off for my summer in Maine. The tool box would travel on the seat next to me, ready for stops along the road, for delicate tuning of the engine, like a cellist listening to a note, as I tightened or loosened a screw in the carburetor.

My mother came down with a cup of coffee. Chuck was moving into my white room. He brought me a book for the trip, *Zen and the Art of Motorcycle Maintenance*. "It seemed an apt topic but," he smiled, "maybe you've already learned the lessons?"

I looked up at the rambling, peeling house and felt so much love for my family.

We were all together and we were getting through. I had learned to do something, not just think. I'd learned I could enjoy talking to people and it didn't have to be intellectual to be satisfying. On Parker Street, we all hit bottom. We didn't know about surviving. We had to learn. Living in poverty with my mother and brother became an important antidote to our years of living in unconscious privilege. I had to expel the passivity of a child raised in a wealthy village, root out the curse of expectations and assumptions about tuition being paid and my needs taken care of. We each wrestled with our legacy of inheritances from my father. My mother was furious, breaking out of her decades of subservience. Wood and I both wrestled with depression and the whisper of suicidal impulses. Our old friend Chuck was our wise counsel who knew where we came from. He helped us emerge from the damage of our entrapment in the glass house.

HUBBARD CAME INTO town from Glendale in the VW bus to say good-bye. At seventeen, he towered over me, his hair growing in from being shaved for swim team. He was finishing high school in a few weeks, after cramming all his courses into three years. His face had a strained, serious look. "I'm getting out of that house and never going back." He was heading south for a job on a fishing boat in the Gulf. He had a line of stitches over his eye. Wood looked at him. "Hey, how'd you get that? The old man deck you one?"

"Well, kind of." He'd been helping our dad empty out the old architectural office on William Howard Taft Road. They had to move all the boxes down the steep stairs. The second floor was packed, and the attic, too. Packed with boxes of rolls of plans, architectural models and books going back to his own father's practice. Rolls and rolls of plans, ink on linen, from our grandfather's magnificent schools and towers. They filled up the VW countless times for the dump.

Exhausted by the stairs, Hubbard and our father started dropping boxes out of the second- and third-floor windows, even though some exploded on impact, causing more work. At one point Hubbard was below, catching empty cardboard file boxes my dad threw down, some with a reinforced frame of metal. One metal edge caught my brother right above the eye. "Blood all over."

Wood laughed, "Yeah, nothing like a head wound to gush a lot of blood. Impressive. So how many stitches did you get?"

Hubbard continued, "We're not there yet." They found some rags to stop the flow a bit, and then he thought they'd go to the hospital. But our father wouldn't stop until he finished the job and unloaded what they saved out at the house in Glendale. "Two or three more hours."

Wood shook his head. "That bastard."

"I'm a kid. I don't know these things. I was worried the emergency room would close." He called the hospital and asked how late they were open. They assured him they were open all night and asked questions. Finally, when our father thought they'd done enough, around ten they went to the ER. A doctor stitched him up and let him watch in a mirror. "But Wood, here's the good part." He had a look of pride, like he'd done something great.

"When we got home, we found the fire department and police had broken into our house."

Wood raised his eyebrows, "No kidding!"

"Really!" The hospital had taken it seriously that a teenager called with a gash on his head and his father wouldn't take him to the hospital. Of course our father went into a rage. He blamed it all on my brother. He severely chastised

Hubbard in front of them all and afterwards. "But I smiled to myself, knowing I was right, and everyone else knew it too. I didn't have to defend myself." He grinned, but his face was tight. "That's how I get by—little moments of revenge."

The brothers looked at each other. Wood patted him on the shoulder. We stood there on the sidewalk looking at my little black sports car and then up at the ramshackle house. Nearly midnight, lights were all on with the Grateful Dead playing on speakers set in an open window. Then Hubbard said, "I gotta say good-bye to Jo. Have a great trip. I'll be heading out soon myself." The three of us hugged. My younger brothers dwarfed me, their strong arms stretched around me.

CALIFORNIA

1980s

*Architecture can't fully represent the chaos and
turmoil that are part of the human personality, but
you need to put some of that turmoil into the
architecture, or it isn't real.*

—FRANK STELLA

YEARS LATER, AFTER OUR FAMILY HAD SCATTERED,
after the glass house was sold, I still hoped the adored father
from my childhood might return. Woodie visited me in California in the early 80s, when I was twenty-seven and he
sixty-seven. San Francisco felt as cool and fresh as the raw
oysters on ice we shared at a sidewalk café. Our conversation
was the slice of lemon, the dash of Tabasco.

He revved his new Renault Fuego up the steepest streets.
We parked at the summit, pointing out our favorite Victorian details in the colorful row houses marching down the
hill. We both disliked the design of the Transamerica Pyra-
mid, no matter how earthquake-resistant. Roaring across the
Golden Gate Bridge, his car sliced stripes of shadow and
light. We gazed up at the orange beams soaring above us. His
enthusiasm flooded the black leather interior; his arm swept
across the dashboard as we raced toward the Marin high-

lands. "I read about this baby in *Car and Driver*. She can do zero to sixty in five seconds, and zero to one hundred in twelve seconds! Want me to give her a run for our money?"

I laughed, "Of course," and sighed with relief.

I'd barely seen him since I'd moved to California, but we'd gotten into a habit of talking nearly every week. Sometimes on the phone he was buoyant. He was learning to use the new computers to draw out architectural plans. He'd say, "Lilibet, you won't believe when I got to sleep last night." On the screen, he played with the plans for our glass house, thrilled now to look at the house from any angle or perspective, to add and change dimensions as he liked right on the screen. He said he often did this, spending long nights in front of the blinking green screen, until he was surprised by the sunrise and staggered off to bed.

Other times his voice from Ohio was despairing. He confessed, "I'm sorry, Missy, I just can't keep going on like this much longer."

Chilled, instantly hooked in, I became the girl who had to make her daddy happy, who couldn't let him get too sad. I pedaled as fast as I could, hurtling suggestions like a kid on a paper route.

Books. "Daddy, I just finished Carl Jung's *Memories, Dreams and Reflections*. He built a circular stone tower where he painted mandalas. Have you ever thought of building a small beautiful building with your own hands?"

Painting. "I remember that morning when I was a kid and I came down to see you'd been up all night painting. There was a watercolor I couldn't believe wasn't Kandinsky. Don't you want to paint again?"

Hours of desperate suggestions. "How about having a roommate, maybe an architectural student? You love talking to young people so much."

He always had a reason why he couldn't. Eventually one of us gave out. Usually he promised. "Okay. I'll make some calls tomorrow. That's a good idea. Thank you so much, Sugar." He said good night the way we always had. "Night, night. Love you."

I answered "Love you" back, and we hung up. Of course, he never made any calls for roommates, or art supplies, or the books I mentioned. But I never stopped trying. But this time he'd said "Yes" when I suggested he come to visit.

The city sparkled as night settled in around us. We walked arm in arm into the buzz of the artsy crowd as we entered a grand old auditorium for an avant-garde performance by Laurie Anderson called *United States*. We found our velvet seats under crystal chandeliers before the room darkened. Laurie Anderson entered the stage, petite in a tux, with spiky short hair like mine. Three enormous screens reverberated with close-up images of her as she played a white lacquered violin, running her magnetic-tape bow across a playback head instead of strings. Her flat voice echoed urgent patterns of sound. Oh—oh—oh—oh. Light streamed from her mouth in the dark. Music beating like a heart flooded us. My dad was turned on, electric, riveted. He patted my hand enthusiastically.

During intermission, he raved, "This is fantastic!" to the gay couple next to us and the punk couple in front of us. The way they laughed with him I knew they thought he was the coolest: this bald older man, in his Brooks Brothers baggy tan suit, white shirt and narrow red bow tie, trying to get the words right from Laurie Anderson's song "Oh Superman."

Driving across the Bay Bridge to Berkeley, we chanted the chorus, copying her haunted voice: *'Cause when love is gone, there's always justice . . . / Oh Superman . . .*

———

WHEN WE GOT back to the stucco bungalow I shared with two roommates, we stayed up late like kids in college, playing the "O Superman" single on the record player. I said, "Wow! Her chorus is just like a section in the *Tao Te Ching* I've been reading." I flipped through pages until I found the passage: *When kindness is lost, there is justice.*

My father murmured as he read the words. Then he said, "Sugar, I'm fading fast, but this has been the best day. I can't thank you enough. See you in the morning." He patted me on the shoulder, taking the book to read. I showed him to the little cottage in the backyard, where he slept under fir and orange trees in the flatlands of stucco cottages tangled in overgrown fuchsias, bamboo, and roses.

The next day we drove towards the Berkeley Hills. I wanted to show him the rose gardens and the view of the Bay. Gripping the wheel in his sports car, we roared up the winding hills. White and beige, palomino-barked eucalyptus trees edged the road, their long narrow leaves waving like delicate brushstrokes as the East Bay cities slipped below us.

I watched his profile as he drove. He was looking older, his neck curving forward, yet gazing ahead with such vitality it was as if he couldn't wait for the next curve in the road. His large chest was snug in his black and red plaid shirt, tucked in firmly with a thick worn leather belt above his khaki pants.

When the change came, it was rapid. He patted my knee as he maneuvered the tight curves past the Botanical Gardens, past the towering cacti, and called me "Lover." I felt uneasy, but pushed the feeling away with his immediate qualifying words, "In my day, we talked that way with our friends."

But a few sentences later, he slipped and called me my mother's name, "We've always loved driving together, haven't we, Jo?" He caught himself with a start, suddenly glaring. His words stumbled. He shifted gears raggedly as he accelerated up the steep, winding Wildcat Canyon. He turned a face of fury to mine for an instant before he jolted the car around the next bend. "Your mother destroyed my life, and you just won't see it!"

My heart broke in an instant. I'd been hoping that after years of careful phone calls that maybe now my father was all right, that he wasn't crazy anymore. But at that moment, as he free-fell over the edge, my heart walled him out, and my body stiffened. I instantly remembered I needed to protect myself. His strident voice lectured, his thick finger pointed as he fired off a barrage of sins we had done against him. "Your mother and you children all conspired to destroy me."

The Renault lurched as he shifted gears. I braced myself in the slippery leather seat, staring ahead, trying to hold us to the road with my eyes. My body grew rigid. I refused to look at him, but his ragged breathing filled the car. I felt claustrophobic, trapped by his voice, bellowing, "Your brothers aren't going to amount to anything. They have no integrity." The tires squealed. He steered too close to a rough rock face with loose stones scattered onto the road. I was frightened but couldn't say anything, couldn't protest or defend my brothers. He would get worse, louder, and even more dangerous. I knew it. All I could do was wait him out.

Slamming jolts at stop signs. Heavy piston brakes grabbed. Rapid acceleration, curves taken too tight. "You bankrupted me, you and your mother's divorce." His large body jammed into the bucket seat was too big for the car. "Your court case for college tuition drove me into the ground." With one hand I gripped the dashboard; with the other I seized the handle above the window. How many times had I endured this kind of ride, praying to arrive safely?

"Please," I whispered to the trees whipping by, "let me survive. Please, I can't die yet." I looked out the car window and felt like someone drowning, scanning for a branch along the edge of a river I could grab onto. My mind started racing through the old fights. A tight turn slammed me against the door. I tried to remember the old protests I used to defend myself. By the time the car careened onto Skyline Drive, I was hooked back into his madness.

I remembered my mother's mantra. "There is no way to reason with craziness. It will make you crazy." But through all these years, I'd never given up on him. I tried to stay connected to both parents. When I visited my dad, in the years after the divorce, my mother lived in a fury, turning away from me, saying, "You have no sense of ethics. Your brother will have nothing to do with him ever again." My brother Wood did not notify our father when his daughters were born and never let them meet him. I couldn't do that. My brother would joke, but looked at me piercingly. "You may be smart," he'd say, "but you sure are stupid." My mother would nod, agreeing. My move to California was the exit from my parents' war zone.

But because I had tried, because I loved my father, here I was, all over again, trapped in the car, trapped by my trying. The engine at high rev, he squealed into a parking spot at Inspiration Point. He fumbled with the key, turning it too far so the engine ground harshly before he could turn it off. He looked at me, his face huge and contorted, hands in fists on the wheel, spit flying from his thin lips. I turned away, staring ahead. I couldn't bear to look at him. He shouted, "You have no integrity. You have to choose between your mother and me. I won't stand this impasse another moment. It's up to you." I was frozen silent, once again the teenager I'd been when we lived in the glass house.

As I stared across the gleaming white hood, down over the sparkling patchwork gypsy skirt of gardens and buildings stretching to the bay, I wanted to cry. This was my new world, where no one knew I was Woodie's daughter, where I was safe, thousands of miles from Ohio. Here the bay was stitched with bridges, glinting in the afternoon light, and beyond the Golden Gate stretched the Pacific Ocean. Somehow I thought being here would protect me from their battles. But I was caught all over again, trying to endure, just like my years in high school when I would stare into the grain of the teak dining room table as my father grilled me for hours.

When Woodie finally stopped shouting I used my voice to soothe, to palliate, to draw him back into the moment. Some of these quiet words caught hold. "We need to get some dinner. There is a performance tonight. You need to get a good rest before you start driving on the rest of your trip tomorrow." He quieted. He shrank. Soon he was a lost old man staring at the cities sprawling beyond him.

———·———

MY FATHER'S LIFE was haunted from the beginning. Soon after he was born in the Victorian house, his mother disappeared into a darkened room for three years. How could a mother lie in bed for years and not come out when she heard her children crying or playing on the stairs or running in the backyard? When I heard these stories as a child, I did not wonder, as an adult might consider: was this post-partum depression, migraines, or something more serious? I did not consider this was similar to what my father sometimes did, staying in bed with the curtains drawn all weekend or sometimes even for weeks. My mother would say he was tired and we needed to be quiet. Families can get used to mysteries, used to hearing stories and not asking about them, not wondering out loud. Until something shifts somehow and we begin to investigate our history, like a detective.

In the early 1950s, my father's first major building, the Cincinnati Public Library, was under construction when my father stopped getting out of bed. His business partner called daily, frantic to talk to my dad. Contractors were demanding answers to questions. My father would turn away when my mother brought him the messages. She finally called Phil Piker, my father's psychiatrist, who advised her. "Carry on life as if nothing is wrong. Bring him meals. Be cheery and upbeat. When people call, say he can't speak to them. Carry on as if everything is fine. It will lift, eventually." And it did. Again and again.

It wasn't until I was in my thirties, flying over the Southwestern desert for a week of outpatient therapy at a treatment center for adults who had experienced severe abuse as children, that I read a magazine article describing new advances in treatment of the mental illness once called Manic Depression, now referred to as "bipolar disorder." I was stunned. My father had a mental illness? How had I not realized this?

Years later, I read a legal deposition taken when my father had been sick in his seventies and had sued a doctor for medical negligence. The court reporter recorded a battle, a lawyer gathering medical history while trying to entrap my father into misleading generalizations. Like a dying bull in the ring, heaving with countless goads in his back, my father lashed back. They skirmished repeatedly while mapping out my father's many hospitalizations over 150 pages of onionskin testimony.

Unexpectedly, my father acknowledged his mental illness—or what he preferred to call his "emotional difficulties"— with candor. He described depressions "that literally rob you of your ability to function at all." He didn't remember when they started. He asked on the record, "Doesn't every teenager get depressed?" However, it was after his first marriage ended and his wife took their young daughter, disappearing for thirty years, that a depression broke him. A young doctor prescribed electroshock convulsive treatments in the late 1940s in Cincinnati. This was when my parents were dating. The treatments scrambled my father's memory, erasing months of memory at a time.

Soon afterward, my father found his way to Phil Piker, trained at a psychoanalytic school in Chicago, who stopped the shock treatments. My father told him he wanted answers, he wanted a cure. He stated in the deposition, "I'll never forget what Phil Piker said to my dying day . . . 'I will never let you down' . . . He said, 'I may not be able to cure you but I will teach you how to live with your problem.'" Phil told my father that emotional problems were causing his extreme reactions because he "took everything with such intensity. . . . These things are not all bad . . . If you didn't have this intense emotional approach to your work, you wouldn't be the hell of an architect that you are."

My father described how he would talk to Phil when he had problems that "were really disturbing me . . . He was marvelous, the way he helped me unravel them. . . . He never gave me any medicine, we just talked." My dad was with Phil the day Phil died, who even then repeated his belief in my father's gifts. I can only wonder, having no idea if medication might have helped my father, whether Phil Piker's decision not to constrain my father's brilliance is what cost my father his family.

In the years after we were all cast out of the glass house, we tried to understand what happened when we lived there. In the first years, we would say he was crazy. It was craziness. Nothing else to say. But when my mother worked as a child protective worker, she attended a seminar on the treatment of Borderline Personality Disorder. She was excited when she called me. "This is what he is." She read me a list of characteristics. Charismatic, manipulative, compulsive liar, can change their personality on a dime, blames others.

From the distance of twenty years, my brothers, mother,

and I began to debate the details, putting together a diagnosis like an addition problem. Bipolar plus rage equals Borderline. The hardest to treat. My youngest brother, Hubbard, emailed me lists from the Internet listing symptoms, convinced our dad was a sociopath. We were like survivors of a war, cataloguing what we had survived. My brother Wood said our father had no empathy, giving examples, like the time he walked by Hubbard with his broken arm and didn't even look at him. My brothers agreed. Our father had only used people. He was incapable of love.

But I couldn't imagine he had never loved us. What about the good times when I was a girl? It couldn't have all been poisoned by madness. I spent years fitting puzzle pieces together from my father's history to try to understand him, as well as to heal myself. As a child with a mother locked away in the dark, he grew up wanting to control women. As an unmothered and untouched child, he became a man desperate for a woman's touch. He became a man who was enraged by illness, or ignored it as if it didn't exist. He became a man who, when his sick daughter was dying, or when his youngest son lay on a kitchen table with a broken arm, walked by, didn't look, or say a word. He left for the office, escaping into the world of architecture.

He was bipolar, a sex addict who fondled a few teenagers, was emotionally intrusive with a few little girls he had fixated on, a mentally/emotionally/spiritually abusive parent; and he was also a charismatic, brilliant architect, receiving the AIA lifetime achievement award for his impact on modern architecture, creating modern buildings amidst huge controversy that impacted a city. He was my father who loved, abused and trained me through intellectual seduction, grooming my mind to be his intellectual companion.

At the core of his self was a damaged individual, and yet I believe he also had a capacity to love. There was a genuine, loving, not-seductive part of him, and a seductive, grooming, not-loving part of him, and he could move between these two places in a moment. He had a natural genius and a natural enthusiasm that people responded to. But his radical vision was not tolerated, and in the battles to manifest his work, he went crazy. A German tyrant father raised him, and he became a tyrant too. The deeper story doesn't excuse the behavior, but I have compassion for the suffering he lived with and compassion for those he harmed.

I REMEMBER THE best times. My father came to my graduation from acupuncture school. I was thirty-one, dressed in a San Francisco-designer white linen dress with a red leather belt and shoes. I loved my white, wide-brimmed hat with the modern touch of a black veil. He was seventy-one, in a summerweight Brooks Brothers seersucker suit and a favorite red and black bow tie. He was proud of me, toasting with the other families, talking avidly with my teachers at this second graduating class of twenty students from one of the earliest schools of acupuncture in the US. It was 1984 and we were standing at the beginning of what would become a tidal wave of alternative health care.

Afterwards, I would be going back to California to begin my practice; he was on his way to visit friends and go sailing.

We had a few days together and drove north. In the Philadelphia art museum, we fell by accident into an exhibit neither of us knew anything about. The paintings were an eruption of brilliant reds, yellows, blues, and metallic luminosity, cubed, built into structures, ribbed lines of hot colors printed on black. Hundertwasser. "In German that means one hundred waters," my father said. We gazed into a golden wheat field becoming a woman's face, with lines of brilliant orange and red houses extending out of her eyes and mouth. "Irinaland over the Balkans." We paused between paintings, exuberant, in the pure pleasure of discovery. "Woodie, look at this next one! It's amazing!" We faced golden onion-shaped domes, doorways with faces, tears in brilliant windows of color. We read the titles out loud like poems. "It Hurts to Wait with Love if Love is Somewhere Else." In that long-ago room we were beginners, no one knowing more or less, no teacher or student, just enthusiasts, father and daughter, alive and breathing in color.

We continued to New York, driving up through the fresh warmth of spring, leaves unfurling, a baby-green lace canopy over us as we drove along Central Park to the Guggenheim. He always said he hated Frank Lloyd Wright, but we both loved the Guggenheim. I'd spent a day there in college walking the ramp, studying the plans, writing a paper for a class on Modern Architecture. We entered the building, took the elevator and emerged at the top in the filtered gallery of light at the top of the spiral. This building was an old friend we'd each made on our own. We walked arm and arm following the pathway, standing at the edge to look down the spiral, pointing out what details we'd discovered. Waiting for us was a show of Kandinsky's The Blue Rider period. We sounded out the words in German, Der Blaue Reiter. We both loved and knew these paintings, but had never seen them in person, only in books. We savored each one, finally agreeing our favorite was the orange-robed horsemen on white leaping horses, crossing indigo mountains, with trees, yellow and deep pink reds, erupting into pure abstraction. We moved in close to study the thick brush strokes of yellow mounding out of the mountains, melting into green and pink-tinged white.

We left slowly, walked arm and arm back to his car. He would continue north; I was meeting friends before taking a plane west. As we hugged goodbye, he said, "Lilibet, I've loved this trip together."

"Woodie, it's been the best."

After he got into his car, ready to drive off, he rolled down the window and said, "Love you."

And I said back as I always had, 'Love you, too."

LAST WORDS

1994

We are a landscape of all we have seen.

—ISAMU NOGUCHI

MY WORK TO BREAK MY BONDAGE TO HIM, TO stand up for myself, and to say no to him continued until the last month of his life when he was dying in 1994.

After years of wandering I had found my way. I was in my sixth year of a busy private practice as an acupuncturist in a small coastal town in Maine. My husband and I designed the passive solar house he built on seventy-five acres, where we lived with our two young children.

My mother had also moved to Maine, and lived two hours south, where she and her second husband were renovating an old Maine Cape. My brothers, Hubbard and Wood and their families, would eventually move to New England, and we all lived two hours away from Jo, the dynamic center of our family. We feasted at her cozy home for Thanksgivings and ate on the back porch in summer while our children played in the yard. Often one of us would turn to another and say quietly, "It's amazing, no one is yelling at us." We'd nod with relief.

Even though I talked weekly with my dad as his health steadily declined, I never knew what a call from him would bring. To distract him from his furious complaints about the people helping him, I'd tell him things he'd like.

"Guess what, Woodie, I'm making applesauce with your favorite apples, Jonathans."

His voice belted out his gasping enthusiasm. "The secret is cooking down the peels separately. That's how you get that incredible red color. You remember, don't you?" He sighed. "We used to freeze over a hundred quarts of applesauce. That wasn't too terrible, was it?"

"No, of course not," I reassured him. I didn't say I would never make my children work until midnight canning and freezing food.

He said, "I don't know what I'd do without you, Missy. This was really great talking tonight."

"It was. Good night, Daddy. Love you."

One winter day I came into my house and heard my father's voice on the answering machine. "Hi Sugar. I was hoping I could talk to you." I stood, poised with water bottles to take to my husband and children cross-country skiing in the meadow.

His voice continued. "I've been doing a lot of thinking." His usually commanding voice was quieter, gentle.

I put down the water and picked up the phone. "Hi, Woodie. I'm glad to hear you."

I pulled the phone cord so I could see the kids at the crest of the hill. Four-year-old daughter Miriam was trying to ski in tracks in the snow. My husband Peter showed eight-year-old Gabriel how to use his poles as he skied downhill.

My father's voice was subdued. "I want to know what I did to you. I don't remember."

I was stunned, silent.

He continued, "Peter once yelled at me, saying that I'd ruined your marriage because of what I did. I'm ready to talk about that." He was waiting, leaving a space for me to speak.

Where to begin? I'd spent years in therapy, filled journals with nightmares and memories. There were years when I couldn't let my husband touch me because his hands turned into my father's in the dark. But my life now was filled with love. I didn't need to blame him or attack him.

Then I knew what to do. I stepped into the professional voice I use in my practice as an acupuncturist as a way to educate someone. I started. "You took nude photographs of my brother and me to chart the development of our bodies. That was a violation of our sexual boundaries."

He had kept the Polaroids in his upper-right bureau drawer, where he dumped his coins at the end of the day. If I closed my eyes I could reach in that drawer and slip out the faded photos. My brother and I stood in the living room, nude children. My brother's eyes stare through the floor. Our faces flat and enduring. Our young bodies held captive on fading blue-green glossy Polaroids.

"You forbade us to close the bathroom door when we took showers. You walked around the house naked, with just a magazine over your groin, when our friends came over. This was a violation of our boundaries."

I wrenched myself out of my childhood to look out the window. Where were the kids? I stretched the phone cord as far as it would go so I could look down the snowy hill. There they were, slowly skiing. Peter was holding Miriam under her arms so she could ski right in front of him and not fall down. Gabe was farther ahead, turning back to wave to his dad.

I breathed, trying to calm the tightness in my belly, before I spoke again. "You made me lie naked and gave me back rubs and then front rubs. That is sexual abuse. I froze my body so I didn't feel anything."

He asked with a saddened voice, "Does it make any difference that I never meant to hurt you?"

I answered, "Even if you didn't mean harm, harm was still done. I've gone to therapy for fifteen years."

His voice was anguished. "Why would you have anything to do with me?"

"Because I love you. I kept working and working on this for years, trying to heal, and still have a relationship with you."

He was in tears. "I'm so sorry. I never meant to hurt you."

I cried too. "I'm sorry too. But the biggest gift you could ever give me is that you asked. You listened, and you said you are sorry."

"I'm so sorry. I feel so bad about this. I love you."

"I love you too."

After I hung up, I felt dizzy and shaken. I picked up the water bottles, put on my snow boots, and walked out into the bright sunlight. I walked through the snow following my family's footsteps to the field just as Peter, with Miriam on his back, skis askew, arrived at the top of the hill. Gabe was beaming because he'd beaten them to the top. I handed them each a bottle of water and put my arms around Peter, and began to cry.

"What's happened?" he asked.

"A miracle," I smiled. "My dad said he was sorry, for everything."

Peter wiped the tears off my cheeks.

My daughter asked, "Why is mama crying?"

"Because I'm so happy."

A WEEK LATER, winter settled back in with a vengeance, ten below zero. The north wind carved the snow in hard chiseled ridges around the house. The woodstove warmed our hand-built home. Miriam lined up her dolls in a row. Gabe built a Lego fort. I was upstairs folding laundry when the phone rang. Before I sensed danger, I said, "Hi, Daddy."

His words throttled me. "You stupid, hysterical, ridiculous woman." His words pinned me like someone holding a knife to my throat. I stumbled to sit in my desk chair, staring at the door to anchor myself. His furious voice bellowed over the phone. "Why have you done this to a dying man? You are a vicious, sick, cruel woman!"

I sat in my bedroom at my desk, staring at the wooden door my husband made from wild cherry cut from our woods. My father's voice blasted into my ear. I stared into the grain of the wood, unable to see the sun-drenched snowy meadows stretching beyond the window behind me. I heard my daughter laughing on the swing we had bolted into the ceiling beam.

I was reeling. I didn't know what to do. He was a sick, dying man. Maybe I had to listen. Maybe I had to be understanding. His mind had played him like a mad piano night and day. His words kept socking me. "You lay this shit on me. It's shit, that's what it is! You are cruel and relentless." His words were jabs, slaps, punches.

———·———

IT TOOK ME half an hour before I remembered: I didn't have to listen to this anymore. I decided no one would ever yell at me again. I interrupted, speaking quietly, "I'm done, Woodie."

"What?" he demanded, startled that I dared speak and break his tirade.

"I'm done. Good-bye." Setting down the phone felt like locking a door. The bond with my father which had always kept me, trying and enduring, had broken. I felt faint and trembled. I lay down and stared at the ceiling. I heard my children talking to Peter as he made blueberry pancakes for breakfast. Slowly the goodness of my life brought me back.

A month later, on Valentine's Day, my father's voice was tender on my message machine, when the kids and I got home from school. "Hello Sugar. I was hoping to talk to you. I miss you." He paused before saying goodbye, the last time I heard his voice. "Love you."

———·———

BY THE TIME my father died a few weeks later, no one from our family was there. He had worn us out. No one spoke of madness. He was Woodie, damned stubborn, unrelenting, unbending, impossible, Woodie. His apartment was like places you read about in the paper, of old men living in mazes of piled newspapers. It was a labyrinth of books, architecture journals, sculptures, and papers, stacked and falling. He was dying and hell if he was going to eat Meals on Wheels. Hell if he was going to let that old woman give him a bath. Hell if he was going to let anyone move him to the hospital. But in the end, when he was screaming in pain, they took him by ambulance into the city to hospice, where they made him comfortable for the last two days.

When my youngest brother, Hubbard, called to check on him, the nurse said, "He's in a light coma, but I'll hold the phone next to his ear so you can talk to him. He can probably hear you."

Hubbard heard the Dave Brubeck they were playing for him, and his rough breathing. When Hubbard began to speak of their years together, Woodie opened his eyes. "I want you to know we love you. Remember that trip when we went to Boston to Legal Seafood, and how you loved plates of raw oysters. Do you remember the time I was sailing so fast and hit a rock and flipped your catamaran in the main channel with everyone watching? And they were supposedly impossible to flip." He continued until he ran out of stories. He paused. "We love you, Woodie." He was quiet and stayed on the line from his office in Boston.

The nurse came back on the line, "Your father just died."

After a long pause, she added, "Yesterday he looked me in the eye and said, 'I'm not afraid to die. It will be a relief.'"

A BLIZZARD SCOURED the windows of my home in Maine when my mother called me. "Your dad is gone." While the wind whirled around the house, I sobbed like a girl who had lost her daddy. Yet after the tears eased, I felt a sudden release of tension in my body. "I don't have to be afraid, anymore. Nothing more bad can happen."

The next morning I began driving before dawn. My husband and two children would follow in a few days. The plows had cleared the blizzard's sprawl across the roads, carving smooth walls of snow three feet deep. The wind on the high ridges kept drifting snow across the back country roads as I drove toward the highway. I barely made it to the plane in Portland. My mother joined me at the airport and we slipped into our seats. We felt suddenly celebratory, called on an unexpected errand. She pulled out of her bag little containers, offering me cool squares of pineapple, a spoonful of her frozen applesauce, sharing a granola bar. She was coming to Cincinnati to be there for her children. She would rejoin the Garber family that had been hers for twenty-five years until my father banished her after the divorce. She wouldn't go to the funeral.

When the plane stopped in Boston for passengers, Hubbard joined us, sliding his long legs under the seat ahead. We laughed and hugged as if we were going to a wedding. The stewardess noticed. "It's so nice to see a family so happy together. Going to something special?"

"Yes," my brother and I smiled curiously. "Our father died."

Her smile froze and she hurried on. Looking into each other's faces, my sixty-year-old mother's beautifully lined face edged with short white hair, my brother's tall forehead and strong-boned face, we reached out for each other's hands, our eyes tearing with a strange confusion of feeling.

My brother Wood had been reached by ship-to-shore radio, miles from land, where he was in charge of a container ship's engine room. He was transported by boat, helicopter, and plane to arrive in time for the funeral. When he arrived, we put our arms around each other and held on tight. I looked at my brothers, both in their thirties. Wood was weary in jeans and a work shirt, his long hair in a ponytail, and Hubbard towered over us with short hair, mustache, and tailored clothes.

Wood told us, "On the ship, they thought I was crying because I missed my father. Hell no. I cried because I never had the dad I wanted, and now he's gone."

Hubbard put his arm around Wood's broad shoulders, comforting him.

———·———

HUBBARD AND I went to the funeral home, both of us taking time to be alone with our father. A man in a black suit led me to a private viewing room and wheeled in a metal table, my father's body covered with a heavy grey cloth, waiting for us, before he was cremated. He closed the door.

I hadn't seen him this long last year as he was dying. I hadn't spoken to him since his voice sliced insults across the line. Yet I felt at home being near him even under this heavy cloth. I uncovered his heavy hand, curled into a fist. I placed my warm hand around his. His skin didn't feel old, it felt new, like when you peel bark off a tree, smooth and never seen. His hand and arm felt heavy, as if it could never be moved, as if it touched bedrock and was part of it. If he was a drowned man, I could never pull him ashore. But this was good: to feel the weight of him, so finite, at the end, when he couldn't hurt us anymore, when it was safe to love him again.

I remembered the stones, how we held stones with our eyes closed on the beach in Nantucket. I pulled a smooth black stone from an island in Maine out of my coat pocket. I took his cold clenched hand and slid the black sea-smoothed stone until it disappeared into his grasp. So he would not be alone when he slipped into the flames.

Sander Hall Implosion, 1991

IMPLOSION

1991

Architecture aims at eternity.

—CHRISTOPHER WREN

ON A JUNE MORNING IN 1991, THREE YEARS BEFORE
my father died, I was working in the garden with my children
playing nearby. I had no idea my father was standing on a
house boat anchored at a precise location in the earth-brown
Ohio River. He mentioned it casually over the phone a week
later, as I spooned oatmeal for my one-year-old daughter. He
said, "We met early at the dock." Bob, the mechanical engineer for Sander Hall, had helped my father aboard, before
motoring downstream until he angled his boat into position,
out of the current. Tugs rumbled by, maneuvering barges
piled with small mountains of glistening coal.

My father, nearly eighty, his back curved over from os-
teoporosis, had brought a bottle of chilled champagne. They
trained their binoculars on the top floors of the mirror glass
dorm that appeared, like a Japanese kite, flying high above
the tree-covered hillside. They checked their watches and
looked up every few seconds.

From that distance the tower had appeared as beautiful as
my father had envisioned it, silvery rose mirrored walls rising

high above the earthly world, where clouds floated over the surface, like the painting I'd seen in his office, a building surrounded with grass and trees. But my father's grand vision had been hijacked by a miasma of circumstances. The tower was inextricably knotted into a collision of 1970s radical social change, wealth and poverty, racial inequality, and battles between administration and students in a roaring fury against the establishment that Sander Hall represented.

———·———

AFTER I LEFT home I'd heard occasional reports on Sander Hall. It was known for an epidemic of arson. Smoke rising up stairwells. Smoke seeping into dorm rooms. Eleven years after it was opened, a panicked girl used her desk chair to smash through the mirror glass wall of her sixth floor room to escape the smoke. Firemen on a ladder lifted her down. The University closed the building.

Studies battled over the fire safety of the dorm. Did it meet state code? What could be done to increase the safety of the building? Add an additional stairwell at the end of the building? Newspaper articles debating the issues stacked up on my aging father's desk. An occasional letter to the editor praised the building and declared it was the students who had been the problem. The university considered changing the tower over to administrative offices. But the price tag for renovation came back nearly the same as for a new building.

The University finally abandoned the building, leaving it to stand empty, a dark derelict tower, a shadow hanging over the University for nine years. Twenty years after the hall opened, in 1991, the President of the University was quoted in *The Cincinnati Enquirer*: "If I didn't know better, I'd say the building was haunted."

———·———

THROUGHOUT MY CHILDHOOD my father always declared, "I'll be an architect until the day I die. It's in my blood." Yet no one could have guessed in the weeks before the ribbon-cutting ceremony for Sander Hall that the financial recession of the 1970s would halt major construction in the U.S. for years. In 1971, Sander Hall looked like the pinnacle of Woodie's success, with the promise of more work to come. His career began with a glass tower that was never built and ended with the completion of a glass tower when he was fifty-eight. He held onto his empty office for a few years, finding consulting work, and finally, he taught a few classes to architectural students at Miami University.

———·———

ON CAMPUS THE crowds started gathering hours before. Some had stayed up all night partying and waiting. They pushed up close to the police barricades. Mid-June, Saturday morning, the University of Cincinnati campus should have been sleepy and quiet on summer school schedule. But surrounding the campus on flat roofs of cheap apartments, students clasped mugs of coffee and munched on bagels. Figures lined the top floors of University buildings. Crowds lined Calhoun in front of bookstores, head shops and the falafel shop where they would put up a framed series of second-by-second photographs of that day. Everyone waited, their eyes tracing the familiar high-rise dorm, Sander Hall, which had stood on the east side of campus since the turbulent early 1970s.

Twenty-seven stories tall, a grid of strong vertical lines with horizontal mirrored panels from an era famed for glass buildings, the dorm reflected two church steeples, pearly clouds, and plumes of airplanes across its glistening surface. On either side of the building, the column of windows was edged with my father's invention, crushed milk-glass panels, made in Xenia, Ohio, sparkling when the sun cut through Midwestern cloud cover. Two years after the tower was completed, a tornado destroyed the town of Xenia and the plant where the panels were constructed. The panels were never used on any other building besides our home and this dormitory.

The only skyscraper outside of downtown, like an arrow on a compass, the gleaming tower could orient you even from miles away. "Oh, there's campus," you would say to yourself. While driving along Columbia Parkway edging the Ohio River, when the steep hills and wooded ravines tucked just right, you could catch a glimpse of the upper half of the tower, just for a moment.

That morning, everybody had their opinions of the building; the same rumors, questions, and curses multiplied like flies, a cacophony of murmurs across every crowded hillside.

"Man, who the fuck ever wanted to live twenty-seven floors up?"

"There were fires in there. I heard someone died!"

"Some people tried smashing open their windows."

"Did anyone jump?"

"Whoever would have designed such a thing?"

"A damned eyesore!"

———

AFTER WE LEFT the glass house our father lived a cursed life, a kind of King Midas, except everything he touched seemed to turn to lead, leaking slow poison, accelerating his disintegration. By the time he sold the glass house for a pittance, he cursed it, glad to be free of "that stone hanging around my neck." His investments tanked. What was left, he used to pay for his dream trip of sailing around the world, yet within a day of setting sail from Florida to Tahiti the seeds of disaster were planted.

He would later document, in his last Literary Club paper, the first half of his ill-fated journey, trapped aboard a forty-foot yacht under the command of an abusive and inconsistent captain who risked their lives and held their passports so they couldn't leave. At the same time a common medication, Inderol, prescribed preventatively to keep his heart steady on the journey, was withering him. After six months at sea he returned, a collapsed skeleton of an old man, repeating every sentence three times, apparently terminally ill until he stopped the medication. He sued the doctor and lost. With his complicated cardiac and mental health history, it was impossible to prove the cause of his collapse.

He would recover slowly, and for a few years began to rebuild a life; learning how to use a computer, he'd stay up till dawn. But years of isolation and depression took their toll, and he began to sink. His teeth were failing, and his dentist convinced him to pull them all out and have implants screwed into the bone. This would turn into a year of torture, sleepless on pain meds and antibiotics, gums swollen and infected, a liquid diet, health robbed again. He wouldn't recover this time, despite the wall of perfect teeth imbedded in his withering face. By the end his spine betrayed him, crumbling and caving in before cancer settled into his colon. This was the man who sat in the middle of the Ohio River that June day, looking up at the tower that had consumed all of our lives.

———·——

SANDER HALL TOOK seven seconds to fall. Young voices cheered what might no longer be cheered, a chilling first practice in watching a modern glass-sheathed building shudder and wobble like a woman fainting or shot. Still managing to keep her dignity as she stayed upright, she sank to her knees before vanishing in a tsunami of dust that pursued the onlookers. Online, you can play and replay four screens showing the single largest implosion in the western hemisphere. Five hundred and twenty pounds of dynamite carefully placed. Six months to plan. Seconds to fall.

———·——

ON THE HOUSEBOAT, they raised their glasses to toast. White dust puffed gossamer between deep green hills where the tower had held the view for twenty years. My father said over the phone to me a week later, "Good riddance." His voice still defiant. Interviews in the paper quoted him saying, "I still believe it was a perfect building. Even with all those fires set, a student never died in it."

Yet I imagined him looking down, tracing his foot along a seam in the deck, muttering quietly, "It's a terrible thing to outlive your buildings."

House that Woodie designed on
Nantucket, Wood playing, 1959

EPILOGUE: NANTUCKET

2011

[Modernism] was revolution then, but it is art now. It is time to stop using modernism as a convenient punching bag, or turning it into trendy kitsch; this was one of the most powerful movements in history.

—ADA LOUISE HUXTABLE

MY MOTHER AND I LEAN ON THE STERN RAILING OF the Gray Lady, a high-speed ferry from Hyannis to Nantucket Island, on an unseasonably warm last day of September. My mother is in her early eighties and I am in my late fifties. This is the first time we have returned to Nantucket since our visit in 1959 to the "upside-down" modern house overlooking the beach. We left our homes in Maine the day before, and drove south from Boston on a crowded highway in a rainstorm. Today a pale blue sky is washed clear of clouds, and the boat fills with day trippers sporting summer white shorts and tee shirts.

As we watch the island slowly expand and grow larger on the horizon, we go over the old story of our visit in 1959. I calculate our ages. "I was five and you were thirty."

She nods. "I don't know how I could have managed without you. Even at three months, Hubbard was such a big heavy baby. You helped me carry our bags. But it was little Wood at three who wouldn't stop running off." She explains about the pea-soup fog that had kept us from flying from Boston to the island the night before. We took a crowded limo to Hyannis where the driver dropped us off at a boarding house. "That lady was shocked when we all slept in one room, but your dad had sent us off on the plane from Cincinnati with hardly any money." I remember that sweaty night traced with fog horns and the smell of salt, my first time near the ocean. On the ferry the next day the fog lifted to a sunny day, like today.

My mom continues, "Little Wood was racing around these bolted seats and you tried to catch him. Other travelers kept an eye on him while I held the baby. Ruth met us at the dock. She drove us straight to the cottage, and we never left that whole week. I could finally rest."

This time, when our ferry pulls into the dock on Nantucket, two architectural historians are waving to us. They are both professors at the University of Cincinnati's College of Design, Architecture, Art and Planning (DAAP) and seem to be in their late forties. Patrick Snadon is tall, lean, and gracious, with a slight accent from his Missouri upbringing. Udo Greinacher looks distinctively European, with steel-edged glasses, and speaks with a softened German accent. I had discovered their collaborative book, *50 from the 50's: Modern Architecture and Interiors in Cincinnati.* I was fascinated by Patrick's insightful comments about how Cincinnati became a leader in Modernism in the US after the war, with the city of seven hills offering spectacular sites for modern houses.

When Patrick wrote that my father's design for the Public Library seemed reminiscent of Le Corbusier's Villa Savoye, I was compelled to write to him and included my chapter on building the model together. Did he know that was my father's favorite house? Patrick responded with enthusiasm and countless questions. He felt my father was Cincinnati's most significant and original Modernist architect and of national stature and importance. Part of the intention of their book was to raise awareness of how many early Modernist buildings had been torn down and were at risk, and to contribute to the appreciation and preservation of a remarkable era in architecture. We began a rigorous and generous correspondence; he answered my architectural questions and I discovered how much I had to offer his research into my father's work.

———

IN THE YEARS after my father's death, my life was filled with my own family and work in Maine. I thought less and less of my childhood in Cincinnati until 2008. It was sixteen years after my father died and the arrhythmia I had inherited from my father was increasing in frequency. I needed to have a surgical procedure called an ablation, to scar areas of the heart that were misfiring. As I recovered, I woke each morning flooded with vivid childhood memories: the wallpaper on the wall next to my bed, my fears of the witch under the bed who might grab my ankles, my little sister faintly breathing in her bassinet. Each day I wrote down what my little-girl self in Ohio wanted me to remember. Each day there were more memories following me. Over the months I remembered when we moved from the Victorian house to the glass house, to leaving home. At first I was bewildered. What is going on? But I just kept writing everything down. The stream of memories continued daily for nearly two years until I had written every memory I had of my childhood, teens, and twenties, filling hundreds of pages. This was how I began to write this memoir about my relationship with my father, and how the rest of our family survived.

After his death in 1994, when my brothers and I cleared his chaotic apartment and desk, we filled a box with his photographs, letters, Literary Club papers, and newspaper clippings and put them away, thinking we might someday deal with them. Hubbard took the box, and it moved with him from house to house, until it was forgotten in an attic. We were a family where none of us had photos of our father displayed. He was a book we had closed with relief and a shudder. After my memories started surfacing, I told Hubbard I wanted the box of our father's papers. But after he passed it on to me, I was afraid to touch it for weeks. Yet after sixteen years, something had happened. I realized the radioactive half-life of my father's fury had faded. I opened the box. At the top of the stack of papers was an oval sepia photograph of a curly-headed child with steady eyes. I delved into the layers, suddenly yearning for my father's handwriting, his notes, his photographs. I would begin to see my father's life as the unwinding of a tragedy: a toddler in a sailor suit during WWI, a lanky teen on horseback, a racing car driver, a young father, a visionary architect, a tyrant, a broken man.

When I first began asking questions about my childhood and our years in the glass house, my mother was amused by my interest, but when the questions stirred up her decades of fury, she called me. "You can ask me about when you were little, but nothing more about when things got bad. I'm waking up with nightmares where I'm still trapped in that glass house." After that, I carefully steered away from any difficult memories with her, or with my brother Woodie. His face weary from his years of working in engine rooms at sea, his eyes sad, he said, "I don't want to go back there. I do everything I can to lock away those bad memories."

My youngest brother Hubbard, from his office in Boston, at first wrote back quick answers. He couched his answers with, "Our father was a bad man. I have no happy memories from my childhood except the months when our dad visited you on the ship." But the emails grew longer, more detailed. One weekend, he spent hours writing all the bad memories he had with his father. After sending them to me, he put his arms about his wife and sobbed. A week later he sent me four more pages. He had remembered the good times with his father. A few months later, for our mother's eightieth birthday, he wrote a ten-page letter filled with his happy memories from his childhood with our mother, baking bread and riding with her in the VW bus.

At Thanksgiving at my brother's house, my mother glared at me. "Why in the world are you writing about the horrid man? Why would anyone want to hear about him?"

I answered, "What I shared with my father was architecture and art."

Her face changed. She looked out the window as if looking back in time. She said, "I forgot. You had a very different relationship with your father than your brothers." She paused. "Okay, now I get it." Later I heard her in the kitchen, telling my sister-in-law, "Elizabeth's book about her dad is focused on architecture." She could accept this. She was willing to answer questions about my father's buildings after that.

When I flew to Cincinnati a year later, I rediscovered the complex, beautiful, and disturbing city I'd left at age twenty. I called my mother daily, saying "You won't believe where I am now!" I loved the familiar parkways and architectural treasures all over the hilly city, art and historical museums, and old friends and cousins. I grieved the swaths of city blocks, burned out, bulldozed or abandoned nineteenth-century buildings, and the obvious polarizations of poverty, race, and wealth. Living in rural Maine for a quarter century, I was shocked by the vast suburban ring, a gorgon knot of highways through industrial complexes, abandoned shopping centers and concentrated housing, without a single building with any integrity or beauty in design. But overall, I spent a week compelled to find buildings and places that had been memorable in my childhood.

On my return to Maine, as my mother drove me to her house from the airport, I was brimming with excitement as I recounted my adventures. I had met with the architectural historians, Patrick and Udo, and spent three days walking through my father's buildings, as they filmed each building and interviewed us speaking with the owners. At the end of my visit, the historians and I discussed which was our favorite Woodie Garber house. The glass house in Glendale we lived in? The Klausmeyer house in Indian Hill, a glass cube on a wooded hillside? Or the Moore house which they had documented before it was demolished a few years ago? Two glass rectangular spaces with a glass bridge connecting them, white stone walls, and a hundred-foot precipice to a creek below. My mother teared up: "I loved that house." That site was now covered with five McMansions.

After I entered my mother's Maine cape, she added wood to the cookstove and served eggplant parmesan, warm from the oven. "The last eggplant from my greenhouse." As we ate dinner, she mused. "If I had to chose which of your dad's buildings was my favorite, I'd say it was the Klausmeyer house on Nantucket. You remember how we entered on the ground floor where he'd put the bedrooms. Upstairs, I loved cooking in the kitchen and looking straight out over the dunes to the ocean." She declared with excitement, "I guess for this project of yours, we'll just have to go visit it!"

AS THE JOURNEY to Nantucket nears, my mother is animated. "What is great about going to the Nantucket house is that I only have good memories about that house." She had been remembering how, after my sister Bria was born, she had been glued to home caring for her until our friend Ruth told her to come to Nantucket. "The ten days on Nantucket gave me a rest and a chance to gain perspective. We never left the house and the beach. Ruth was so good with you children, telling stories, giving you scarves for dress-up. And then we'd play on the beach. We were so happy. I think that was when I learned that I could face my life. I could face what would happen with Bria and everything that would come after that."

On Nantucket fifty years later, we walk the cobblestone streets to have lunch with Patrick and Udo before driving to see the upside-down house. I have been in contact with Eleanor, the new owner, who purchased the cottage for her children's families to enjoy. She is excited to meet us. Udo will film an interview with her as well as our exploration. When he asks my mother if he could interview her, she asks, "But what do I know?"

We drive across the island, following directions, until we reach a warren of sand-drifted lanes where, dwarfed by recent elaborate summer cottages, we find the modest wind-worn modern cottage that shocked the island when it was built in the early 1950s. After we tour the house with Eleanor, the new owner, Udo sets up his video camera and mic to face a comfortable chair in the long great room. He invites my mother to sit. She asks with a trace of impatience, "What do you want me to say?" Patrick and I leave them to begin. We lead Eleanor downstairs to the far bedroom to ask her questions about the line of bedrooms nestled into the sand dunes on the ground floor of the house. We learn that this house is one of barely a handful of modern houses on the island. Planning boards got rigid, and required strict designs to ensure the same design style across the island. Houses are now required to have a complex cottage roofline, and no walls of windows overlooking the sea.

Occasionally we hear the murmur of voices above. Patrick and I begin measuring the layout of each wall, hallway, closet, window, doorway. Since there are no longer any working drawings of this house, they want to take measurements. Back at the University of Cincinnati design studios, they will create a new set of plans and have their students create a model. This is the beginning of creating a retrospective show of my father's legacy as an architect. As we work, Patrick is sorting out the details of the house through the lens of an historian and what this now-small summer cottage built sixty years ago means in terms of the history of modern architecture.

When I hear the pushing aside of chairs and footsteps, I go upstairs and my mother smiles to me. It's time for a walk on the beach. I hand the tape measure to Udo. As my mother and I take off our shoes and socks on the deck, I ask, "How did it go?"

She looks animated. "He took me completely by surprise He asked how I met your father." She doesn't look mad as I might have expected from the past; she is slightly flushed, like a schoolgirl who is telling about a crush. I suddenly realize I have never heard the story of how my parents met.

"So what did you say?"

"I told him the story of how he spilled beer on my pants at a party."

"He did! Why?"

"Because he was jealous of my date."

"What! I've never heard that story!"

"Oh, it's just a silly story." She laughs as she looks out to the beach. "I realized as I was answering his questions that what I remember are the funny moments and the times that scared me. But I'll tell you later. I have to put my feet in those waves."

We follow the narrow worn path between the sharp-edged grasses up and over the dune to the beach beyond. This path is exactly the same, what my five-year-old self knows by heart, from our ten days of happiness in this house filled with light overlooking the beach. As my mother and I step down the hill, she says, "Feel how the sand is so thick and textured." We step around the scatter of broken shells in the wind-tossed sand, making our way down to the ocean-packed slope. The soft rumble of waves became as familiar as breathing when we stayed in this house above the beach. We roll up our pants, and follow the edge of the sea. We hold hands, Jo feeling a little uncertain of her balance as the water pulls the sand away from under our toes.

We search the beach, picking up shells. I pass her a worn moonshell. She hands me a flat square stone—"It's your favorite color"—and holds it next to my coral t-shirt. It is the sand-dry smoothness, lingering on my fingertips, that suddenly reminds me of walking this same beach with my father, passing stones to each other. I look down and pick up a round gray stone, just like the stone he and I shared. I walk ahead, smoothing it between my fingers. I close my eyes and feel its coolness, and hear the ocean murmuring beside me. I feel the company of my father long ago, and my mother now. I hold the stone and try to imagine a color to the stone as my dad had encouraged. But I don't want to see another color. As I walk along the packed warm sand, I like the gray stone simply how it is. I put it in my pocket, and take my mother's arm before we walk back to the house to say goodbye.

CREDITS

————

Permission for Quotations

Photo Credits and Permissions:
page number for each photograph

————

Formal portraits of W. Garber and Garber Family, photo credit Jerry Morgenroth: 5, 26

1968 Garber house photos: photo credit George Stille: 22

Photos of Sander Hall: photo credit George Stille: 150, 176

Proposed Schenley Building drawing by W. Garber, originally published Progressive Architecture, Oct. 1945: 34

ACKNOWLEDGMENTS

Everything begins with my mother Jo and my brothers Woodie and Hubbard, who risked re-entering the pain to answer my countless questions, who allowed me to write about them, and were willing to read drafts of this book. We could not have emerged without each other. My gratitude to their wives, Anita and Anna, and my niece Bianca, for reading and commenting on drafts, and supporting my brothers in the pain this book stirred up.

My gratitude goes to my children, Gabriel and Miriam, who always encourage me. I am grateful to their father, Peter, my ex-husband, for helping me heal and for his unfailing friendship. I am grateful to my Garber and Woodward cousins for countless emails uncovering family history, and especially Francie and John Pepper who let me stay with them on research trips to Cincinnati. My brothers and I are forever indebted to Francie for overseeing my father's care as he was dying.

It took decades of work to heal from my childhood. I couldn't have written this book without thirty years of skill and loving support from these three remarkable women: my acupuncturist, Vicki Pollard; my mentor, Alexandra Merrill; and my therapist, Judith Grace.

My old friends, Alvin McClure and Chuck Krumroy, helped me remember vivid details from the 1970s in hours of delightful conversations. I'm grateful for reconnecting with old friends as I wrote: Linda Findlay, who lived across the field from the glass house; Kimble Perry and Pogo (Roy) Stevens, from the year on the Ship; and my friends Lee Smolin and Professor Greg Nagy, from my time at Harvard.

I re-entered the world of architecture as I spent years immersed in research, rereading Le Corbusier, studying commentary on Modernism, and reconstructing my father's rapidly disappearing legacy of buildings. I became friends through lengthy correspondence with a University of Cincinnati architecture professor dedicated to documenting my father's work, Patrick Snadon, along with his colleague Udo Greinacher, who is photographing and filming their research. We spent several days documenting Woodie's work in Cincinnati and Nantucket. The Mexican architect owner, Ana Gomez, generously showed us her remarkable post-modern renovation of the "Glass House" in Glendale. I am grateful for Eleanor O'Neill and family, who let us spend hours exploring the "upside-down" house in Wauwinet on Nantucket.

I researched and explored many of my father's buildings not mentioned in this book. I want to thank those who assisted me: Wendy Gradison in correspondence about her family's house in the Smokey Mountains; Geoff and Marilyn Stokes, Gregory Spaid, and Kemp Roelofs for my visit to the Roelofs house in Gambier, Ohio; Will Sawyer for my visit to their island cottage built for Miss Mary Johnston near Pt. au Baril, Ontario; the staff at Christ Church Glendale, where I explored the Woodie's modern addition before it was demolished; the staff at The University of Cincinnati's College of Nursing & Health, before Woodie's design was updated beyond recognition; the renter of the house in Indian Hill, Ohio built for the Klausmeyer family; and a worker who let us explore the remarkable design of what was once the Johnson Harding printing plant off Red Bank Road in Cincinnati.

Additional architectural assistance came from Beth Sullebarger, Susan Rissover, and especially Jayne Merkel's writings, research, and support for Cincinnati Modernist architecture. I'm grateful to the UC architectural librarian Elizabeth Meyer for archiving boxes of my father's materials and scanning copies of articles and photographs for me. I am profoundly grateful for my father's last architectural student and friend, Mike Dingledine, who stored boxes of invaluable materials for twenty years in the belief that someday someone would be interested in Woodie's work.

I wrote many architects who had once worked or studied with my father. When I sent out emails with the subject line titled "A Question from Woodie Garber's daughter," I received emails back from a taxi in NYC, and from offices and homes in Oregon, Ohio, and Georgia. I deeply appreciated my long conversation with Bob Frasca, who had been my father's coop student for two years, "hanging out" with my parents from when I was a baby to a toddler. He was enthralled with the passionate commitment of my father's teaching and for Woodie taking his students to Mexico in a VW Bus to see Félix Candela's buildings in the early 1950s. I also heard from Woodie's old architectural partners and colleagues who had made peace with their painful dealings with my father. Charles Shoenberger wrote extensive notes about his experiences working with Woodie. My deep gratitude to Hayden May and his wife Cynthia for our long family friendship since the 1960s and for our day spent walking through Proctor Hall, talking about Sander Hall, and lunch afterwards at Lenhardts.

I'm grateful for the generous research of R. Dale Flick, librarian for The Cincinnati Literary Club, who searched through decades of archived papers to find and send me copies of my father's papers that I didn't have. I also thank the Glendale Historical Society for maintaining the records from the Glendale Literary Club, where I found detailed reports on meetings at my grandparents' and parents' homes.

So many writing teachers encouraged me. The unwinding of memory took years and patient mentoring. It took years as well to move from writing poetry to finding my voice as a prose writer. During my MFA at Stonecoast at the University of Southern Maine, I worked with the poet Tim Seibles in the Writing about Race Seminar (with Patricia Smith & Richard Hoffman). Tim encouraged writing the hard truths about race in memories of my childhood and teens in southern Ohio. Richard Hoffman supported my writing of the painful memories of childhood abuse from his having done the same. Two week-long writing seminars at Haystack under the skillful teaching of Baron Wormser (in addition to a year of mentoring) as well as Meredith Hall deepened the process of re-entering memory. Seminars with Debra Marquart, Suzanne Stempek Shea, and rigorous critique from Jaed Coffin propelled my writing.

A two-week artist residency at Virginia Center for the Creative Arts gave me a community of memoir writers and a writing friend, Annette Gendler. During a month at Jentel's Artist Residency on a cattle ranch near the Big Horn mountains in Wyoming, I experienced a depth of concentration I've never known that propelled me into memory, allowed me to complete the first draft, and gave me shared walks and conversations in the foothills with the remarkable artist Christel Dillbohner. Working with editor Nina Ryan helped me focus the memoir on my relationship with my father. I continued working on self-created retreats in the studio on Great Spruce Head Island, thanks to Anina Porter Fuller and the Porter family, and in Rose Cottage on Bear Island, thanks for the Fuller family.

Through this entire process my stalwart friends kept reading and giving feedback, a chapter or manuscript at a time. I am forever grateful for their thoughtful attention: Linda Buckmaster, Martha Derbyshire, Annette Gendler, Alexandra Merrill, Lauren Murray, Vicki Pollard, Coleen O'Connell, Diane Brott Courant, and Barb Klausmeyer. Many other friends and family members read and commented on the numerous drafts. I am so grateful for their generous encouragement.

Near the end, when I despaired of ever finishing, Monica Wood's skillful teaching and her referral to Polly Bennell helped me transform the manuscript. Polly's skillful coaching directed me to the hero's journey, and to map the three-act structure through the memoir. I could not have made it to the end without our work together. My writer friend Elizabeth IlgenFritz and I traded chapters and writing struggles for years. She was my skillful copyeditor, and her sudden early death propelled me to make sure my memoir would be published after I'd almost given up on it. My husband's friends, Alan and Gail Venable, were encouraging readers and editors for a last edit. My old friend Maya Christobel appeared at the last moment with great ideas for the cover.

I am grateful for my former literary agent, Wendy Strothman, who over seven years looked at the manuscript four times before accepting it, and asked tough questions that needed to be answered. She believed in this project, and worked diligently as she tried to find the right publisher.

I am so grateful my book found a home with She Writes Press. I deeply appreciate their dynamic publisher, Brooke Warner, who encourages a fine community of supportive and responsive writers. Thanks to Cait Levin for overseeing the editing process, and Julie Metz for her elegant cover design. I felt comfortable from the start with my sensitive and thoughtful publicist, Caitlin Hamilton Summie, who has helped me steadily through the process of bringing my book out into the world.

Finally I thank my husband Dirk, who appeared in my life three years ago. Fortunately, he missed the six intense, consuming years of birthing this book! Now he brings his steady loving support to my life as I bring this story out into the world.

BOOK GROUP

DISCUSSION

QUESTIONS

1. This memoir explores not only a family's life but also the life of their modern home. How do you think the family changed when they moved into "The Glass House"? Do you think that living in the house worsened the father's mental instability?

2. How aware are you of the design and architecture of your home and where you live, and do you have a sense of how it influences your life?

3. Was it shocking for you to imagine what happened when the students moved into the mirror glass dormitory, Sander Hall, on the University of Cincinnati campus? It's hard to remember the radical disruption of American culture that happened in the late 1960s and early 1970s. Can you imagine a college where the students would commit acts of arson multiple times a week in their dorm?

4. You can watch a video of the implosion of Sander Hall described in Implosion on YouTube: https://www.youtube.com/watch?v=Euuoof1TN-U. After reading this book, how did you feel watching the building collapse? Have you ever thought about architects and their feelings about the buildings they design?

5. This book follows the descent of a creative brilliant man into a violent, abusive father and then his emerging into a more stable older man struggling with depression. Has this book affected how you think about mental illness and how it affects a family?

6. Was it hard to imagine that the author at nineteen could reach a point of such desperation that she would decide she had to kill her father to save her family? Did this memoir help you to understand the emotional torture that can happen in a family held hostage by a parent with a mental illness?

7. What do you think of the author's mother, Jo? Is it difficult to imagine her not defending her children for so long? This is not only a coming-of-age story for the author but also for the author's mother, who grew up alongside her children, and who waited until she was finally brave and financially stable enough to leave her marriage and create a safe home for her children. Do you think it was wise to wait for so long? What did you observe about how she changed once she moved out?

8. What do you think of the author's brothers: the middle brother, Wood, living with his mother, and the younger brother, Hubbard, with his father? How did sending Wood and Elizabeth away to the school on the ship affect them and the family?

9. So often when people think of mental illness they think of the negatives, but in the book you could also see how Woodie was filled with intensity that led him to race cars, study wines, enthuse over jazz, and design gardens, as well as become a world-class architect. The author describes her father "as the most alive person she'd ever known," and yet in a moment, he could flip into a raging tyrant. What do you think of his psychiatrist's decision not to give him medication that would have tamped down his creativity but might have saved him from harming his family?

10. Was it difficult to understand the author's loyalty to her father as she tried, for years, to help him as he struggled with depression and rage? What do you think of her not calling back the last time he called?

For more information about the author and her family, the buildings her father designed, and information about Modern architecture and design, you can go to:
www.elizabethgarber.com

About the Author

Elizabeth W. Garber is the author of three books of poetry, *True Affections: Poems from a Small Town* (2012), *Listening Inside the Dance* (2005), and *Pierced by the Seasons* (2004). She collaborated with Michael Weymouth, combining her poetry and essays with his paintings and photographs, to create *Maine (Island Time)* (2013). Three of her poems have been read on NPR by Garrison Keillor on *The Writer's Almanac*, and her poem "Feasting" was included in his *Good Poems for Hard Times*. She was awarded writing fellowships at the Virginia Center for Creative Arts and the Jentel Artist Residency Program in Wyoming.

Garber studied Greek Epic in the Mythology and Folklore Department at Harvard and received a BA from Johns Hopkins, a MFA in creative non-fiction from University of Southern Maine's Stonecoast Masters Program, and a Masters in Acupuncture from the Traditional Acupuncture Institute. She has maintained a private practice as an acupuncturist for over thirty years in mid-coast Maine, where she raised her family. Visit her at:

www.elizabethgarber.com.

SELECTED TITLES FROM SHE WRITES PRESS

She Writes Press is an independent publishing company
founded to serve women writers everywhere.
Visit us at www.shewritespress.com.

The Sportscaster's Daughter: A Memoir by Cindi Michael. $16.95, 978-1-63152-107-2. Despite being disowned by her father—sportscaster George Michael, said to be the man who inspired ESPN's *SportsCenter*—Cindi Michael manages financially and heals emotionally, ultimately finding confidence from within.

The Coconut Latitudes: Secrets, Storms, and Survival in the Caribbean by Rita Gardner. $16.95, 978-1-63152-901-6. A haunting, lyrical memoir about a dysfunctional family's experiences in a reality far from the envisioned Eden—and the terrible cost of keeping secrets.

Fourteen: A Daughter's Memoir of Adventure, Sailing, and Survival by Leslie Johansen Nack. $16.95, 978-1-63152-941-2. A coming-of-age adventure story about a young girl who comes into her own power, fights back against abuse, becomes an accomplished sailor, and falls in love with the ocean and the natural world.

The S Word by Paolina Milana. $16.95, 978-1-63152-927-6. An insider's account of growing up with a schizophrenic mother, and the disastrous toll the illness—and her Sicilian Catholic family's code of secrecy—takes upon her young life.

Veronica's Grave: A Daughter's Memoir by Barbara Bracht Donsky. $16.95, 978-1-63152-074-7. A loss and coming-of-age story that follows young Barbara Bracht as she struggles to comprehend the sudden disappearance and death of her mother and cope with a blue-collar father intent upon erasing her mother's memory.

Don't Call Me Mother: A Daughter's Journey from Abandonment to Forgiveness by Linda Joy Myers. $16.95, 978-1-938314-02-5. Linda Joy Myers's story of how she transcended the prisons of her childhood by seeking—and offering—forgiveness for her family's sins.